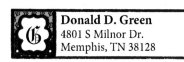

From the Editors of
American Herit

SPANISH WORD
HISTORIES
AND
MYSTERIES

ENGLISH WORDS THAT COME

FROM SPANISH

Houghton Mifflin Company
Boston • New York

Visit our website: www.houghtonmifflinbooks.com

Spanish word histories and mysteries : English words that come from Spanish / from the editors of the American Heritage Dictionaries.
    p. cm.
  Includes index.
  ISBN-13: 978-0-618-91054-0
  ISBN-10: 0-618-91054-9
  1. English language--United States--Foreign words and phrases--Spanish. 2. Spanish language--Influence on English. I. Houghton Mifflin Company. II. American Heritage dictionary.
  PE1582.S7S636 2007
  422'.461--dc22
                                    2007022646

Manufactured in the United States of America

MP 10 9 8 7 6 5 4 3 2 1

Table of Contents

Editorial and Production Staff

Vice President, Publisher of Dictionaries
Margery S. Berube

Vice President,
Executive Editor
Joseph P. Pickett

Vice President,
Managing Editor
Christopher Leonesio

Project Editor
Patrick Taylor

Editor
Catherine Pratt

Art and Production Supervisor
Margaret Anne Miles

Production Associate
Darcy Conroy

Database Production Supervisor
Christopher Granniss

Text Design
Catherine Hawkes, Cat & Mouse

Introduction

In modern times, English speakers have tended to take pride in the multicultural melting pot that is English vocabulary—a single page in the dictionary, opened at random to the letter *K,* can feature words from Chinese, Greek, Hawaiian, Japanese, Latin, Malay, Swahili, and the aboriginal Australian language Guugu Yimidhirr. This exotic mixture of languages is fascinating, but in some ways, it gives a misleading impression. Most of the words on the average page in the dictionary are in fact borrowed from the familiar languages French and Latin or else directly inherited from Old English. After these three languages, however, Spanish is one of the most important ingredients in English vocabulary.

Today, Spanish is the most widely spoken language in the United States other than English—people speaking Spanish can be heard all around the country, in all kinds of places and in all kinds of situations, on the airwaves and on television. Many of the readers of this book, written in English, will probably speak Spanish as their first language, or as one of their first languages. Because of the widespread use of Spanish in America, it is natural that Spanish has an influence on contemporary American English vocabulary. However, the Spanish influence on English is in fact centuries old, and Spanish words can be found in all areas of English vocabulary and in the most unexpected corners of an English dictionary. Beginning with medieval loanwords in the 1300s and 1400s, ranging across the maritime and mercantile borrowings of the 1500s, 1600s, and 1700s, to American words from the Old West in the

1800s and the language of Latino music in the 1900s, a great deal of the wealth of words in English is a borrowing of the linguistic treasures of Spanish.

When the peoples of the world sit down at the dinner table, it is likely that more families will converse in Spanish than English. More people in the world probably speak Spanish as their first language than English—despite the fact that millions of people learn English as a second language in order to participate in international business or exchange the results of scientific research conducted around the world.* Spanish is the official language of Argentina, Bolivia, Chile, Colombia, Costa Rica, Cuba, Dominican Republic, Ecuador, El Salvador, Guatemala, Honduras, Mexico, Nicaragua, Panama, Peru, Spain, Uruguay, and Venezuela, and it is one of the two official languages of Paraguay, Puerto Rico, and the African nation of Equatorial Guinea. The vastness of the area over which Spanish is spoken results from the immense influence of the Spanish Empire that flourished in the 1500s, 1600s, and 1700s and included the greater part of North and South America as well as the Philippines and scattered territories in Africa.

The roots of the Spanish language are in Latin, the language that began as the local dialect of the city of Rome but expanded across much of Europe with the help of Roman conquests. Nowadays, Latin is often described as a dead language, but reports of its demise, to borrow a phrase from Mark Twain, are an exaggeration—it is alive and well in Latin America, where the largest Spanish-speaking populations now live. During the last days of the Roman Empire, in the 400s, Latin was the language of everyday life across a vast area of Europe, including Spain. From the Portuguese coast of the Atlantic to the mountains of Romania, when parents

---

* For example, according to the July 2006 estimates of the Central Intelligence Agency Factbook online at https://www.cia.gov/cia/publications/factbook/geos/xx.html (consulted 12 March 2007), 5.05 percent of the world's population learns Spanish as a first language, while 4.84 percent learns English.

conversed with their children in the farmyards and in the fields, they spoke in Latin. When friends chatted in the streets and taverns of Roman cities, they spoke in Latin. And when the Roman Empire finally disintegrated, and writing was forgotten by all but a few clerics, people did not just stop speaking Latin. They kept on talking as they had before, but the words, sounds, and grammar of their everyday spoken Latin changed a little bit with every passing generation, as happens in all living languages. Over the centuries, the cumulative effect of such small changes in pronunciation, vocabulary, and grammar will completely transform any living language. In the modern world, we can observe evidence of the same sort of changes in action when we hear completely unfamiliar accents in films only fifty years old, or when our grandparents use some quaint bit of slang from their youth, or when our own children use new expressions that are completely unfamiliar to us.

In this way, through the build-up of small changes, the everyday Latin spoken in Spain during the late Roman Empire slowly developed into Spanish, while in other areas of Europe, different sets of changes transformed Latin into the other Romance languages like Portuguese, French, Italian, and Romanian. Many of the Spanish words discussed in the pages of this book are the direct descendants of Latin words. The same Latin words also have direct descendants in French and Italian, and English has often ended up borrowing the same Latin word twice, once in its Spanish form and once in its French form. The entries in this book for words such as *caldera* and *salsa* attempt to point out the hidden connections between English words of Spanish and French origin that result from this twofold borrowing of words of Latin origin.

Not all Spanish words, however, are descended from Latin. In 711, the southern part of the Iberian Peninsula was conquered by Muslims from North Africa. The society of North Africa at this time included people of both Arab and Berber heritage, as it still does today, and historians often use the term *Moors* to refer to peoples of the medieval Muslim North Africa as a whole. (The Berbers, by the way, are the indigenous inhabitants of Northwest Africa and the Saharan oases who were converted to Islam during the great expansion of Islam in the 600s. They speak languages distantly related to the Semitic languages, including Arabic and Hebrew.) The areas in Spain conquered by the Moors soon broke apart into several small independent kingdoms, but for convenience, historians usually refer to the entire area in Spain that was under Moorish rule by the Arabic name *Al-Andalus*. (Al-Andalus is also the source of the modern Spanish name for this region, *Andalucía*.) The Moors brought the Arabic language to Al-Andalus, where it was spoken alongside the dialects descended from Latin that would eventually become Spanish. Many Christians and Jews also lived in Al-Andalus, and although there were occasional periods of persecution by Muslim authorities, for the most part the followers of different faiths lived alongside each other in relative peace and tolerance. Together they achieved a great level of prosperity, and visitors to Al-Andalus marveled at the many well-watered gardens and groves of the land and sang the praises of its beautiful architecture and splendid cultural achievements.

During this period of Muslim rule, a very large number of Arabic words entered Spanish, and these borrowings are found in all areas of vocabulary, from building materials (*adobe*) to music (*guitar*). These borrowings were carried to the Christian north of Spain along with the influence of the cultural advances of Al-Andalus. Many of the inhabitants of Al-Andalus spoke a Romance dialect descended from Latin and closely related to Spanish, and as the Christian rulers of northern Spain began to conquer the Muslim kingdoms of Al-Andalus one by one, these Romance dialects were eventually absorbed into Spanish, and they too contributed to the Arabic element in Spanish vocabulary. This book discusses several Spanish words of Arabic origin that subsequently made their way into English, including *adobe, albatross, alcove, alfalfa, barrio, hazard, loco, mundungus,* and *sarabande.*

Spanish words have entered English continuously since medieval times up to the present day, although during certain periods, more Spanish words flowed into English than at others. A few words of Spanish origin, like *hazard,* came into English by way of French during the medieval period, but the speed of borrowing began to step up after 1492, a momentous year that figures more than once in the pages of this book. Not only did Spanish ships arrive in the Americas in that year, but the last Muslim kingdom in the south of Spain also fell to the forces of Ferdinand of Aragon and Isabella of Castile. This event helped consolidate the kingdom of Spain, whose power would eventually spread the Spanish language around the world. Ferdinand and Isabella's political gains were not all made through conquest, however—they also managed to betroth their daughter Catherine of Aragon to the future Henry VIII, a story told in this book at the word *farthingale.*

When Columbus stumbled upon the Americas in his search for a westward passage to India, he revealed the existence of a rich world previously unknown to Europeans. The first indigenous people of the Americas that the Spaniards met were the Taíno, and the Taíno language furnished words for many of the plants and animals that were new to the Spanish. These Taíno words continued to be used in Spanish even when the Spaniards conquered the mighty empires of the Aztec and the Inca, as well as vast areas in the rest of the Americas, where a great many languages besides Taíno were spoken.

Many English words relating to plants, animals, and the natural world of the Americas ultimately come from indigenous languages like Taíno, Nahuatl, and Quechua, but these terms have usually been filtered through Spanish before reaching English. *Cassava, hurricane,* and *savanna* are among the English words that refer to nature and the enviroment and that come from Taíno by way of Spanish. Words of Nahuatl origin in this group include *avocado* and *chicle,* while words of Quechua origin include *condor, llama,* and *puma.* Many English names for basic foodstuffs native to the Americas have reached English through Spanish, among them *potato* and *tomato.* Other words refer to man-made items originating in the indigenous cultures of the Americas, such as *barbecue* and *hammock* from Taíno and perhaps *jerky* from Quechua. Spanish also borrowed words from many of the other indigenous languages spoken in the Americas besides Taíno, Nahuatl, and Quechua, and some of these have also made their way to English, including *abalone* and *jojoba*.

When trying to describe the unfamiliar things that they encountered in the Americas, the Spaniards also put their own words from Spain to new uses, and English has received some of these words as well. The reptile called the *alligator,* the fish called the *barracuda,* and the large rodent called the *nutria* are all known in English by names made from words used in Spain before the conquest of the Americas. The English word *chocolate* comes from Nahuatl by way of Spanish, but *vanilla* originates in a Spanish word with purely Roman roots.

Although the familiar song from the 1700s commands Britannia to rule the waves, it was Spain that ruled the world's oceans from the early 1500s through the 1600s, after the conquest of the Americas. Spain's military and mercantile domination of the seas during this period has left a significant mark on English maritime vocabulary, with *armada, cargo, embargo,* and even *breeze.* It was not just the material wealth and natural resources of the Americas that Spain exported to the rest of the world during this period, however. At the same time, the culture of Spain itself also contributed to the artistic traditions of other European countries. English words from Spain relating to the fine arts include *guitar, passacaglia,* and *sarabande,* and the word *compliment* reflects the Spanish influence that began to be felt on courtly manners from the time of the Renaissance onwards.

Most of the area west of the Rockies that is now part of the United States was once part of the Spanish Empire. When Mexico declared its independence from Spain in 1810 (independence that Spain would not recognize until 1821), these Spanish possessions in North America became Mexican territory. At the time, the region had only a very sparse population. Spain, and later Mexico, had made attempts to encourage settlement, but frontiersmen and settlers from the United States had moved into the area as well. The land eventually became part of the United States as a result of the Mexican-American war, which was widely denounced by many Americans at the time. Mexicans today still mourn the loss of the territory that now forms the American states of California, Arizona, New Mexico, and Texas.

As they rode into these areas formerly part of Mexico, English-speaking cowboys picked up much of their distinctive lingo from the Spanish that had long been spoken on the ranches in the region—the word *ranch* itself is one of many words typical of the Old West that come from Spanish. Others discussed in this book include *arroyo, bonanza, canyon, hoosegaw, loco, mustang, mesa, quirt, rodeo,* and *vamoose.* The cowboy's life was full of words ultimately from Spanish, from the *lariat* or *lasso* in his hand to the *ten-gallon hat* on his head.

In the last few decades, the cultural influence of Latin America has made itself felt all over the United States, not just in the states adjoining Mexico or in Florida, across the Straits of Florida from Cuba. *Fajitas,* served with *salsa* made from fresh *cilantro,* are featured on menus in Minnesota, and barbecue enthusiasts can buy *mesquite* wood for grilling in Maine and Michigan, far from where the mesquite bush actually grows. Similarly, the popularity of Latin American musical genres has brought many other Spanish words into English, including *mambo, merengue,* and *tango,* in addition to *salsa* music, named after the sauce.

This book attempts to show that when speakers of one language borrow a word from another language, this borrowing often occurs for a reason—the speakers of the borrowing language feel a need for a new word when they encounter a new object or idea, or when social pressures and historical circumstances otherwise motivate the borrowing. This book attempts to illustrate these historical circumstances vividly, by quoting from important authors and notable writings from the past. Often these passages are presented with the original spelling and grammar used by the authors of the 1500s, 1600s, and 1700s, to give readers a taste of what Spanish and English looked and sounded like during the time when vast numbers of Spanish words were flowing into English. Quotations from Spanish are presented in indented text set in italic type, and English translations of the quoted passages follow in indented text set in Roman type.

The social pressures, scientific advances, and other forces that motivate the borrowing of words are not merely things of the past, however. On April 1, 2000, the date of the last census, there were 35,305,818 people who described themselves as Hispanic or Latino in the United States, out of a total population of 281,421,906. (Although many members of Latin American communities in the United States prefer to identify themselves as *Latino,* the United States Census Bureau uses the term *Hispanic* in addition to *Latino* in its description of population groups. Unlike *Latino,* the term *Hispanic* can also be used to describe Spanish-speaking people of Iberian, rather than Latin American, origin.) When Hispanics or Latinos of African and non-African descent are counted together, the census confirmed that Hispanics are the largest minority group in the United States. Of course, not all people in the United States who identify themselves as being of Hispanic or Latino descent will speak Spanish as their first language like their parents, grandparents, great-grandparents, or even their more distant ancestors. Many people from families that have lived in the United States for generations take pride in the heritage of their Spanish-speaking ancestors even if they do not always use the language in daily life.

Nevertheless, as the size, as well as the political and cultural importance, of the Latino community in the United States increases, the influence of Spanish on English vocabulary will undoubtedly increase as well, and many more Spanish terms will be added to the English dictionaries of the 21st century. Economic resurgence and development in the countries of Latin America, as well as in

Spain, may also add new vocabulary of Spanish origin to the English lexicon. These new words will join hundreds of others that have been at home in English for decades and even centuries, and whose surprising and fascinating stories are told in the pages that follow.

—Patrick Taylor
Project Editor

Pronunciation Key and Other Symbols

Symbol	Examples	Symbol	Examples	Symbol	Examples	Symbol	Examples
ă	pat	îr	deer, pier	o͞o	boot	y	yes
ā	pay	j	judge	ou	out	z	zebra, xylem
âr	care	k	kick, cat,	p	pop	zh	vision,
ä	father		pique	r	roar		pleasure,
b	bib	l	lid, needle	s	sauce		garage
ch	church	m	mum	sh	ship, dish	ə	about, item,
d	deed, milled	n	no, sudden	t	tight,		edible,
ĕ	pet	ng	thing		stopped		gallop,
ē	bee	ŏ	pot	th	thin		circus
f	fife, phase,	ō	toe	*th*	this	ər	butter
	rough	ô	caught,	ŭ	cut	N	French *bon*
g	gag		paw	ûr	urge, term,		(boN), *blanc*
h	hat	ôr	core		firm, word,		(blän)
hw	which	oi	noise		heard	KH	German *ach*
ĭ	pit	o͝o	took	v	valve		Scottish
ī	pie, by	o͝or	lure	w	with		*loch*

In this book parentheses are placed around these symbols when used to indicate pronunciations. For example, the Castilian Spanish pronunciation of the letter *z* is indicated as (th), while its pronunciation in American and Andalusian Spanish is indicated as (s).

Spanish has inherited many words from Latin and borrowed words from a wide variety of other languages, especially Arabic and the indigenous languages of the Americas. Modified letters are used in this book to represent the special sounds of these languages. In Latin words, the letters *a, e, i, o,* and *u* sound much as they do in Spanish, while the letters *ā, ē, ī, ō,* and *ū* have the same vowel qualities but are pronounced approximately twice as long.

Arabic has many sounds very different from those of English or Spanish. The long vowels of Arabic, *ā, ī,* and *ū,* are pronounced roughly like Spanish *a, i,* and *u* but twice as long. In Arabic words, the symbol *š* represents the sound (sh). The symbol (') is used to represent the sound of the Arabic letter *'ayn,* made by constricting the throat. The symbol (') is used to represent the sound called a glottal stop. It is the sound in the middle of English *Uh-oh!* The letter *ḥ* represents an Arabic sound that to English speakers sounds like a raspy *h* made deep in the throat. The letters *ḍ, ṣ,* and *ṭ* sound roughly like English *d, s,* and *t* but with an added quality that "darkens" or "deepens" vowels around them. The letters *ṯ* and *ḏ* represent (th) and (*th*), while *q* represents the Arabic consonant *qāf,* which to English speakers sounds like a *k* made deep in the throat.

xiv

abalone

Abalones are marine molluscs of the genus *Haliotis* that in general resemble large snails, except that they have an ear-shaped shell with a row of holes along the outer edge. Abalones use these holes for respiration, reproduction, and excretion of waste. The interior of their shell is covered with a colorful, opalescent layer of mother-of-pearl that is often used  for making jewelry. Abalones are prized as food in many parts of the world, and they were once extremely abundant on the coasts of California. Since the 1970s, however, Californian abalone populations have crashed because of overharvesting that has brought several abalone species near the brink of extinction.

The word *abalone* comes from American Spanish *abulón,* and *abulón* in turn comes from *aulun,* the word for the red abalone (*Haliotis rufescens*) in Rumsen, one of the languages spoken by a group of indigenous peoples of California known as the Ohlone or Costanoans. Just as much as the great material wealth of the Americas enriched Spain in the 1500s, 1600s, and 1700s, the indigenous languages of the Americas have enriched the Spanish language with thousands of words, and *abulón* is just one of these.

The history of the word *abalone* allows us to trace the broad history of the whole region now called California. Before the arrival of European settlers, the indigenous inhabitants of the San Francisco Bay area, the Ohlone, had long taken advantage of the rich harvest of abalones as one of their staple food sources. Spain began to establish Franciscan missions and settlements of Europeans in California only in the middle of the 1700s, even though the region had long been part of the Spanish Empire—the Spanish had ignored the fertile potential of the land until Russia and Great Britain began to cast envious eyes on the territory. It was during this period of early settlement that the Ohlone word must have entered Spanish as *abulón*.

When missions were established in the San Francisco Bay Area, however, many Ohlone died from European diseases, such as measles, to which they had no resistance. Many Spanish settlers also treated the Ohlone cruelly and forced them to work in the fields and on ranches. When Mexico became independent from Spain in 1821, California became part of Mexico, and after the Mexican-American War (1846–1848), the United States took control of the region. But the inhuman treatment of the indigenous Californians continued until the languages of the Ohlone peoples eventually became extinct. For this reason, only sketchy records of Rumsen and the other Ohlone languages survive, but field notes taken by an ethnologist in 1884 and preserved in the archives of the University of California, Berkeley, allow us to determine that the word comes from Rumsen.

acequia

In the Southwest of the United States and in parts of Texas, an irrigation ditch or canal is often called an *acequia,* pronounced (ə-sā′kē-ə). Like so many of the distinctive terms relating to everyday life in these parts of the United States, the word comes from Spanish. The Spanish word *acequia* itself comes from Arabic *al-sāqiya*. *Al* is the Arabic word for "the," while *sāqiya* means "irrigation ditch" or more literally, "one who gives someone something to drink." *Sāqiya* is derived from the Arabic verb *saqā*, "to give to drink."

Many other Spanish words of Arabic begin with the letter *a* and include a trace of the Arabic definite article *al*. These are discussed at the entries for the words *adobe* and *alcove* in this book.

achiote

The achiote (whose scientific name is *Bixa orellana*) is a tropical American evergreen shrub or small tree with heart-shaped leaves and lovely rose-pink or white flowers. It produces spiny pods, each of which contains around forty to fifty dark red seeds about the size of grape seeds. Each seed is surrounded by an aril (outer seed covering) that is the source of annatto, a yellowish-red dyestuff used to color foods like margarine and cheese. The seeds are also one of the main components of *recado rojo*, the popular Mexican red spice paste containing a variety of other ingredients such as oregano, cumin, coriander, allspice, and garlic. In themselves, achiote seeds have hardly any flavor, but their rich color makes any cooked dish look more appetizing—just as saffron makes paella look even more tempting or turmeric makes curry look tasty. The indigenous peoples of the Americas used the seeds to make cosmetics and body paint, and this has given the achiote another name, the *lipstick tree*. Both the tree and the seeds are also called *annatto* as well.

The English word *achiote* comes from Spanish, and the Spanish word comes from the word *āchiotl* in Nahuatl, the language of the Aztec Empire. The English word *annatto,* on the other hand, is thought to originate in one of the Carib languages, the family of indigenous languages formerly widely spoken in the islands of the Caribbean, northern South America, and the eastern coast of Central America.

Any person who has ordered a cheddar cheeseburger in the United States has probably eaten achiote without knowing it, since achiote is the natural colorant most often used to give cheddar a yellow-orange color. In traditional cheesemaking, however, the color of cheese depends on the plants that the cows have eaten, not on added colorings. In spring and summer, for example, cows may eat more fresh plants rich in beta carotene—the common natural orange pigment that gives color to carrots and many other vegetables—and the cheese made from their milk at that time often has a rich, appetizing orange color. In the winter, the cows often eat only hay and silage, which contains fewer natural pigments, and so the winter cheese is creamy white. To imitate the appetizing seasonal orange color and to give their product a uniform, recognizable look, cheesemakers began to add colorants like marigold petals to their cheese. After the arrival of Europeans in the Americas, the use of annatto as a coloring spread around the world, and the cheddar cheese sold in supermarkets in the United States is now usually colored with the natural annatto pigment derived from achiote seeds.

adobe

From the ancient Egyptians along the Nile to modern Americans in the Desert Southwest of the United States, many groups of people living in hot, dry areas have built their houses with thick walls of adobe bricks. Adobe bricks are made by mixing earth—usually earth composed mostly of sand and clay—with straw and water. The mixture is shaped into bricks that are then dried in the sun. Thick walls of adobe will keep the interior of a house cool in the daytime, but they will also gradually release heat soaked up during the day to warm the house during cold desert nights. Appropriately enough, our term for this building material ideally suited to the desert comes, by way of Spanish and Arabic, from the ancient Egyptian word for "brick."

In the hieroglyphic writing system, this word was written as *ḏbt*. The hieroglyph (or combination of hieroglyphs) transcribed with the letter *ḏ* in this word probably originally had a sound like English (j) in *jay*, but its pronunciation seems to have changed over the long history of the Egyptian language. The ancient Egyptian writing system also had no straightforward way of writing vowels, and when Egyptologists wish to give a spoken form to the word *ḏbt*, "brick," they will insert vowels according to certain conventions and pronounce it as (jĕ-bĕt).

As the ancient Egyptian language developed into Coptic, the language of medieval Christian Egypt, *ḏbt* became *tōbe*. After the Muslim conquest of Egypt beginning in 639, Coptic *tōbe* passed into Arabic as *ṭūba*. (In transcriptions of the Arabic alphabet into Roman letters, the *t* with a dot represents the Arabic letter *ṭā*, which has a sound like English (t) but with a characteristic "deep" or "dark" quality.) From Arabic, the word made its way into Spanish as *adobe*.

The appearance of the initial letter *a* in Spanish *adobe* requires some explanation. In Arabic, the word for "the" is *al*. However, when the definite article is placed in front of a noun beginning with a consonant that is made with the front part of the tongue (like *s*, *n*, *t*, or *ṭ*), then the *l* of *al* will become identical to that consonant. The phrase "the brick" is thus pronounced *aṭ-ṭūba*. This entire Arabic phrase passed into Spanish as a single noun, *adobe*, meaning just "adobe," not "the adobe."

Adobe is just one of the many Arabic words that entered Spanish after the Islamic conquest of the Iberian peninsula beginning in 711. The Spanish language kept its rich heritage of Arabic words even after the region was gradually reconquered by Christian rulers, and *adobe* was later spread to the Western Hemisphere with the expansion of Spain's imperial power. The word begins to appear in English in the 18th century, at first in descriptions of buildings in Spanish-speaking areas of the Western Hemisphere.

aficionado

When the Spanish word *aficionado,* "amateur, fan," was borrowed into English in the middle of the 1800s, it was at first used only to describe aficionados of bullfighting, the archetypal spectacle of Spanish culture. Later on in English, however, people began to use the word to describe ardent practitioners or enthusiasts of any other sort of activity.

In Spanish, *aficionado* is grammatically a masculine word, and its corresponding feminine form is *aficionada.* A female fan would always be *una aficionada* in Spanish, and this specifically feminine form *aficionada* is sometimes heard in English, too, when the fan in question is female. English, however, is a language in which grammatical gender plays a less important role than it does in Spanish. Many English words like *devotee, amateur,* and *fanatic* can be used to describe both men and women, and the word *aficionado,* for the most part, joined this group when it was borrowed into English. Since English does not consistently show the masculine gender of nouns and adjectives with the ending -*o*, as Spanish does, there is nothing in particular about the word *aficionado* in English that suggests that the word cannot be used of women just as well as men. Many, perhaps even most, English speakers would find nothing strange about sentences like *She is a big aficionado of mountain-climbing* or *My girlfriend is a huge Rolling Stones aficionado.*

The Spanish word *aficionado* is, in origin, the past participle of the verb *aficionar,* "to inspire affection." This verb is also used in the reflexive form *aficionarse* with the meaning "to become fond of, take a liking to, become a fan of." *Aficionar* is derived from the noun *afición,* "fondness, liking," and *afición* comes from Latin *affectiō. Affectiō,* "inclination, fondness," is, of course, also the source of the English word *affection.*

albatross

The majestic birds called *albatrosses* live mostly in the Southern Hemisphere and make their nests on remote islands. They are very efficient fliers—a talent that helps them range widely over the open ocean, swooping down to eat fish, crustaceans, and squid. One albatross species, the Royal Albatross (*Diomedea epomophora*) often has a wingspan of eleven feet or more, the largest that is regularly recorded for any living bird.

The English word *albatross* comes from *alcatraz,* the Spanish and Portuguese word for the large sea birds called *gannets* in English. Gannets are common sea birds in coastal regions, and the main species of gannet of the northern Atlantic has white plumage with black wingtips. In the 16th century, English sailors picked up the Spanish and Portuguese word for the gannet in the form *alcatras* and began using it to describe a variety of other sea birds that they encountered as they sailed into the southern oceans. An early form of the English word, *alcatras,* was used of the frigate bird, a large bird of tropical seas with black plumage and a throat pouch like a pelican's. Eventually English *alcatras* was modified to *albatross* and began to be used of the very large birds of the open ocean now called *albatrosses*. (Gannets and albatrosses especially resemble each other in their long, graceful wings.) The reason for the change of *c* to *b* in English *albatross* is something of a mystery, but it may be an attempt to make etymological sense out of the earlier form *alcatras* by associating it with the Latin word *albus*, meaning "white"—the plumage of many albatross species is a luminously pure white.

In English, the word *albatross* is also used with the meaning "a constant, worrisome burden or liability" in such expressions as *an albatross around one's neck*. For instance, a political commentator could describe an unpopular, lame-duck politician as *an albatross around the neck* of a certain political party. Such expressions make allusion to "The Rime of the Ancient Mariner," a poem by Samuel Taylor Coleridge first published in 1797 and later revised. At the beginning of the poem, a ship is driven off course and loses its away among the icebergs around Antarctica. An albatross appears, however, and soon afterwards the ship finds its way out of the icy desolation. The ship's crew welcome the bird's company, perhaps believing that it is the soul of a lost sailor that has taken wing as an albatross. But one of the sailors shoots the albatross with his crossbow, and a curse descends upon the ship. To punish the sailor who murdered the bird, the other sailors hang the bird's carcass around his neck.

> *Ah wel-a-day! what evil looks*
> *Had I from old and young;*
> *Instead of the Cross the Albatross*
> *About my neck was hung.*

The sailor bears this burden as the ship is pursued over the seas by supernatural forces.

The Spanish and Portuguese word *alcatraz*, "gannet," is itself of Arabic origin. It comes from the Arabic phrase *al-ġaṭṭās*, literally meaning "the diver." (In *al-ġaṭṭās*, the letter *ġ* represents the Arabic letter ghayn, which has a sound very much like the sound of the letter *g* in such Spanish words as *hago,* "I do," *pagar,* "to pay," and *según,* "according to," but unlike any sound found in English. The letter *ţ* represents a special sound of Arabic like a *t* pronounced with a particular dark quality resonating deep in the throat.) *Al* means "the" in Arabic, while the word *ġaţţās* can refer not only to human divers but also to diving sea birds. Gannets are in fact remarkable divers. They hover and flap several meters above the surface of the water until they spot a fish beneath the waves. They suddenly dive straight down, tuck their wings close to their body, and plunge into the water at amazing speed to seize their prey.

The island in San Francisco Bay now known as *Alcatraz,* the site of the federal prison that once held Al Capone, was originally named *La Isla de los Alcatraces,* "The Islands of the Gannets." This name was bestowed upon it by the Spanish explorer Juan de Ayala, the head of the first European expedition to reach the San Francisco Bay region. The prison also held Robert Franklin Stroud, the famous "Bird Man of Alcatraz," who served twelve years for manslaughter on the island. The birds associated with Stroud, however, were canaries rather than gannets or albatrosses. After Stroud had found some injured sparrows in the prison yard and had nursed them back to health, the prison warden allowed him the space and materials to raise hundreds of canaries. Stroud even wrote two books on bird diseases while serving his sentence. The prison was closed in 1963, and the rocky isle of Alcatraz is now home to a thriving colony of sea birds, including the gannets that gave their name to the island.

albino

The word *albino* is used to describe a person or animal whose body does not produce normal amounts of the pigment melanin and thus has very white hair and skin. Albinism occurs when an individual inherits two copies of a gene for the condition from his or her parents. The English word comes from Spanish *albino*, which was originally used to describe albino people living in sub-Saharan Africa. Spaniards visiting Africa were struck by the appearance of the occasional albino individual they saw living among the usually dark-skinned peoples of Africa. *Albino* first appears in Spanish around 1570, but it does not enter English until about 1770, when it is also used of albino people from Africa.

The Spanish word *albino* is derived from *albo,* a poetic word for "white." *Albo* comes from the Latin word for "white", *albus.* The English word *albumen,* "white of an egg," is related to the Latin word *albus.* And the word *album,* as in *photo album,* comes from Latin *album,* literally "something white." In English, *albums* were originally blank books in which people collected signatures and other mementos—later, *album* came to mean any miscellaneous collection, such a sheaf of musical compositions.

The everyday word for "white" in Spanish, *blanco,* does not come from Latin. Instead, it is a borrowing from a language in the Germanic family, the family of languages that includes English, Dutch, German, and the languages of Scandinavia. As Roman power waned in western Europe before the Empire finally collapsed in AD 476, various tribes speaking Germanic languages moved into Roman territory and began to take over the government. They brought with them a large number of Germanic words that became part of the everyday spoken Latin of the Roman cities and villages. One of these words was a word for "white," which replaced Latin *albus* in everyday spoken Latin. As spoken Latin gradually evolved into the modern Romance languages, this Germanic word for "white" shows up as *bianco* in Italian, as *blanc* in French, and as *blanco* in Spanish. The French word *blanc* was also borrowed into

Middle English, and it eventually appears in Modern English as *blank*. From the point of view of history, at least, Spanish *blanco* and English *blank* are the same word.

alcove

The English word *alcove* comes from the Spanish word *alcoba*. The first known occurrence of the word in Spanish is found in a document dating from the very early 1200s, where it refers to a room in which things are weighed publicly. In a text dating from the time of the great Spanish king, Alfonso X el Sabio ("Alfonso the Wise," who lived from 1221 to 1284), the word was used to refer to the cupola of a building. Later, in the 1500s, the word came to refer to a sleeping alcove added on to the side of a room in which a bed could be placed. The word was then borrowed into French as *alcôve,* and from French it was borrowed into English.

Alcoba comes from the Arabic phrase *al-qubba,* made up of the word *al,* "the," and the word *qubba,* "vault, vaulted chamber." *Alcoba* itself is just one of over four thousand words in Spanish that were borrowed from Arabic during the period from the early 700s to the early 1400s, when a large portion of southern Spain and Portugal were under Muslim control. Within the frontiers of the various small Muslim kingdoms that succeeded each other in this area over the centuries, Muslims, Jews, and Christians lived in harmony, and the arts and sciences flourished with a brilliance unknown elsewhere in Europe at the time. Hundreds of new ideas and products flowed into Spain from the Islamic world, and with them came hundreds of new Arabic words used to name them.

As a result of this process, Spanish has many hundreds of words beginning with the letters *al–* just like *alcoba,* and the majority of these are from Arabic. In addition, under certain circumstances, the *l* in the Arabic definite article often became another consonant such as *d* or *t* or *s,* and then the phrase consisting of the definite article and its following noun was borrowed into Spanish without an *l.* Because this process disguises the Arabic definite article somewhat, even more Spanish words contain a trace of the Arabic definite article than might appear at first glance. (The process is explained in greater detail at the note for the word *adobe* in this book.) Since Spain was also the route by which many of the innovations of the Islamic world entered Europe, English borrowed a large number of the Spanish words containing the Arabic definite article.

alfalfa

Alfalfa is one of the most important crops grown as hay for animals. Alfalfa makes the most nutritious kind of hay of all commonly grown feed crops, and hay can be cut from alfalfa fields several times a year. Like all plants in the bean family, alfalfa also improves the land in which it is grown by adding nitrogen to the soil. The plant grows about a foot or a foot and a half high and has leaves divided into three cloverlike leaflets. It also has clusters of blue-violet flowers resembling  the flower heads of red clover, a common roadside plant in the United States. In England and many English-speaking countries besides the United States, alfalfa is more often known as *lucerne,* a word from French. The common name in the United States, however, is usually *alfalfa,* and *alfalfa* comes from Spanish.

   The alfalfa plant is native to Iran, and it is in Iran that the word *alfalfa* begins its journey into English. *Alfalfa* began as the

Persian word *aspist*, meaning "clover." The Persian word entered Arabic as *faṣfaṣa*, when the valuable new crop began to spread from Iran. (The sound of the Arabic consonant *ṣ* resembles the regular *s* of Spanish or English but with a characteristic dark or deep quality.) The Arabic word then entered Spanish during the Muslim conquest of Spain, and *faṣfaṣa* at first shows up in early Spanish with a variety of spellings, such as *alfaz*, *alfalz*, and *alfalfez*. Later on, the usual form of the Spanish word settles down as *alfalfa*. *Alfalfa* first begins to appear in English in the middle of the 1800s.

The *al–* at the beginning of *alfalfa* is a trace of the Arabic definite article, "the." Spanish often borrowed Arabic words with the definite article still attached, and this phenomenon is discussed further at the entries for *adobe* and *alcove*.

alligator

A few days after Easter in 1513, the Spanish conquistador Juan Ponce de León and the other Spaniards accompanying him on his expedition spotted the shores of what they believed to be a large island. Ponce de León bestowed the name *la Pascua Florida* on this territory. In Spanish, the Easter season is called *Pascua florida*—*Pascua* means "Easter" in Spanish, while *florida* means "flowery, full of flowers." Later on, of course, Florida turned out not to be an island but rather a peninsula connected to a vast continent. Gradually, the Spanish began to maintain relations with the indigenous peoples of the area and to convert them to Christianity, and in 1559, the Spanish established Pensacola, the first European settlement in all the territory that is now the United States. (Spain eventually ceded Florida to the United States in 1819.) During the initial period of their exploration of Florida, the Spaniards must have encountered a monstrous reptile, probably much larger than any crocodiles that they might have seen elsewhere on their voyages. The Spaniards called this creature simply *el lagarto,* "the lizard." It was, of course, the American alligator.

The modern range of the American alligator lies entirely within the United States and extends from North and South Carolina through Georgia, Florida, Alabama, Mississippi, Louisiana, Akansas, and Oklahoma all the way to southern Texas. One of the first Englishmen to see this animal, *el lagarto,* in the flesh was probably Job Hortop, a sailor and gunman who was part of an English expedition to the Americas in 1567. Hortop had many adventures on his voyage, and he was eventually captured and forced to work as a galley slave by the Spanish. After twenty-three years away from England, he finally returned home and published an account of his sufferings in 1591, called *The rare travailes of Job Hortop.* Hortop described the interesting animals and plants he had seen on the expedition, and he included for the benefit of his fellow Englishmen the following portrait of *el lagarto* (here presented in Hortop's original 16th-century spelling):

> *In this Island called River de hatch, we were troubled sore with mostrous allagartaes, which use those partes. They are formed in this manner: it hath a head like a hog, bodied like a serpent and ful of scales on the backe, everie one being as broad as a sacer, his taile long and full of knots, there bee some five and twentie foote long by the rule. One of which we slewe.... We haled the monster on shore, which was four and twentie foot long measured by the carpenter's ruler: this monster was verie wide between the chappes [jaws], and the teeth was uglie and sharpe.... This monster will devour both man and beast and carrie horse and man cleane away.*

Not bothering to separate the definite article *el,* "the," from *lagarto,* "lizard," the English adopted the whole Spanish phrase *el lagarto* as the noun *alligator.* Later, Spanish borrowed the English term *alligator* back as *aligátor,* in order to differentiate the animal from the many species of *cocodrilo,* "crocodile."

Alligators differ from crocodiles in the shape of their heads and in their dentition. Alligators have a shorter, broader head than crocodiles, and when an alligator closes its jaws, only the upper row of its teeth can be seen, projecting downwards over its lower jaw. In crocodiles, both upper and lower rows can be seen when the jaws are closed, projecting down over the lower jaw and up over the upper jaw.

armada

The Spanish word *armada*, "navy, a naval fleet," was borrowed into English in the first half of the 1500s, when the Spanish Empire was expanding over the Americas and Asia, and the Spanish navy was establishing itself as the supreme power on the seas. In English, the Spanish word *armada* was originally borrowed as *armado*. Just as in the case of words like *tomato* (from Spanish *tomate*) or *potato* (from the combination of Spanish *batata* and *papa*), the final vowel of *armada* was replaced by -*o* by English speakers who had limited knowledge of Spanish but were familiar with the fact that many Spanish nouns end in -*o*. However, the correct Spanish form of the word eventually replaced *armado*.

Even though the word *armada* was known in English before the Anglo-Spanish War (1585–1604), the conflict between England and Spain during this period must have helped impress the term in the minds of the English. King Philip II of Spain sought to prevent England from supporting the Protestant cause in the Netherlands (which were then a part of the Spanish Empire) and even to restore the Catholic faith to England itself. At the time, England was ruled by Queen Elizabeth, a protestant and the head of the Church of England.

The roots of this conflict between England and Spain went deep. In 1553, Queen Mary had ascended to the English throne and restored Catholicism as the state religion of England after the reigns of her Protestant father, Henry VIII, and her brother, Edward VI. Soon after her accession, in 1554, Mary married the Spanish prince Philip, who was soon to be King Philip II of Spain. This alliance was a strategic triumph for the Spanish— through this diplomatic marriage, rather than by war, Spain hoped to assert permanent control over England and ensure that Catholicism remained the religion of the country even after Mary's death. But the English themselves worried that England might become just another province of the Spanish Empire. Many of the remaining Protestants in England still hated Catholicism passionately. Protestant nobles also fretted that they might have to return the property that they had seized from the Catholic Church when Henry VIII had created the Church of England. Eventually, however, things worked out in the Protestants' favor. Mary loved Philip intensely, but Philip was not attracted to his wife. The couple was unable to conceive, and Philip left for Spain a little over a year after their wedding, never to see his wife again. When Mary died in 1558, her Protestant sister Elizabeth ascended to the throne and restored the supremacy of the Church of England, and Spanish hopes for a peaceful way to gain control over a securely Catholic England were dashed.

Philip therefore turned to force of arms. In 1588, he assembled a vast fleet of around 130 warships in order to transport an army for the conquest of England. The fleet was called *la Grande y Felicísima Armada* ("the Great and Most Fortunate Warfleet") or *la Armada Invencible* ("the Invincible Warfleet") in Spanish, but was known in English simply as *the Spanish Armada*. The Armada, however, suffered from bad planning and simple bad luck. It sailed into the English Channel in an attempt to pick up an army in the Spanish Netherlands, but it was constantly harried by the English navy. The Spanish sailors had been trained for close combat, but the English refused to engage them in this way. Eventually, the English forced the Armada to sail into the North Sea, and pursued it all the way up to Scotland. The Armada rounded the northern tip of Scotland and encountered a terrible storm, nicknamed the *Protestant Wind,* off the coasts of Ireland. Many ships were wrecked, and in the end, only 67 of the vessels, crammed with starving sailors, limped their way back to Spain. The expenditures for the Armada of 1588, for subsequent armadas assembled later, and for other campaigns against the English eventually bankrupted Philip II, and when he died, the Anglo-Spanish War simply petered out under his son Philip III. But the word *armada* was securely established in English.

The Spanish word *armada* is in fact closely related to the English word *army. Armada* comes from Latin *armāta,* the feminine singular of *armātus,* "armed, equipped with arms," from the verb *armāre,* "to arm." As French slowly evolved from the spoken Latin of the region of the Roman Empire that is now France, *armāta* became Old French *armee,* "armed force, army." The Old French word was borrowed into Middle English and eventually developed into Modern English *army.*

Queen Mary's mother, by the way, was Catherine of Aragon, daughter of the great pair of Spanish monarchs, Isabella of Castile and Ferdinand of Aragon. Catherine's story, another tale of the intertwining relations of Spain and England, and of the Spanish and English languages, is told in this book at the note for the word *farthingale.* See also the following entry, *armadillo.*

armadillo

Armadillos are found only in North and South America, and the first Spaniards who reached the shores of the Americas needed to find a new word for these animals. *Armadillo* literally means "little armed one" in Spanish in reference to the bony plates that protect its body from predators. In a book entitled *Historia medicinal de las cosas que se trae de nuestras Indias Occidentales* ("Medical Study of the Things that are Brought from our West Indies") that described the unfamiliar items that were imported to Spain from the Americas, Nicolás Monardes (1493–1588), a Spanish physician, describes the strange appearance of the armadillo as it seemed to the Spaniards of the day (Monardes's text is here quoted in its original 16th-century spelling, which omits many of the accents used in Modern Spanish, as in the word *está*):

> ...*un animal estraño, que esta todo encubertado de conchicas, hasta los pies, como un cavallo, que esta encubertado de armas; por do le llaman, el Armadillo. Es de tamaño de un Lechon, y en el hocico paresce a el. Tiene una cola larga, y gruessa, come de lagarto. Abita dentro de la tierra, como Topo.*

> ...a strange animal, which is all covered with little plates, all the way to its feet, like a horse that is covered with armor; from this, they call it the *armadillo*. It is the size of a hog, and has a snout like one, and it has a long, thick tail, like a lizard. It lives under the earth, like a mole.

Some species of armadillo can roll themselves into a tight ball impenetrable to predators, but the species of armadillo that lives in the southern United States, the nine-banded armadillo *Dasypus novemcinctus,* cannot roll itself up completely.

The Spanish word *armadillo* is the diminutive of *armado,* "armed," and *armado* in turn is the past participle of the verb *armar,* "to arm, provide with weapons." The verb *armar* comes from

a nine-banded armadillo

Latin *armāre,* "to arm," and *armāre* is derived from Latin *arma,* a plural noun meaning "tools, weapons." In the same way that Latin *armāre* evolved into *armar* in Spanish, *armāre* also evolved into the verb *armer* in French. The French word was borrowed into English as the verb *arm,* meaning "provide with weapons."

The English noun *arm,* "weapon," also comes from Latin *arma,* "weapons," by way of French *arme.* The English noun *arm* meaning "limb of the upper part of the body," however, does not belong to this family of words descended from Latin *arma*—instead, this *arm* comes from Old English *earm.*

arroyo

An arroyo is a gulch cut into the land by a stream that runs only intermittently. At the bottom of a dry arroyo, the path that the stream takes when the arroyo is full of water is often traced with a layer of rounded stones or gravel left by the rushing current. Besides dry streambeds, the word *arroyo* can also be used of running brooks or creeks.

The English word *arroyo* is most common in the English of the American Southwest, and like many of the words used to describe the landscape of the region, it is of Spanish origin. The Spanish word *arroyo* means basically "stream" but also "street gutter." The further origin of Spanish *arroyo* itself is uncertain, but is probably somehow related to the Latin *arrugia,* a word which occurs only a few times in all of Roman literature. An *arrugia* seems to have been a shaft or series of tunnels in a gold mine.

In Roman times, gold mining was one of the most important industries in the area that is now Spain. In a vast book summarizing the scientific knowledge of his time, the Roman writer Pliny the Elder (AD 29–79) says that Spanish gold miners literally moved mountains of rubble into the sea in order to get at the gold in their land. The miners would dig a series of galleries under a mountain and then cause it to collapse, and then they would search the rubble for veins of gold and wash the debris in streams of water to find gold nuggets. Pliny notes the vast quantities of rock that ancient Spanish miners broke apart and moved: *the earth flows down to the sea, and the shattered mountain is washed away, and the shores of Spain are extended far out into the sea.* Pliny also lists several technical Latin mining terms, including *arrugia,* that are thought to be from the languages spoken in Spain before the arrival of the Romans, and the Spanish word *arroyo* may descend from this pre-Roman mining word from Spain. Although the distance in meaning between *arrugia,* "gallery in a goldmine," and *arroyo,* "stream," may seem rather great, it is possible to think of links between the two concepts. The same technology used to rearrange the landscape and bring water to wash the gold could be used to create channels and canals to bring water from mountain springs and streams to towns and farming areas.

avocado

Avocados are the fruit of a tree native to the American tropics. The word for the fruit comes from Spanish *aguacate,* and it begins to be mentioned in English-language writings during the 1600s. At first, the word is spelled in a variety of ways, such as *avogato, avocato, avigato,* and *albecaco,* but eventually the spelling settles down as *avocado.* In Spanish, the word *avocado* was in fact found as a variant of the standard form *aguacate,* but it is now obsolete.

The Spanish word *aguacate* itself is one of the many words that Spanish has borrowed from Nahuatl, the language of the

Aztec Empire that ruled central Mexico at the time when the Spanish began to conquer the Americas. *Aguacate* comes from the Nahuatl term for the avocado, *āhuacatl.*

The Nahuatl word *āhuacatl* ends with the extremely common Nahuatl suffix *–tl* that is added to a large number of nouns in the language. (Even the name of the language, *Nahuatl,* ends in the suffix.) The grammar of the Nahuatl language is quite different from that of English, Spanish, and many other European langauges, and it makes extensive use of suffixes to perform various grammatical functions. If no other suffix is added to a noun, a default suffix *–tl* is often added to many nouns. The Spanish had trouble pronouncing this *–tl* at the end of the word, and when they borrowed one of these Nahuatl nouns that took the ending *–tl,* they often substituted a *–te.* A similar substitution is discussed at the entry for *tomato* (from Spanish *tomate*) in this book.

In English, the avocado is sometimes also called by the name *alligator pear.* English speakers trying to make sense out of early English forms of the word as *avogato* and *avocato* must have been reminded at once of pears and of the leathery brownish-green skin of the alligator when looking at the avocado, and they then transformed *avogato* into *alligator pear.* The term is now somewhat old-fashioned and rare, however.

Although the pebbly skin of the avocado may have reminded English speakers of an alligator, it reminded Nahuatl speakers of something else entirely. The Nahuatl word *āhuacatl,* besides meaning "avocado," also means "testicle." When growing on a tree, the fruit also often dangles down in suggestively shaped bunches of two or three. Among early European visitors to the Americas, avocados eventually acquired a reputation for stimulating lust in anyone who ate them.

Nowadays, avocados are commonly served in the form of guacamole, a thick paste of mashed avocado combined with seasonings. The Spanish word *guacamole* is also a borrowing from Nahuatl—it comes from Nahuatl *āhuacamolli,* a compound of the Nahuatl words *āhuacatl,* "avocado," and *molli,* "sauce."

Nahuatl *molli* is also the source of the Mexican Spanish word *mole,* which refers to any of various spicy sauces of Mexican origin. Many kinds of *mole* served with meat an poultry are made from a base of onion, chilies, nuts or seeds, and unsweetened chocolate, but there are as many kinds of *mole* as there are cooks and dishes. Nowadays, the word *mole,* still pronounced (mō′lā) as in Spanish, is also used in English, as the richness and variety of Mexican cuisine grows more popular in all parts of the United States.

balsa

The balsa tree, whose scientific name is *Ochroma pyramidale,* grows in tropical South America, Central America, and Mexico. The tree grows very rapidly, and its wood is the softest and lightest of all the different kinds of wood used in woodworking and industry. A piece of balsa wood can be over 90 percent air. The wood is so light, in fact, that a thick log from a balsa tree can be carried by a single person. Nowadays, the wood is popular as a material for model airplanes. In the past, however, balsa wood was also extensively used in flotation devices, and this offers a clue to the ultimate origin of the word.

The English word *balsa* is a borrowing of the Spanish word for this tree. In Spanish, the word *balsa* originally meant "raft" and "barge." Taking advantage of the excellent buoyancy of balsa wood, South Americans would tie together balsa logs to make lightweight rafts to transport goods down rivers easily. Since the tree provided the best wood for making a *balsa* or raft, the word *balsa* eventually became the name for the tree itself.

The ultimate origin of the Spanish word *balsa,* "raft," is more than a little obscure, however. It is perhaps related to another Spanish word *balsa,* which means "pond" or "waterhole." Most Spanish words are of course descended from Latin, and it is usually easy to find the Latin ancestor of a Spanish word by rolling back the changes that occurred as the everyday spoken Latin of Spain gradually evolved into the Spanish language. But for *balsa,* "raft," and *balsa,* "pond," there is no known Latin term from which they could descend. In fact, some other very common, everyday words in Spanish seem to have come from the languages originally spoken in Spain before the arrival of the Romans. *Perro,* "dog," and *barro,* "mud," are two other words in Spanish that seem to have pre-Roman origins. Of the various languages that must have been spoken in Spain before Roman times, only Basque has survived until today. As for the others, we can learn about them only from some short, poorly understood inscriptions and from the words they have given to Spanish, like *balsa.*

barbecue

The idea of sleeping on a barbecue sounds a little crazy to speakers of English in modern times—it would be very uncomfortable, even when there is no fire blazing underneath. When the word *barbecue* first began to appear in English during the late 1600s, however, it could refer not only to a wooden rack for drying or smoking meat but also to a wooden construction used as a sleeping platform. The English buccaneer William Dampier (1652–1715), who is the first person known to have circumnavigated the globe twice, is also one of the first English authors to use the word *barbecue.* According to Dampier's account of an expedition into the area that is now Panama, he and his men were forced to camp on swampy ground near a river:

> *The twelfth* [day] *in the morning we crossed a deep river.... We built huts upon its banks and lay there all night, upon our barbecues, or frames of sticks raised about 3 foot from the ground.*

The thirteenth day, when we turned out the river had over-flowed its banks, and was 2 foot deep in our huts.

In reports and travelogues from the West Indies written in English, other English travelers and writers of the 1600s use the word *barbecue* to describe a rack for smoking meat—this sense of the word is much closer to the common meaning that the word has today, "an apparatus for roasting meat over coals." In the 1700s, *barbecue* comes to refer to a festive social occasion at which meat is roasted outdoors over a fire.

The English word *barbecue* is a borrowing of the Spanish word *barbacoa*. *Barbacoa* can refer to any sort of apparatus for roasting meat in the open air, but a *barbacoa* can also be a rough or makeshift bed made by weaving together flexible sticks. Spanish borrowed the word *barbacoa* from the language of the Taíno, the indigenous inhabitants of the Greater Antilles (Cuba, Hispaniola, Puerto Rico, and Jamaica) and the Bahamas. The Taíno were the first people encountered by Christopher Columbus when his expedition reached the Americas, and the Spanish apparently found the Taíno drying pieces of meat and fish by putting them on frameworks of sticks laid over posts above a fire. The Taíno word that the Spanish borrowed as *barbacoa* probably referred to this sort of framework of sticks.

barracuda

Barracuda are fierce-looking fish that live mostly in tropical seas like the Caribbean. They have a projecting lower jaw, and their large mouth holds two rows, one behind the other, of fanglike teeth of varying length. Barracuda are noted for being fast swimmers, suddenly sprinting through the water to seize smaller fish in their jaws. Some species of barracuda can grow over six feet long, and many sports fishermen enjoy the challenge presented by the size and strength of barracuda. Small barracuda are good to eat, but the flesh of large barracuda sometimes causes a kind of poisoning called *ciguatera* (this word is the subject of a separate note in this book, by the way).

The English word for the fish is a borrowing of American Spanish *barracuda*. Although the origin of the Spanish word remains unclear, it is interesting to note that it looks like the feminine form of a Spanish adjective formed with the extremely common suffix *–udo* that means "provided with" or "characterized by." This suffix can be seen in such adjectives as *peludo,* "hairy, hirsute" (from *pelo,* "hair"), *cornudo,* "horned, having horns" (from *cuerno,* "horn"), and *barrigudo,* "paunchy, pot-bellied" (from *barriga,* "belly"). In Spanish, adjectives are frequently used by themselves as nouns, so *barracuda* could originally have been "the one who is *barracuda.*" However, if the *–uda* of *barracuda* is the feminine form of the suffix *–udo,* then what might the *barrac–* part of the word be?

The solution to this problem may come from the region of the city of Valencia on the Mediterranean coast of Spain. Historically, the people of Valencia and the countryside around it have spoken a dialect of the Romance language Catalan, rather than Spanish. (Spanish and Catalan are not mutually intelligible, even though the two languages sometimes resemble each other quite closely, since they both descend from Latin. If anything, Catalan is more similar to the various Romance languages traditionally spoken in southern France, like Provençal, than it is to Spanish.) It so happens that in Valencian Catalan, there is a word *barracó* meaning "a tooth that sticks out in front and overlaps the others." Although we do not know the exact route taken by the Valencian word on its way to the Caribbean where barracudas live, the Catalan people have always been closely tied to the sea and involved in trade and fishing in the Mediterranean region. It is therefore easy to imagine a sailor from Valencia on a Spanish ship carrying his local words to the other side of the world, where *barracó* was then used as the base of an adjective ending in *–udo*. In this way, the word *barracuda* may be based on the Valencian word and make reference to the fish's fearsome jawful of long teeth—the barracuda is simply "the snaggletooth."

barrio

In Spanish, the word *barrio* means simply "neighborhood." In the United States, however, the word *barrio* is most often used to describe a Spanish-speaking neighborhood within a city. To English speakers, the term *barrio* usually calls up images of densely populated urban centers, such as East Harlem in New York City—the part of Manhattan often called simply *El Barrio* and historically the center of the Puerto Rican population in the city.

The Spanish word *barrio*, however, ultimately comes from a word meaning something quite different from a populous city neighborhood in a modern city. Spanish *barrio* is derived from the Arabic noun *barr*, meaning "land, open country." The Arabic adjective corresponding to this noun is *barrī*, meaning "of the land" and by extension "on the outside" (of the city walls or district limits, for example). In medieval times, when Muslim rulers governed the south of Spain, both Arabic and Old Spanish were spoken in the streets of the thriving towns in the region, where Christians, Muslims, and Jews lived together side by side in peace. During this period, the Arabic word *barrī*, "of the land," was applied to villages and hamlets that lay in the territory surrounding a town or city. As medieval towns outgrew their original walls and overflowed into the surrounding countryside, these villages or *barrios* were enveloped by the expansion and became neighborhoods of the town itself.

bastinado

A *bastinado* is a beating with a stick or cudgel, especially on the soles of the feet. The word has been around in English since the 1500s—Shakespeare uses it three times, as in the passage from Act 5, Scene 1 of the comedy *As You Like It* quoted below. Touchstone, the clown of the court of a duke, falls in love with a shepherdess, who is also being wooed by a local rustic. Touchstone warns his rival to stay away from her and tries to overwhelm him by a blustering display of vocabulary, rather than force:

> *Abandon the society of this female, or, clown, thou perishest;*
> *or, to thy better understanding, diest; or, to wit, I kill thee,*
> *make thee away, translate thy life into death, thy liberty into*
> *bondage: I will deal in poison with thee, or in bastinado, or in*
> *steel.*

The English word *bastinado* comes from Spanish *bastonada,* "a blow with a stick." The Spanish word is in turn derived from *bastón,* "stick, cane," in the same way that words like *patada,* "kick," and *palmada,* "slap," are derived from *pata,* "leg, paw" and *palma,* "palm." The word *bastón,* "stick," itself is a descendant of Vulgar Latin **bastōnem.* Although this word is not found in any classical Latin writings, people in Roman Spain and the rest of the Roman Empire must have used the word in the everyday conversational Vulgar Latin that they spoke in the fields and streets. The Vulgar Latin word has descendants in the other Romance languages, like Italian *bastone* and Old French *baston,* both meaning "stick, wooden rod." As Old French developed into Middle and Modern French, the consonant *s* was dropped when before another consonant, and Old French *baston* developed into Modern French *bâton.* English borrowed the French word as *baton* in the

1500s. In this way, *bastinado* and *baton* are etymological cousins.

blue blood

The English expression *blue blood,* meaning "an aristocratic pedigree" as well as "a member of the aristocracy," is in origin a translation of the Spanish expression *sangre azul* (made up of the words *sangre,* "blood," and *azul,* "blue.") The Spanish phrase makes reference to the fact that veins can sometimes be seen as lines of blue running under the skin of people with fair complexions.

The year 1492 was a crucial one in the history of Spain—and of the world—for several reasons. Not only did Ferdinand of Aragon and Isabella of Castile sponsor Columbus's voyage to the new world in that year, but they also conquered Granada, the last of the Muslim kingdoms of southern Spain. This event ended a long period of artistic splendor and religious tolerance in the Muslim-controlled Spain, where Christians, Jews, and Muslims had lived side by side in relative peace for centuries. After the Christian conquest of Muslim Spain, many Muslims and Jews were compelled to accept Christianity, and these converts were often viewed with suspicion and contempt by Christian authorities. Since many of the Spanish Muslims and Jews were ultimately of North African origin, they often had quite dark skin in which the blue lines of veins were not visible. Fair skin, on the other hand, was thought to be typical of the Christian nobility that now controlled Spain. *Sangre azul,* or *blue blood,* thus came to be considered to be proof of Christian ancestry—without any admixture of the Muslim or Jewish elements that were widely thought to be foreign to Spain after the Christian reconquest.

In English, the first known occurrence of the expression *blue blood* is found in *Helen,* by the Irish writer Maria Edgeworth, first published in 1834. Edgeworth's works describe the strained relationship between the wealthy landowners of Ireland and their impoverished tenants. In one chapter of *Helen*, a talented and widely admired man named Horace Churchill attends a social occasion but does not make any effort to impress or amuse his fellow guests, including a Spanish nobleman:

> Some of the neighbouring families were to dine at Clarendon Park. Mr. Churchill abhorred country neighbours and country gentlemen. Among these, however, were some not unworthy to be perceived by him; and besides these, there were some foreign officers; one in particular, from Spain, of high rank and birth, of the sangre azul, the blue blood, who have the privilege of the silken cord if they should come to be hanged. This Spaniard was a man of distinguished talent, and for him Horace might have been expected to shine out; it was his pleasure, however, this day to disappoint expectations, and to do "the dishonours of his country." He would talk only of eating....

To judge from the context in which Edgeworth uses the phrase, *blue blood* was still primarily associated with Spain and the Spanish aristocracy in the author's time.

Human blood, by the way, is never actually blue—not even in the veins of kings, queens, dukes, or duchesses. When blood is filled with oxygen in the lungs and pumped by the heart through the arteries, it has a bright red color. After the oxygen in the blood has been used up in various parts of the body, however, it turns a duller and darker red. When this dark blood returns to the heart through the veins, it appears blue or blackish when seen through the other pigments of light-colored skin.

Linguists have a special term for words and expressions like *blue blood* that are translations of words or expressions in another language—they call them *calques* or *loan translations*. (The word *calque* means "copy made by tracing" in French, and it is related to the Spanish verb *calcar*, "to trace.") Another

English expression calqued on a Spanish phrase is discussed at the entry in this book for *moment of truth*.

bodega

When doing our daily shopping, we would not go to an apothecary to find the same things that we would look for in a fashionable boutique or a bodega—as little groceries are often called in some cities in the United States. Yet all three words—*apothecary, boutique,* and *bodega*—ultimately come from the Greek term *apothēkē,* meaning "storehouse." The differences between the modern words arose as the Greek word traveled by different routes through Latin, French, and Spanish before finally reaching English.

In the days of the Roman Empire, at the eastern end of the Roman realm, Greek was the one language that everybody had in common. People from many different ethnic groups—Anatolians, Armenians, Syrians, Jews, and Egyptians in addition to Greeks and Romans—rubbed shoulders in the streets of the bustling cities on the eastern shores of the Mediterranean Sea, and they all spoke Greek to one another. Greek merchants were also known for their mercantile savvy, and for these reasons, the languages of the Mediterranean world (including Latin in ancient times and French, Italian, and Spanish in more recent days) have borrowed a good deal of their business vocabulary from Greek. The Romans, for example, borrowed the Greek word *apothēkē,* "storehouse," into Latin as *apothēca.* Then, by the addition of the Latin suffix *–ārius,* the Romans formed the new word *apothēcārius,* meaning "clerk, warehousekeeper." In medieval times, *apothēcārius* came to refer primarily to a person storing and selling medicines and drugs, and it was with this meaning that the word was borrowed into English as *apothecary.*

Also in medieval times, the Greek word *apothēkē,* "store-house," was borrowed into Old Provençal, the Romance tongue that was the main language spoken in the southern half of France at this time. In Old Provençal, *apothēkē* developed into the form *boutica,* "small shop." The Old Provençal word was then borrowed into French as *boutique,* and from French, the word at last reached English in the 1700s.

Meanwhile, as the everyday spoken Latin of Roman Spain slowly evolved into Spanish, Latin *apothēca* became *bodega,* which originally meant "wine cellar" or "wine shop" in the Spanish of Spain. Later, in the Americas, the meaning of the word was extended to include shops, like small groceries, that sell other sorts of provisions. Spanish *bodega* was used with this extended meaning in the parts of the United States where Spanish is widely spoken, and the word eventually entered American English. In this way, the ancient word *apothēkē* has continued to have a very successful life in the modern world— on a single city block in the United States, three different descendants of the Greek term may be read on the signs for the apothecary, the clothes boutique, and the corner bodega.

bonanza

On hearing the word *bonanza,* most Americans probably recall familiar stereotypes from the Old West—the hard-scrabble life of gold miners working their claim and the saloon lowlifes and gunslingers who lived off the miners' lucky strikes. The Spanish word *bonanza,* however, first arose among the Latin-speaking sailors who plied the Mediterranean in the days of the Roman Empire.

Una bonanza, in Spanish, was originally a sailor's term for a period of calm seas and gentle winds. The Spanish word has relatives in the other Romance languages, like Italian *bonaccia* and

French *bonace,* both meaning "a calm at sea." The ancestor of these Romance terms was the word **bonacia* in Vulgar Latin. (Vulgar Latin was the everyday variety of Latin spoken by the people of the late Roman Empire, including the sailors who manned the decks of the ships that crisscrossed the Mediterranean in Roman times.) **Bonacia* was created by blending the Latin adjective *bonus,* "good" (the source of Spanish *bueno,*) with the Latin noun *malacia,* "calm seas." Latin *malacia* itself was a borrowing of Greek *malakiā,* a noun derived from the adjective *malakos,* "soft, mild" and literally meaning "mildness." When speakers of Vulgar Latin heard the *mal–* in *malacia,* however, they were probably not reminded of the Greek word *malakos,* "mild," but rather of their own word *malus,* "bad" (the source of Spanish *malo*). Such associations would certainly have made no sense in the context of calm seas—why call sunny skies and favorable winds "bad times"? For this reason, the *mal–* in *malacia* was replaced by the *bon–* of *bonus,* "good."

Eventually, the word *bonanza* began to be applied in Spanish to times of peace and prosperity in general, just as the English expression *smooth sailing* can be used to describe any situation presenting favorable conditions. In particular, *bonanza* came to refer to a rich vein of gold, silver, or ore in a mine that could be worked profitably for a long time, and this was the sense in which the Spanish word first reached English. Spanish had already been spoken for a long while in California and the Southwest when these regions were part of the Spanish Empire and later Mexico, after this country won its independence from Spain. When settlers from the United States began to cross the Rocky Mountains and trickle into the sparsely settled Mexican territories, the word *bonanza* entered English as it mixed with Spanish in these regions. A mine was said to be *in bonanza* when a rich vein had been tapped and it was producing abundantly. Later on in English, *bonanza* began to be used of any period of prosperity or opportunity for gain.

bonito

In English, the word *bonito* can refer to any of several species of fish, found in various parts of the globe, that are closely related to but generally smaller than tuna. Bonitos are important food fish, and one species of bonito found in the Pacific, also called the *skipjack tuna,* is used to make one the fundamental ingredients of Japanese cuisine, the fish broth *dashi.*

The English word *bonito* comes from the Spanish name for the fish, *bonito.* Of course, this word is identical in form to the Spanish adjective *bonito,* meaning simply "pretty." In all probability, the Spanish name for the fish comes from this adjective—perhaps a *bonito* was originally just a "pretty little tuna" in Spanish.

booby trap

The word *booby* meaning "a stupid person" probably sounds a bit old-fashioned to most speakers of American English. It is not much used nowadays outside of the extremely common expression *booby trap*—a device designed to be triggered when an unsuspecting victim disturbs a seemingly harmless object. Although often used of devices equipped with bombs, a booby trap can also just be a prank designed to take advantage of a naïve person or to make someone look foolish—that is, like a *booby.* This word *booby* is ultimately the same as the English word *booby* that refers to sea birds of the genus *Sula,* tropical birds with long, graceful wings. Boobies catch fish by flying above the water until they spot some prey, whereupon they plunge at great speed beneath the waves to seize it in their beaks.

The Spanish term for the booby is *pájaro bobo*—literally, "stupid bird." The Spanish adjective *bobo* in this expression means "foolish, stupid," and *bobo* is probably the source of the English word *booby* both in the sense "a stupid person" and in the sense "bird of the genus *Sula.*" But how did the adjective *bobo* come to be applied to the sea bird?

The answer is given by Gonzalo Fernández de Oviedo y Valdés (1478–1557), a Spaniard who made several visits to the Americas in the years around 1500. Oviedo wrote an account of the Americas, *Historia general y natural de las Indias* ("General and Natural History of the Indies"), that provides a great deal of priceless information about life in the Western Hemisphere as it was in the period soon after the arrival of the Spaniards. Oviedo's work was widely read throughout Europe and helped inform Europeans about the vast, unfamiliar world across the Atlantic. Oviedo took notes about the unfamiliar flora and fauna of the Americas, and he gives us the following description of the booby (Book 14, Chapter 1):

> *Hay otras aves que se hallan en la mar océana, que se llaman* pájaros bobos. *Estos son menores que gaviotas. Tienen los pies como ánades, e pósanse en el agua cuando quieren. Hállanse, viniendo de España, cuando las naos son a ciento e menos leguas de las islas primeras destas Indias que he dicho; e viénense estas aves a los navíos e siéntanse en las gavias y entenas, e son tan bobas y esperan tanto, que las toman muchas veces a manos, con un lazo en la punta de un dardo u otra asta corta. …No son buenos de comer, e tienen mucho bulto en la pluma en respeto de su poca carne; desuéllanlos los marineros e cómenlos cocidos o asados.*

There are some other birds that are found out on the ocean that are called *pájaros bobos* [literally, "stupid birds"]. These are smaller than seagulls. They have feet like ducks', and they come to rest on the water when they please. When coming from Spain, they appear when the ships are a hundred leagues or less from the first islands [to be reached] of the Indies that I have mentioned. These birds come to the ships and sit on the topsails and the lateen sails, and they are so stupid and so slow to react that they often can be taken by hand, with a loop of rope on the end of a spear or other short pole.... They are not good to eat, and most of their bulk is just feathers when one considers how little meat they have. The sailors skin them and eat them boiled or roasted.

The Spanish word *bobo* comes from Latin *balbus,* "stammering, stuttering." Latin *balbus* itself probably originates as an onomatopoeic imitation of the sound of lips flapping, just like the English word *babble.*

breeze

Nowadays a cool breeze can be enjoyed almost anywhere in the world, but when the word *breeze* first appeared in English in the late 1500s, it originally referred to the northeast trade winds of the mid-Atlantic Ocean. The trade winds are the steady, gentle winds that blow in tropical latitudes. In the Northern Hemisphere, these winds blow from the northeast, while in the Southern Hemisphere, they blow from the southeast. The winds are caused by the flow of air from areas of permanent high pressure lying around 30° north and south towards

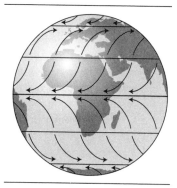

global wind patterns

areas of permanent low pressure lying around the equator: as the air flows from the north and south towards the equator, it is deflected to the west by the rotation of the Earth. This change in direction is one manifestation of the Coriolis effect, the same phenomenon that can be seen in the counterclockwise rotation of hurricanes in the Northern Hemisphere versus the clockwise rotation of cyclones in the Southern Hemisphere.

The northeasterly trade winds played an important role in spreading the Spanish language around the world in the 1500s, since the winds filled the sails of ships as they left the shores of Spain, Portugal, and West Africa and crossed the Atlantic to the Caribbean and South America. (When returning to Europe, the ships would then sail north and follow the Gulf Stream with the prevailing westerlies—the steady winds blowing from the southwest between 30° north and 60° north.) To refer to these convenient winds that brought them to their colonies, the Spanish used their word *briza*, "northeast wind." (Nowadays, this word is more often spelled *brisa* in Modern Spanish.) *Briza* also came to refer to the light wind, typical of tropical coasts, that blows in from the sea during the day and out from the land to the sea at night. Eventually the word *briza* came to refer to any light wind.

In the late 1500s, when the English began to sail the *briza* to North and South America just like the Spanish, they borrowed the Spanish name for the wind as *breeze*. For example, Sir Walter Raleigh uses the word in a work entitled *Discoverie of the large, rich, and beautiful empyre of Guiana* and dating from 1595. He describes the difficulty in sailing against the steady northeasterlies when military reasons required doing so: *By sea, if any man invade to the eastward, those to the west cannot in many months turn against the breeze and eastern wind.* Like such other words as *cargo, flotilla,* and *galleon,* the word *breeze* is thus one of the numerous Spanish maritime terms that English borrowed when it was Spain, not Britannia, that ruled the waves.

Spanish *briza* itself is related to words in the other Romance languages like Italian *brezza*, "cold wind," and French *bise*, "cold north or northeast wind." The French word, without an *r* after the *b,* is thought to be closer to the original form of the word, which probably entered Vulgar Latin or the early Romance languages from a source in the Germanic family of languages. The medieval Germanic languages, for example, have words like Old High German *bisa* meaning "northeast wind." The origin of the *r* in Spanish *briza,* however, remains one of the outstanding mysteries of Spanish etymology.

bronco

A bronco is a horse, either a mustang or a semiwild horse used to running the range freely, that has not been broken to the saddle. Cowboys often shorten the word *bronco* to just *bronc.* It takes a great deal of skill, stamina, and sheer strength to bust a bronc—that is, to make the bronc accept a rider on its back—and the elemental confrontation between cowboy and bronc is one of the great themes in the songs and stories of the Old West. When a rider tries to mount a bronc, the horse will kick, rear up on its hind legs, and do everything in its power to buck the rider off, and the sight of the furious bucking bronc makes bronc riding one of the most exciting events at modern rodeos.

Bronco comes from Spanish *bronco,* an adjective with the general meanings "rough" and "coarse." When used of a voice, *bronco* can mean "hoarse" or "harsh," and when used of a person, it can mean "surly." In Mexican Spanish, it also means "untamed" when used to describe a horse. If we take the etymology of Spanish *bronco* all the way back to Latin, however, it becomes a little complicated. *Bronco* probably comes from a Vulgar Latin word **bruncus* meaning "a knot in a tree." Knots in wood are of course natural defects that lower the value of the material and make it difficult for woodworkers to shape and carve. The Vulgar Latin word itself may have developed from a cross between two different Classical Latin words, *broccus* and *truncus. Broccus* was an adjective meaning "projecting," used of the teeth of horses, while *truncus* meant "stump of a tree"— a rough and intractable object. *Truncus* is of course the source of Spanish *tronco*, "tree trunk," and also, by way of French *tronc*, of English *trunk*.

See also *mustang.*

buckaroo

The iconic figure of the cowboy has gone by many other names in American English, including *buckaroo, cowhand, cowman, cowpoke, cowpuncher, vaquero,* and *waddy,* and two of these words, *buckaroo* and *vaquero,* come from Spanish. The territory that is now Texas, New Mexico, Arizona, Nevada, Utah, and California, as well as parts of Colorado and Wyoming, was once part of the Spanish Empire, and it became part of Mexico when Mexico achieved independence from Spain. (Mexico declared independence in 1810, but the Spanish government only recognized Mexican independence officially in 1821.) Mexico was forced to cede this vast territory to the United States after the Mexican-American War (1846–1848), but even after that, Mexicans drifted north and Americans drifted south of border, and the Spanish and English languages continued to mix.

Throughout the early 1800s, Spain and Mexico had tried to increase settlement in the sparsely populated grazing lands that are now the American Southwest. English speakers from the United States also began to venture out into the Spanish-speaking regions to the west, and it was during this period, around the late 1820s and early 1830s, that *buckaroo* and *vaquero* began to appear in English. From the point of view of etymology, *buckaroo* and *vaquero* are in fact the same word. In Spanish, *vaquero* simply means "a man who deals with cows"—that is, a cowboy. It is derived from the word *vaca,* "cow," by means of the suffix *-ero.* When *vaquero* was borrowed into English in southwest and central Texas, the pronunciation of the word stayed as close to the original Spanish pronunciation as English speakers could manage, and it kept the original Spanish spelling.

In California, however, the Spanish word *vaquero* was Anglicized to *buckaroo.* (The same change of a Spanish *o* to an English *oo* can be seen in several other English words discussed in this book, such as *calaboose* and *vamoose.*) Craig M. Carver, noted American dialectologist and author of *American Regional Dialects,* points out that the two words *vaquero* and *buckaroo* also reflect cultural differences between cattlemen in Texas and California. The Texas vaquero was typically a bachelor who hired on with different outfits, while the California buckaroo usually stayed on the same ranch where he was born or had grown up and raised his own family there.

buoyant

The word *buoyant* is probably a borrowing of Spanish *boyante,* an adjective derived from the verb *boyar,* "to float." The verb *boyar* is in turn a derivative of the noun *boya,* "buoy," and *boya* comes from a source in one of the Germanic languages and is akin to the Dutch word *boeie,* "buoy."

The English word *buoy* itself is ultimately from this Dutch word *boeie.* English may have borrowed *boeie* directly from Dutch, but the Dutch word was also borrowed into French as *bouée,* and English may have then borrowed the word from French. It is usually difficult for linguists to trace the history of maritime words like *buoy*—in the past just as in the present, the crews of trade vessels often included men from various countries, and the lively mix of languages in port cities encouraged the exchange of words. Once a maritime word caught on along the coast of one country, sailors could rapidly carry it to the four quarters of the world.

In English, the Spanish borrowing *buoyant* originally had spellings like *boyent* without the *u*, but the spelling of the adjective was soon influenced by the noun *buoy*. In Modern English, the word *buoyant* is usually pronounced (boi′ənt), but the pronunciation (bo͞o′yənt) is also heard. These pronunciations probably reflect variations in the pronunciation of the noun *buoy*. Sailors most often pronounce *buoy* as (boi), while (bo͞o′ē) is heard from landlubbers.

busker

Buskers are musicians who *busk*—that is, perform music in public places like street corners and subway station platforms, usually with their instrument cases open beside them so that people passing by can toss a little money in if they like the music. The verb *busk* has been used with this meaning since at least the mid-1800s, when it usually referred to musicians circulating around taverns and offering to play songs. But when *busk* first appeared in English in the mid-1600s, the verb was originally used of ships changing tack repeatedly. (By changing tack, or first sailing diagonally to one side of the wind and then diagonally to the other side of the wind, a ship makes a zigzag course that gradually moves it in a direction directly opposite the direction of the wind—in effect, sailing against the wind.) The verb was also used of pirate ships prowling the seas for plunder. The modern sense of the verb probably developed from the notion of musicians playing and singing while moving about in search of an audience that might toss them a few coins.

Busk is a borrowing of a French verb *busquer*, meaning not only "to search for" but also "to prowl" and "to filch." In contemporary French, this verb is nearly obsolete, but it was once quite common, especially in the expression *busquer fortune,* "to seek one's fortune." *Busquer* itself is a borrowing, perhaps of Italian *buscare,* "to search for." But ultimately both the French verb and the Italian are from Spanish *buscar,* "to search for." Spanish *buscar* itself has an unexpected etymology—it is related to other Spanish words like *bosque,* "wooded area, woods." *Buscar* probably originally meant something like "to go about looking for firewood." *Bosque* and *buscar* are ultimately part of the same family of words referring to wood and trees that also includes the English word *bush.*

cabana

In Spanish, the word *cabaña* means simply "hut" or "cabin," and can be used of the rough shelters built to house the shepherds of Spain when they drive their flocks into the mountains in the summer. In the warmer climes of Latin America, however, *cabañas* can also shelter people from the sun on the beach. English has borrowed *cabaña* as a word to refer to such shelters on a beach or near a swimming pool.

In English, the word is often spelled simply *cabana* without a tilde over the *n*. Many words from the modern European languages have been stripped of their accents and other diacritical marks in the process of being borrowed into English. Consider, for example, the French words *café* and *naïve,* which often lose the acute accent and dieresis (¨) in English and are written as *cafe* and *naive*. In all probability, *cabaña* lost its tilde in the same way. In other instances, the word entering English from another language has been respelled to capture the sound of the word without actually using the letters and diacritical marks of the original language. Such is the case of *cañon,* nowadays more often spelled *canyon* in English. The spelling *cabana* probably motivated the corresponding pronounciation (kə-băn′ə) in English, although many people use the pronunciation (kə-bän′yə), which more nearly approximates the pronunciation of Spanish *cabaña*.

The Spanish word *cabaña* descends from the Latin word *capanna*, "hut." The first occurrence of *capanna* is found only very late in the history of Latin literature, in the writings of St. Isidore of Seville (or in Spanish, *San Isidoro de Sevilla*), one of the greatest scholars of medieval times. Isidore, who lived from around AD 560 to 636, compiled a huge encyclopedic work written in Latin and treating a vast number of different subjects. In this work, Isidore uses many hundreds of Latin words not found in the earlier Latin literature dating from Roman times. These words are simply the everyday words of the Spaniards of Isidore's time that he has remade into Latin by adding the appropriate Latin grammatical endings. His work is thus a fascinating snapshot of the Latin of the early middle ages as it was starting to evolve into the modern Romance languages. Isidore remarks, for example, that countryfolk call a small house a *capanna,* the word that later shows up in Spanish as *cabaña.* (As Latin evolved into Spanish, *nn* became *ñ*. We can see another example of this change in the development of Latin *annus,* "year," which became Spanish *año*.)

It was not only the countryfolk of Spain that used the Late Latin word *capanna.* Peasants in other parts of the early medieval world must have used it as well, for it later appears—in altered form—in other Romance languages besides Spanish. For example, in the region that is now the south of France, the everyday spoken Latin of the people slowly developed into the language called Old Provençal, and *capanna* there shows up as Old Provençal *cabana.* This Old Provençal word was then borrowed into Old French as *cabane.* Later, the French word was borrowed into Middle English, where it was used to describe the simple shelters of hermits and solitary monks in the wilderness. By extension, the word came to mean "small room," and it eventually developed into Modern English *cabin.* From the point of view of history, the English words *cabaña* and *cabin* are thus the same word.

The development of the Spanish letter and sound *ñ* is discussed further at the entry for the word *tilde* in this book.

cafeteria

The English word *cafeteria* comes from the Mexican Spanish word *cafetería,* "a small, simple restaurant." The word first begins to be used in English in the 1800s. In the wider Spanish-speaking world, the original meaning of *cafetería* was "an establishment selling coffee and other beverages." Today, Spanish *cafetería* is also used to mean "a restaurant or dining area where people serve themselves or move along a series of counters to have food put on a tray," the sense that the word has in English.

Spanish *cafetería* was made from the Spanish noun *café,* meaning "coffee" (and also "café, coffeehouse") through the addition of the suffix *–ería*. This suffix makes nouns meaning "place of business," like *papelería,* "stationery shop," from *papel,* "paper," or *zapatería,* "shoe store," from *zapato,* "shoe." The suffix comes from the Latin suffix *–ārium* used to make words nouns with such meanings as "thing related to a certain other thing" or "place related to a certain activity." The Latin suffix can also be seen in English words made from Latin elements like *planetarium* and *aquarium.*

This similarity between English *coffee* and Spanish *café,* "coffee," obviously suggests that the two are related, and in fact both words descend from the Arabic word *qahwa,* "coffee." Coffee trees are native to Ethiopia, and it was from there that the habit of drinking coffee first spread to the Arab world over a thousand years ago. Most scholars believe that the Arabic word *qahwa* originally referred to wine but was transferred to the new beverage when its popularity increased. *Qahwa* was later borrowed into Turkish as *kahve,* and it was from Turkish that the word eventually reached the languages of Europe as the habit of drinking coffee began to spread west in the 1500s.

Kahve was first borrowed into Italian as *caffè,* "coffee," and the Italian word then passed into Spanish as *café.* Italian *caffè* was also borrowed by the French as *café* and the French word is the source of the English word *café.* *Café* first begins to appear in English in the very late 1700s and early 1800s as part of descriptions of France. The English word *coffee,* on the other hand, is perhaps borrowed directly from Turkish, although the Italian word may have contributed to the development of the English word as well. *Coffee* first appears in the late 1500s and early 1600s, as part of travelers' descriptions of the Ottoman Empire, the empire of the Turks with its capital at Constantinople. The Ottoman Empire was at the height of its magnificence at this time, and coffeeshops were an institution all over the Ottoman world. In 1650, a Jewish entrepreneur from Lebanon, then part of the Ottoman Empire, opened the first coffeehouse in England. It was located in Oxford, where many late-night intellectual debates were no doubt fueled by the new stimulant beverage. By 1700, thousands of coffeehouses had sprung up in London and elsewhere in England.

caiman

Caimans are tropical American reptiles that closely resemble their near relatives, the alligators. The black caiman, for instance, is the largest crocodilian living in the Amazon basin. It regularly grows be over twenty feet in length, larger than the American alligator (the largest American alligator ever recorded was nineteen feet long). There are also other, smaller species of caiman. Caimans and alligators differ from crocodiles in the shape of their head, and the lower teeth of caimans and alligators are not visible when they close their mouths, since the teeth fit into special sockets in their upper jaws. The lower teeth of crocodiles, on the other hand, project out visibly over their upper jaw when they close their mouths.

The indigenous peoples living in the tropical regions of the Americas were of course very familiar with the crocodiles, caimans, and alligators living around them. The word *caiman* ultimately comes from the language of the Caribs, one of the indigenous peoples inhabiting northern South America, the Lesser Antilles, and the eastern coast of Central America. In Carib, the word *acayuman* apparently referred to a kind of marine crocodile. The Spanish borrowed this word as *caimán,* and the Spanish word reached English in accounts of the Americas written in the 1500s. The first known use of the word *caiman* in English is found in a work from 1577 entitled *Joyfull newes out of the newe founde worlde,* a translation by the Englishman John Frampton of a treatise by the Spanish physician Nicolás Monardes called *Historia medicinal de las cosas que se traen de nuestras Indias Occidentales* ("Medical Study of the Things that are Brought from our West Indies").

The Cayman Islands, a group of three islands lying south of Cuba and northwest of Jamaica, get their name from caimans. On one early map dated to 1523, the islands are labeled the *Lagartos,* or the "Lizards" in Spanish. *Lagarto,* "lizard," was one of the words the Spanish used to describe alligators and crocodiles, fearsome animals of the Americas that were new and unfamiliar to them—the Spanish word *lagarto* is also the ancestor of the English word *alligator.* Later on, by the 1530s, the islands had come to be called the *Caymanas* or the *Islas Caimán.* In 1586, the English commander and adventurer Sir Francis Drake visited the islands and noted that the islands were full of *great serpents called Caymanas, like large lizards, which are edible.*

See also *alligator.*

calabash

A *calabash* is a bottle, bowl, ladle, or other container or utensil made from the gourd produced by the calabash vine (*Lagenaria siceraria*), a member of the same botanical family that includes cucumbers, melons, and pumpkins. The calabash vine is found all around the world in tropical regions, and it has been domesticated in both the Eastern and Western Hemispheres for many thousands of years. The gourds produced by the calabash vine are edible when small and green, but when they are allowed to mature and dry out, their outer skin and flesh becomes very hard and strong. The dried gourds can then be used to make vessels of various kinds. Calabash gourds are also used to make the body of the instrument called a *guiro*, the subject of a separate note in this book.

English *calabash* is a borrowing of the French word *calebasse*, "gourd," and *calebasse* comes from Spanish *calabaza*. Scholars have long disputed the origin of Spanish *calabaza*, but it is likely that the word is related to Spanish *galápago*, "tortoise"—both calabashes and tortoises have hard shells. *Galápago* is familiar to English speakers in the name of the Galápagos Islands off Ecuador, noted for their giant tortoises.

calaboose

That tramp was wandering about the streets one chilly evening, with a pipe in his mouth, and begging for a match; he got neither matches nor courtesy; on the contrary, a troop of bad little boys followed him around and amused themselves with nagging and annoying him.... An hour or two afterward, the man was arrested and locked up in the calaboose by the marshal— large name for a constable, but that was his title.

In this passage from chapter 56 of *Life on the Mississippi,* a work published in 1833, Mark Twain uses the word *calaboose,* an informal synonym of *jail* from the South and West of the United States. *Calaboose* is pronounced (kăl'ə-bōōs'), and nowadays people often use the word with humorous intent, conscious that it is slightly quaint or even antiquated. *Calaboose* may in fact even date back to colonial times—according to the *Dictionary of American Regional English,* the first known use of the word *calaboose* is in a work dating from 1792, which refers to the *Callibouse in Mobile.* The word *calaboose* comes from Spanish *calabozo,* literally "dungeon," and the term may thus be a legacy from the days when much of the territory around the Gulf of Mexico, including Florida and Texas, was part of the Spanish Empire.

For a word similar to *calaboose,* see *hoosegow* in this book.

caldera

A *caldera* is a large crater formed by a volcanic explosion or by the collapse of a volcanic cone. *Caldera* literally means "cauldron" in Spanish, and by extension, the Spanish word was applied to volcanic craters, in which steaming lakes of sulfurous water or even pits of bubbling lava can sometimes be seen. *Caldera* first begins to be used in English in the 1600s.

The Spanish word *caldera* comes from Latin *caldāria,* "pot for boiling," and *caldāria* is in origin the feminine of the Latin adjective *caldārius,* "suitable for warming." *Caldārius* itself derives from the Latin adjective *calidus,* "warm." *Calidus* is also the source of the Spanish word *caldo,* "broth"—from an etymological point of view, *caldo* is simply "the warm stuff."

The English word *cauldron* is in fact closely related to the Spanish word *caldera.* As the spoken Latin of Roman France developed into Old French, the adjective *caldārius* also served as the base for the Old French word *chaudron,* "cauldron." In the northern parts of France and part of the area that is now Belgium, *chaudron* had the variant form *cauderon.* (The Latin consonant *c* developed into Old French *ch* in the central part of France, including the area of Paris, but *c* simply stayed *c* before *a* in northern French dialects. The Norman Frenchmen who conquered England in 1066 spoke mostly these northern dialects, and so French words borrowed into Middle English times, after the Norman conquest, often have *c* in words like *caudron,* rather than the *ch* still seen in Modern French *chaudron.*) The northern form *cauderon* was borrowed into Middle English as *caudroun,* and *caudroun* was eventually respelled as *cauldron* under the influence of the spelling of the original Latin word *caldāria.*

Spanish *caldera* also has another—rather surprising—relative in English: *chowder.* In the dialects of central France, where Latin *c* had become *ch* before *a,* Latin *caldāria,* "pot for boiling," became *chaudière.* French Fishermen brought this word to Newfoundland, Québec, and Acadia when they settled these areas in the 1600s, and since the sea was the main source of sustenance on the coastal French colonies, the *chaudière* simmering in their kitchens usually contained cod or clams. By the middle of the 1700s, *chaudière* had spread into the kitchens of English-speaking Newfoundlanders and New Englanders, where it became their word for thick seafood soup, *chowder.*

canasta

Canasta is a card game for two to six players requiring two decks of cards. Individual players or partnerships try to score points by laying down combinations of cards that have the same rank according to the rules of the game. Canasta was invented in Montevideo, Uruguay, in 1939, and enthusiasm for the game spread like wildfire to Argentina, Chile, Peru, and Brazil in the 1940s. Canasta fever took hold of the United States in 1946 and eventually spread around the world.

The story of the invention of canasta the game is told in an article by Michael Scully that appeared in the issue of the magazine *Coronet* from February, 1953. Sr. Segundo Santos and his friend, Sr. Alberto Serrato, liked to play bridge together at the Jockey Club, a tony dinner club in Montevideo. Sr. Santos often stayed up late playing the game, and eventually it began to take a toll on his health, so he switched to rummy and cooncan, games that take less time to play. However, he found these substitutes unchallenging—they involved too much luck and not enough skill and judgment. So he and his friend set about finding a way to blend rummy and bridge, and they eventually worked out the rules of canasta and introduced it to their bridge circle.

When asked what he called the new game, Sr. Santos realized that he had not given it a name yet. His eyes fell on the *canastillo,* or small metal tray, that they had borrowed from a waiter to hold and organize the various piles of cards used when playing the game. "*Canastillo!*" he replied. Later, the name became just plain *canasta*—the word *canastillo* is the diminutive of *canasta,* "basket." *Canasta* also came to refer to the combinations of cards of the same rank that players try to lay down during the game to score points.

Spanish *canasta* comes from the Latin word for "basket," *canistrum,* which is also the source of the English word *canister.* Although *canister* nowadays most often refers to a cylindrical metal container, the word originally referred to a basket in Middle English. The Latin word *canistrum* itself is a borrowing of Greek *kanastron,* "basket." *Kanastron* is derived from the Greek word *kanna,* "cane, reed," since baskets can be woven out of reeds. Latin also borrowed this Greek word *kanna* as *canna,* and Latin *canna* is the source of the Spanish word *caña,* "reed, cane" (as in *caña de azúcar,* "sugarcane"), as well as the English word *cane* (as in *sugarcane*).

canyon

The word *canyon* begins to appear in the early 1800s as English explorers from the United States like Zebulon Pike began to push west and enter the territory in the Rocky Mountains and the Desert Southwest, all of which was part of the Spanish Empire at the time. Pike, for example, explored the area that is now Colorado ("The Red Land," in Spanish), and the mountain there called Pike's Peak is named after him. On their expeditions, Pike and the other explorers had to cross the many deep gorges cut by streams and rivers, and they picked up the local Mexican Spanish word for such gorges, *cañón,* along on the way. At first, the Spanish spelling *cañón* was quite common in English, but this was later replaced by the Anglicized *canyon.*

Scholars are divided about the origin of the Mexican Spanish word *cañón,* meaning "canyon." *Cañón* has other meanings in Spanish, such as "tube," "chimney flue," "organ pipe," "barrel of a gun," and "cannon." In these senses, *cañón* is the augmentative of the word *caña,* "stem, reed, shaft," formed with the common Spanish augmentative suffix *–ón.* (An augmentative is a word formed from another word that indicates a large—especially an excessively large—version of the thing denoted by the original word.) It is possible that the sense of Mexican Spanish *cañón,* "canyon," developed from the sense "big tube"—perhaps the original idea was that a narrow canyon channels water like a pipe.

However, the great Catalan scholar of the Spanish language, Joan Coromines i Vigneaux, has pointed out evidence suggesting that the word *cañón* meaning "canyon" has a separate origin from the word *cañón* meaning "tube." In the 16th century, the word *callón* was used in the same sense as modern *cañón*, and *cañón* may have developed from an alteration of *callón*. *Callón* itself looks like the augmentative of *calle*, "street, lane." A *cañón* was thus originally the way a river or stream took as it rushed between cliff walls.

caramel

The English word *caramel* makes it first appearance in English in the 1720s and like so many words dealing with food and fashion in English, *caramel* was borrowed from French. The French word *caramel,* however, is a borrowing of older Spanish *caramel,* nowadays *caramelo*. The Spanish word is in turn a borrowing of Portuguese *caramelo,* which means both "icicle" and "caramel." In the late 1300s and early 1400s, sugar growing and production became an important industry in the Algarve, the southernmost region of Portugal, and in Andalusia, the southernmost region of Spain. Christopher Columbus reportedly brought some cuttings of cane plants to the Americas on one of his voyages, and in the 1500s, sugar production greatly increased in the Portuguese colonies there. At the time, sugar was produced in conical piles that look like icicles, and the Portuguese therefore applied their word *caramelo,* "icicle," to the hard lumps. The word also came to refer to hardened, porous burnt sugar, such as that used in preparing Iberian desserts like caramel flan. The word spread to Spanish, French, and English and eventually came to refer to various confections with the appealing taste of burnt, or *caramelized,* sugar.

The Portuguese word *caramelo,* "icicle," comes from the Latin word *calamellus,* "little tube, little cane, little reed," and makes reference to the reedlike thinness and shape of icicles. *Calamellus* is in turn a diminutive of Latin *calumus,* "cane, reed." The Spanish word for "icicle," *carámbano,* is from an unattested Vulgar Latin word **calamulus,* another diminutive of *calamus,* "reed."

The two-syllable pronunciation of the English word *caramel* with a vowel like that of the word *car* in the first syllable, as (kär′məl)—rather than as (kăr′ə•měl) or (kăr′ə•məl)—appears to be an American innovation. Although the origin of this pronunciation is somewhat obscure, it is only in the 20th century that dictionaries and pronunciation manuals begin to notice and criticize it. Many people still disapprove of the pronunciation (kär′məl), even though it is very widespread in American English.

cargo

In the 1500s, Spanish ships sailed to and fro across the seas as part of the first truly global trade network, the vast Spanish Empire on which the sun never set. These ships not only brought goods around the word, but carried Spanish words into many languages around the world. *Buoyant, embargo, galleon,* and *cargo* are among the Spanish words in English that relate to ships and commerce.

Cargo, meaning "goods loaded onto ships," first appears in English in the 1600s. The form of the English word probably comes from the borrowing and mixture of two distinct but related Spanish words, *cargo* and *carga. Cargo* means "load" or "burden" and also "responsibility," while *carga* has the meaning "cargo" in its strict nautical sense, as well as other senses like "payload (in an aircraft)" and "electric charge." Spanish *cargo* and *carga* are in fact related to the English word *charge.* All three words are ultimately descended from the verb *carricāre,* "to load," in Late Latin, as historians call the Latin language as it was spoken and written from around AD 200 to around 700.

As the spoken Latin of Roman Spain slowly evolved into Spanish, the Late Latin verb *carricāre* developed into Spanish *cargar,* "to load." Alongside the verb *cargar,* two nouns corresponding to the verb also came into existence—*cargo* and *carga.* In the same way, as the spoken Latin of Roman Gaul slowly evolved into Old French, the verb *carricāre* became Old French *charger,* "to load," and the noun *charge,* "load, burden," also came into existence beside the verb. The Old French noun *charge* was then borrowed into Middle English and developed into the Modern English verb *charge.*

The change of *c* before *a* to *ch,* as seen in the development of Latin *carricāre* to *charger,* is a change that occurred regularly on the way from Latin to French. Knowledge of this change can help English speakers studying the Romance languages to recognize hidden connections between English words and their ancestors and cousins in the Romance languages. For example, the same correspondence between a *c* in a Spanish word like *cargo* and a *ch* in an English word of French origin like *charge* can be seen in such pairs of words as Spanish *cantar,* "to sing," and English *chant* (from French *chanter*), both ultimately from Latin *cantāre,* "to sing." In early Old French, by the way, the letter combination *ch* was pronounced as (ch). In Modern French, however, *ch* is now pronounced (sh). The *ch* in Old French *charge* was in fact still pronounced as (ch) when English borrowed the word in medieval times, along with hundreds of other vocabulary items. English *charge* thus faithfully preserves a pronunciation quite close to the original Old French pronunciation of the word.

cassava

Cassava is the large tuberous root of a shrubby tropical American plant (*Manihot esculenta*). The cassava plant produces very high yields per unit of land, and the roots themselves are very high in calories. For these reasons, cassava is now grown all around the world in tropical regions, and many people in developing countries depend on cassava for most of their calories. However, the roots of cassava must be processed in various ways before they can be eaten—they contain cyanide. In some varieties of cassava, the levels of cyanide are low enough that it can be destroyed simply by cooking, while other varieties contain much more. The roots of these varieties are usually ground up, and then the ground cassava is washed and squeezed out in several changes of water in order to remove the cyanide. The cassava is then dried and toasted to produce a kind of coarse flour or meal that can be used in a variety of ways.

The English word *cassava* comes from *casabi,* the older form of the Spanish word *casabe* meaning "bread or cake made from cassava flour." *Casabe* is itself a borrowing of the word for this sort of bread in the language of the Taíno, the indigenous people of the Bahamas and the Greater Antilles. It was the Taíno who met Christopher Columbus when he arrived in these islands in 1492, and the Spaniards subsequently helped spread the Taíno word around the world until it finally became the word for the cassava plant itself in English.

Cassava and cassava products also go by several other names in English, and these are discussed at the word *yuca.*

castanet

Castanets are percussion instruments consisting of a pair of slightly concave pieces of wood or ivory joined by a connecting cord. They are held in the palm of the hand with the cord draped over the thumb and played by clapping them together with the fingers. The basic idea of castanets is ancient—the Greeks and Romans had similar, slightly larger instruments that consisted of a pair of

flat pieces of wood held in one hand and clapped together—called *krotala* in Greek and *crotala* in Latin, these instruments were especially associated with erotic and ecstatic dancing. In more recent times, the Mediterranean tradition of castanet playing has continued most notably in the music of Spain. Among performers of flamenco music in the region of Andalusia in southern Spain, castanets are called *palillos*, literally "little sticks." The other common Spanish name for the instruments is *castañuelas*, literally "little chestnuts." Castanets are usually made from dark-colored wood and the rounded pieces therefore resemble chestnuts, or *castañas*, in Spanish.

Usually two pairs of castanets are played at the same time, and one pair is larger and shaped to produce a lower pitch than the other pair. The lower-pitched pair, called the *macho* ("male"), is held in the left hand and plays the basic rhythm, while the high-pitched pair, called the *hembra* ("female"), is held in the right hand and embellishes the rhythm with more complex patterns.

The English word *castanet* is a borrowing of Spanish *castañeta*, an older word meaning "castanet" that is also derived from *castaña*, "chestnut," but is now less common than *castañuelas*. *Castañeta* may have reached English after first passing through French as *castagnette*, rather than being borrowed directly from Spanish. *Castanet* first begins to appear in English in writings from the 1600s that describe music and dancing in Spain and the West Indies.

The Spanish word *castaña* is the direct descendant of Latin *castanea*, "chestnut." In the same way that Latin *castanea* developed into Spanish *castaña* as the everyday spoken Latin of Roman Spain evolved into Spanish, *castanea* also became Old French *chastaigne* as the spoken Latin of Roman France evolved into French. Old French *chastaigne* was borrowed into Middle English as *chesten,* and up until the 1500s, *chesten,* with no *nut* at the end, was the word for "chestnut" in English. In the 1500s, however, *chesten* began to be used less and less on its own and was followed more and more frequently by the word *nut,* until the two words eventually fused together as *chesnut.* This was the preferred spelling of the word from the middle of the 1500s until the beginning of the 1800s, when the spelling *chestnut* finally prevailed. In this way, the origin of the word *chestnut* has nothing to do with wooden chests or with the part of the body called the chest—instead, *chestnut* is the etymological cousin of *castanet.* Both words descend from Latin *castanea,* one by way of French and the other by way of Spanish.

cedilla

The cedilla (¸) is a mark placed beneath certain consonant letters to modify their pronunciation. In English, it is most often used under the letter *c,* in order to indicate that the letter *c* is pronounced as (s) when preceding an *a, o,* or *u,* as in the word *façade.* The majority of words in English that use the cedilla are of French origin, since the cedilla is an important part of the French spelling system. The cedilla is also used in other languages, such as Turkish, where the letter *ç* has the sound (ch) and the letter *ş* has the sound (sh). The word *cedilla* itself, however, comes from Spanish. Those who are familiar with the spelling system of Modern Spanish will probably wonder why this should be so—Modern Spanish does not use the cedilla.

In medieval times, however, the cedilla had an important role in the Spanish spelling system. In Old Spanish, the letter *z* represented a voiced sound (dz) similar to the last two sounds in English *bids*. The word now spelled *vecino*, meaning "neighbor," was regularly spelled *vezino* and pronounced as if spelled *vedzino* in Modern Spanish spelling. The letter *c*, when before *i* or *e*, represented the voiceless counterpart to this sound, (ts), similar to the last two sounds in English *bits*. The word *cesta*, meaning "basket," for example, was pronounced as if written *tsesta* in Modern Spanish spelling. Before the letters *a*, *o*, and *u*, however, *c* was regularly used to represent the sound (k). In order to show that *c* should be pronounced as [ts], a little *z* was added underneath the *c*, indicating that the *c* should have a pronunciation somewhat like the *z*. The words now spelled *alzo*, "I raise," and *cazar*, "to hunt," for example, were spelled *alço* and *caçar* and pronounced as if spelled *altso* and *catsar*.

The name *cedilla* refers to this small *z* put beneath the *c* to indicate the pronunciation (ts). *Cedilla* is the diminutive of *ceda*, the Spanish name of the letter *z*, now often also called *zeta* in Modern Spanish. The Old Spanish word *ceda* is from Late Latin *zēta*, the name of the Greek letter ζ, and the Greek letter ζ is in fact the source of the letter *z* in the modern Roman alphabet. *Zed*, the British name for the letter *z*, comes from Old French *zede*, which is from Late Latin *zēta* just like the Old Spanish letter named *ceda*.

As the Spanish language developed between 1400 and 1600, the sound (dz) represented by *z* and the sound (ts) represented by *c* and *ç* were merged into one. In Modern Spanish spelling, therefore, the *c* before *i* and *e* has come to have exactly the same sound as *z*. In the standard Spanish of Spain, *z* and *c* before *i* and *e* are pronounced like English (th), while in southern Spain and Latin America, they are pronounced just like (s). As the merger of Old Spanish (dz) and (ts) progressed over the centuries, there was less and less reason to use the cedilla in Spanish—the sound (th) before *a*, *o*, and *u* could simply be represented by *z*. The cedilla gradually fell from use, and orthographic reforms eliminated its use from Spanish entirely. Other medieval languages, like French and Italian, also made use of a small *z* to modify the sound of *c,* and although it is no longer used in Italian, almost every paragraph written in Modern French will usually contain a cedilla or two.

The shape of the cedilla will probably not remind many modern readers of *z,* and in fact, the cedilla derives from the variant of the letter *z* used in Visigothic Spain and in other parts of medieval Europe. After the collapse of the Roman Empire, the area that is now Spain became part of the Christian kingdom of a Germanic tribe called the Visigoths. When Muslim forces conquered the southern part of the Iberian peninsula in 711, the rest of the Visigothic kingdom fell apart into multiple small kingdoms with shifting borders, such as the kingdoms of Leon, Asturias, Castile, and Aragon. The cultural traditions of Christian Visigoths survived in these kingdoms, however, and the shape of the cedilla is based on ʒ, the usual shape of *z* in the style of handwriting used by Visigothic and medieval Spanish scribes, as well as by scribes in other parts of Europe.

cero

The cero is a kind of mackerel (*Scomberomorus regalis*) that lives in the western Atlantic Ocean. It has silvery sides, a dark blue back, and sawlike projections running along the ridges of its back and underside from its dorsal fin to its tail, like many other mackerel species. A popular fish among sports fishermen, it can grow well over a meter and a half in length and is good to eat. The name of this fish comes from the American Spanish name for the fish, *sierra. Sierra* literally means "saw"—without a doubt, the name of the fish makes reference to the sawlike appearance of its back and underside.

See also *sierra.*

chicle

Chicle, pronounced (chē′klā) or (chĭk′əl), is the principal ingredient in the traditional recipe for chewing gum. It is made from the sap of a tree native to Mexico and Central America called the sapodilla. The process of making chicle begins by scratching the bark of the sapodilla trees. A milky sap or latex then oozes out of the wounds, and it is collected in buckets much like maple sap is collected for making maple syrup. The sap is then boiled in vats, where it must be stirred constantly in order to develop the right consistency. After the preparation of the chicle, sugar and flavorings are added to make the finished chewing gum. The ancient Maya peoples were apparently the first to make chicle, and chewing chicle has been a tradition in Mexico and Central America ever since. The word *chicle* itself comes from Nahuatl, the language of the Aztec empire. In Nahuatl, chicle is called *tziktli,* meaning "sticky substance." (The group of consonants written *tz* in Nahuatl is pronounced (ts), by the way.) The Nahuatl word was adopted into Spanish as *chicle* after the Spanish conquest of Mexico, and the word first begins to appear in English in the 19th century.

By an odd twist of history, the word *chicle* probably came into the English language with the help of General Antonio López de Santa Anna, the leader of the Mexican forces that tried to suppress the rebellion of American settlers in the northern Mexican state of Texas in 1835. The clashes between Santa Anna's forces and Texan militias would eventually lead to the formation of the Republic of Texas, which later on joined the United States as the twenty-eighth state in 1845. It was Santa Anna who in 1836 captured the Alamo mission, a stronghold of the Texan militia, and put all of the Texan defenders there to death. He was eventually captured by Texan forces and signed a peace treaty recognizing the independence of Texas. Santa Anna returned to Mexico and enjoyed a great deal of political success, but he later fell from favor. He was eventually driven into exile in the United States, and in 1869 he wound up staying on Staten Island at the house of an inventor named Thomas Adams. Santa Anna suggested that his contacts in Mexico could supply Adams with plenty of chicle that might be used as a cheap substitute for rubber in boots and tires. Adams worked hard to find a way of transforming chicle into a satisfactory rubber substitute, but all of his attempts failed.

daguerreotype of Antonio López de Santa Anna

Adams knew that people in Mexico and Mesoamerica had long chewed chicle. In the United States at the time, however, various natural resins like mastic gum and spruce gum were chewed for pleasure and for freshening the breath, and chewable confections made from paraffin wax were also popular. One day in a drugstore, Adams realized that chicle would make better chewing gum than these other products, so he concocted a batch of chicle chewing gum. It sold well, and the Adams family went into the chewing gum business in 1871. Chicle-based gum soon became the most common kind of gum.

Not surprisingly, the trademark *Chiclets* for the popular brand of candy-coated gum comes from the word *chicle*. Chiclets are just one of the products invented by the team of gum-making brothers extraordinaire, Frank and Henry Fleer, who went into the chicle gum business in the 1880s. Frank developed the first bubblegum in 1906, while Henry, after perfecting the process of coating chicle gum with candy, first marketed Chiclets in 1910. Nowadays, however, most commerical chewing gum is made not from chicle, but from artificial gum bases manufactured from petroleum. Nevertheless, some traditional candy-makers still market all-natural chicle gum, and chicle production is currently being encouraged as a way for Mexicans and Central Americans to use the resources of their rainforests in a way that that both preserves the environment and benefits the local population.

chili

Why are hot peppers called *chilies* in English, when they are the hottest of spices and not *chilly* at all? *Chili* comes from Spanish *chile,* and Spanish *chile* in turn comes from Nahuatl *chīlli,* "chili." (In English, the word *chili* is also the short form of the name of the Tex-Mex dish *chili con carne,* a slight modification of Spanish *chile con carne,* literally "chili with meat.") Although chilies are used extensively in different styles of cooking around the world today—chilies are the source of heat in the cuisine of Korea, Indonesia, Thailand, and India, to name but a few countries—chilies are native to the Americas and were unknown to the rest of the world until the time of Christopher Columbus.

When he set sail to the west in 1492, Columbus hoped to find a direct trade route to Asia, the source of silk and spices. Ever since the days of the Greeks and Romans, Europeans had eagerly imported Asian spices like pepper, cloves, and cinnamon, despite the fact that they were very expensive. The spices were brought westward from islands of Southeast Asia to Europe by complicated trade routes over land and sea, and on the way, they passed through the hands of middlemen who jacked up the price at every step. The better to sustain these high prices, traders even told fantastic stories about the ultimate origin of their wares—cinnamon, for example, was said to come from the nests of giant birds who gathered it from distant lands.

In order to get around these middlemen, Columbus hoped to reach the Spice Islands of Southeast Asia by sailing west—he did not know, of course, that whole continents stood in his way. When he reached the Americas and visited the islands now called the West Indies, Columbus found that the people living there seasoned their food with the extremely hot, hollow, pod-like fruits of a certain plant. The Taíno people of the West Indies called this plant *ají* and today, *ají* is still the word for "chili" in many varieties of Spanish in the West Indies and Central America. The spicy *ají* helped convince Columbus that he had in fact reached Asia by sailing west, and when he returned to Spain, he took some of this new sort of pepper back in order to bolster his claim that he had found a western passage to Asia. Eventually the chili pepper plant would spread from the Americas to the rest of the world, carried by Portuguese and Spanish trade routes.

Chili peppers and words for them are also discussed at the entry for *pimiento* in this book.

chocolate

On his fourth voyage to the Americas, lasting from 1502 to 1504, Christopher Columbus sailed past the islands of the Caribbean to reach the mainland of Central America. Off the coast of what is now Honduras, Columbus's men seized a large canoe from one of the local peoples. It was filled with Mesoamerican trade goods, and when the local people unloaded the canoe for them, Columbus's men were surprised at the care they took in handling what seemed like mere beans. Little did they know that they were the first Europeans to learn of the existence of cacao beans and chocolate.

At the time of the arrival of Europeans in the Americas, the various civilizations of Mesoamerica had been preparing and eating the beanlike seeds of the cacao tree for many centuries. One of the most popular ways of processing and serving cacao beans was as an unsweetened frothy drink flavored with vanilla and chilies. Pedro Mártir, the early chronicler of the voyages of Columbus and the conquest of Hernán Cortés, wrote down the early impressions that cacao beans and chocolate made on the Spaniards: *By itself, it is not worth eating, because it is somewhat bitter, although it is soft like the nutmeat of an almond, but grinding it up it is kept as a powder, and throwing some of that powder in water and stirring it up a little, one obtains a drink fit for a king.* The indigenous peoples of Mexico and Mesoamerica were so fond of this beverage that they even came to use cacao beans as money. As Pedro Mártir says, *Oh what a fortunate kind of money that offers to humankind a delicious and useful beverage, and that frees its possessors from the hellish scourge of avarice, since it cannot be buried or kept for a long time!*

In Nahuatl, the language of the Aztec Empire, the word for the beverage made from the ground cacao seeds has two variant forms, *chocolātl* and *chicolātl*. The form *chicolātl* is typical of eastern Nahuatl dialects, and the linguists Karen Dakin and Søren Wichmann have recently proposed that *chicolātl* is the original form of the word. *Chicolātl* itself looks like a compound of the Nahuatl words *chicolli*, "long hooked stick (such as used for cutting fruit)" and *ātl*, "water." In Aztec times, the *chicolātl* beverage was stirred into a froth by means of a special stick or beater with elaborate carvings or a bundle of sticks at the end. The person preparing the *chicolātl* would the hold the handle of the stick upright in the container by pressing it between the palms of the hands, and the stick would be spun by rubbing the palms back and forth. The modern people of Mexico and Central America still froth *chicolātl* in this traditional way today. Words related to Nahuatl *chicolli* mean "stirring stick" in other languages belonging to the Uto-Aztecan language family like Nahuatl. The Nahuatl word *chicolli* may have been used to describe the traditional beating stick at some time in the past, and the compound *chicolātl* would thus originally have meant "beater-water."

In the past, many scholars thought that the Nahuatl word *chocolātl* was a compound of Nahuatl *xococ,* "bitter," and *ātl,* "water." The original Mesoamerican and Aztec drink was unsweetened, and would have been as bitter as baking chocolate. However, there is no other example of *x,* pronounced (sh) in Nahuatl, changing into *ch,* as the hypothetical derivation of *chocolātl* from *xococ* would require. The lack of such parallel examples makes this derivation extremely doubtful.

The Spanish borrowed *chocolātl* (rather than the original form *chicolātl*) as *chocolate,* pronounced (chō-kō-lä'tä). The Spanish version of chocolate, as consumed in Europe, was originally a bitter beverage just like the indigenous American drink, but sometime in the late 1500s the chili peppers were replaced by sugar. The popularity of *chocolate* gradually spread from Spain to the rest of Europe, although it remained an expensive drink for the upper classes at first. When the word *chocolate* begins to appear in English in the very early 1600s, it still referred to the chocolate beverage modeled on the ancient way of consuming chocolate in the Americas—not to solid chocolate.

Nowadays, of course, when we hear the English word *chocolate,* we probably think of solid chocolate molded into bars and other shapes rather than a beverage. Solid chocolate is actually the result of a complicated process in which the components of the cacao bean are separated and then put together again in varying proportions, and this process was only perfected in the 1800s. In order to make solid chocolate, pure cocoa butter is first extracted from ground roasted cacao beans. The cocoa butter is then mixed with sugar, some finely ground roasted cacao beans, and vanilla. The mixture then undergoes a lengthy grinding process called *conching,* that reduces the cocoa and sugar particles in the cocoa butter to an extremely small size. *Conching* helps improve the texture and flavor of the chocolate. The mixture is then heated and cooled repeatedly in carefully controlled stages in a process called *tempering.* Tempering makes sure that the microscopic masses or crystals of cocoa butter in the chocolate are of the right size, and this gives solid chocolate its particular physical properties—it holds its shape and snaps satisfyingly when broken, but melts just below human body temperature when put in the mouth. Solid chocolate like this still goes by the name *chocolate,* even though the ancient speakers of Nahuatl would hardly recognize their *chocolātl* beverage in it.

cigar

The indigenous peoples of the Americas have used tobacco for thousands of years, and the words *cigar* and *cigarette* probably have their ultimate origin in an indigenous American language—in this case, one of the Mayan languages of Central America and southern Mexico. Although the Maya are often discussed together as a group, there is actually a great deal of diversity among the Maya peoples. This diversity already existed during the climax of classical Mayan civilization, the age of the huge city-states and temple complexes that lasted from around AD 200 to around 900. The descendants of the temple builders still live in the same region today, and currently about six million people speak Mayan languages.

In the Yucatec Maya language of southern Mexico, the word for tobacco is *may,* but in the Quiché Mayan language of Guatemala, the word for tobacco is *sīk'.* (The symbol *k'* represents a consonant that sounds to English speakers like a *k* pronounced with a great deal of force.) In the Q'eqchi' Mayan language of Guatemala and Belize, the verb *sik'ar* means "to smoke." The Spanish word *cigarro,* "cigar," probably comes from a source akin to these words in one or more of the Mayan languages. From Spanish, the word passed into the other languages of Europe, and it begins to enter English in the 1700s, at first in the spelling *seegar.*

Cigarro was also borrowed into French as *cigare,* and in the 1830s, the word *cigarette,* literally "little cigar," begins to appear in French as a designation for small rolls of paper containing shredded tobacco. According to the *Oxford English Dictionary,* the earliest known mention of cigarettes in English dates from a few years later. In a work from 1842 entitled *Pilgrimage to Auvergne,* the popular travel writer Louisa S. Costello made the following comment about the fashion for cigarettes in France: *The habit of smoking cigarettes...is quite* la grande mode [the height of fashion] *of late with certain French ladies.* The usual Spanish word for "cigarette," however, is *cigarrillo. Cigarrillo* literally means "little cigar" and is the diminutive of *cigarro* made with the suffix *–illo.* English has borrowed *cigarillo* specifically as a designation for a small slender cigar. Such small cigars are often called *cigarritos* in Spanish.

ciguatera

Ciguatera is poisoning caused by eating fish and other marine animals whose flesh is contaminated with a chemical (called *ciguatoxin*). Although incidents of ciguatera are found worldwide in warm seas, in the Americas ciguatera is only common in the Caribbean region. The effects of ciguatera include not only nausea and vomiting but also a range of neurological problems like headaches, extreme fatigue, memory loss, and hallucinations. Ciguatoxin is produced by certain species of algae, and it is concentrated in the flesh of marine animals that eat the algae. Larger animals then eat the animals that ate the algae, and with every step up in the food chain, the poison becomes ever more concentrated. Ciguatera is most often caused by eating large predatory fishes like barracuda.

The word for this ailment comes from American Spanish *ciguatera,* which is in turn derived from *ciguato,* the word for a person suffering from such poisoning. (In some varieties of American Spanish, *ciguato* can also be used as a slang word meaning "foolish person" or "idiot," reflecting the mentally debilitating effects of ciguatoxin poisoning.) *Ciguato* is in turn derived from the American Spanish word *cigua,* "sea-snail." *Cigua* was perhaps borrowed from one of the indigenous languages that were originally spoken in the Antilles and the rest of the Caribbean region and that became extinct as the islands were colonized by Spain.

cilantro

In English, a distinction is often made between *coriander,* the seeds of the coriander plant used in pickling spice, curries, and other spice mixtures, and *cilantro,* the fresh, fragrant leaves of the same plant that are an essential ingredient in the cuisine of many regions of Latin America, as well as of India, China, and Southeast Asia. In Spanish, however, *cilantro* means simply "coriander"—the plant, its seeds, and its frilly, aromatic leaves.

The seeds and leaves of coriander have completely different flavors. The seeds have long had a place in the various cooking styles of Europe—coriander is native to Southwest Asia and North Africa. The plant and seeds have gone by the name *coriandre* or *coriander* since medieval times in England, but since the leaves were seldom if ever used in English cookery, there was no need for a separate name for them.

However, in the 20th century, even people with no Latin American heritage began to acquire a taste for fresh coriander leaves as the popularity of Mexican and Caribbean food spread throughout the United States. The word *cilantro* was adopted from Spanish into American English at this time and is often used with the specific meaning "fresh coriander leaves."

Cilantro and *coriander* are in fact the same word, from an etymological point of view. English *coriander* comes from French *coriandre,* which itself comes from Latin *coriandrum.* The Latin word, like so many other Latin words for herbs and foods, is a borrowing from Greek, and the Greek word *koriandron* is probably borrowed from some language of the Mediterranean region that has long since become extinct. In Spanish, the Latin word *coriandrum* at first became Spanish *culantro,* a form of the word that is still used today. A variant *cilantro* developed from *culantro,* and this is perhaps the more common form of the word for "coriander" in Spanish today.

In Latin America, *culantro* is often used as a name for another herb, which has the scientific name *Eryngium foetidum.* (The scientific name of coriander is *Coriandrum sativa.*) Cilantro and culantro resemble each other closely in scent and flavor—although culantro is stronger—and both plants belong to the botanical family Apiaceae, the same family that includes parsley, dill, anise, cumin, caraway, fennel, carrots, parsnips, and celery. Culantro, however, has spearlike, serrated leaves that are a few inches long, completely unlike the fine, frilly leaves of coriander, which are borne in threes. Although *Eryngium foetidum* is not yet well known in the English-speaking world, it is often seen in supermarkets catering to Latin Americans and Southeast Asians, where it is sold under such names as *long coriander* as well as *culantro.*

cockroach

If asked to guess the origin of the word *cockroach,* many English speakers might at first divide it into *cock* and *roach,* especially since everyone knows *roach* as another way of saying *cockroach.* Is a cockroach then just a big and dominating roach, like a rooster among hens?

In fact, the word *cockroach* has a far different origin. It is a borrowing of the Spanish word *cucaracha,* "cockroach." There are many species of cockroach, but they were confined to warm climates before the invention of central heating. The great expansion of Portuguese and Spanish maritime trade in the 1400s and early 1500s probably did not just raise awareness of the existence of cockroaches among Europeans—the ships probably helped begin the spread of the cockroaches themselves. The species called the American cockroach is now 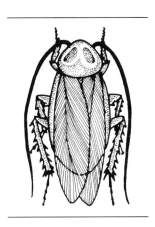 thought to have originated in Africa, but it had so thoroughly colonized the Americas that it was thought to be native there by the time scientists got around to classifying cockroach species. The scientific name of the American cockroach is even *Periplaneta americana,* "the American one that wanders around."

An early form of the word *cockroach* in English is found in the writings of Captain John Smith, the English adventurer who helped found the British colony of Virginia in 1607. In a work first published in 1624, Smith describes the insects on the islands of Bermuda:

Musketas and Flies are also too busie, with a certaine India Bug, called by the Spaniards a Cacarootch, the which creeping into Chests they eat and defile with their ill-sented dung.

Smith's spelling of the Spanish word is perhaps influenced by *caca*, the word for "excrement" in the baby-talk of many European languages, including Spanish and English. Later the form taken by the Spanish word *cucaracha* in English was influenced by another word, *cock*, "rooster," and the modern form *cockroach* was born. (This phenomenon, the alteration of a word resulting from a mistaken assumption about its meaning, is called *folk etymology* by linguists.) The Spanish word *cucaracha* has nothing to do with roosters, however. It is thought to be related to *cuca*, a word for a common kind of caterpillar in Spain.

The Spanish word *cucaracha* is also familiar to the English-speaking world as the title of the Mexican popular song *La cucaracha*. The origin of *La cucaracha* is disputed, but it dates from at least the time of the Mexican Revolution, a period of great turmoil in Mexico that began in 1910 and eventually, in 1917, resulted in the adoption of the current Mexican constitution guaranteeing the rights of the working class and rural populations. *La cucaracha* belongs to the traditional Mexican genre called the *corrido*, and over the years, many different verses have been sung to the well-known melody of the song. One of the most famous stanzas that has been set to the music is the following:

La cucaracha, la cucaracha
Ya no puede caminar
Porque no tiene, porque le falta
Marihuana que fumar.

The cockroach, the cockroach
It can't walk anymore
'Cause it doesn't have, 'cause it's got no
Marijuana to smoke.

Supposedly, this stanza refers to Victoriano Huerta Márquez, a harsh military dictator who proclaimed himself president of Mexico and was bitterly opposed by Mexican revolutionary forces under such leaders as Emiliano Zapata and Pancho Villa. Huerta was a drunkard and apparently a heavy smoker of marijuana as well, and he is said to have walked unsteadily. Even today, Huerta is despised in Mexico and often referred to as *el Chacal,* "the Jackal," not *la Cucaracha.*

cocoa

Chocolate and cocoa powder are made from the seeds (or "beans") of the cacao tree, whose scientific name is *Theobroma cacao.* (*Theobroma* means "food (*brōma*) of the gods (*theoi*)" in Greek.) The cacao tree grows wild in the rainforests of Central and South America, although nowadays West Africa is the largest producer of cacao beans. The cacao tree depends on bats for the pollination of its flowers, and so its flowers hang down from the trunk and lower limbs of the tree, where it is easier for bats to land, rather than from the ends of the smaller branches. The flowers develop into bright orange-red, oblong fruits that measure up to a foot in length and hang directly off the trunk and lower branches. The fruit has an outer layer of pulp that is sour-sweet and good to eat, and within this layer of pulp are the seeds that are the raw material for chocolate and cocoa powder.

In order to produce chocolate and cocoa powder, the seeds are removed from the fruit and put in bins where they are fermented for up to a week or more—it is this fermentation process that produces the unique flavor and aroma of chocolate. The seeds are then dried and roasted and used to make all the various chocolate and cocoa products.

The English word *cacao* comes from Spanish, and the

Spanish word *cacao* is a borrowing of Nahuatl *cacahuatl,* "cacao." Nahuatl was the language of the Aztec empire, and it is still spoken by well over a million people in Mexico today. Like many of the other indigenous peoples of Central America and southern Mexico at the time of the arrival of the Spaniards in the Americas, the speakers of Nahuatl drank a beverage made from ground cacao seeds and water. The recipe for the beverage also included such ingredients as chilies, vanilla pods, and the oily ground seeds of the kapok tree—but no sugar, so it was quite bitter. In Nahuatl, this beverage was called *chocolātl,* a word unrelated to *cacahuatl.* (The ending *–tl* is a suffix frequently added to nouns under certain grammatical circumstances in Nahuatl; it's the same *–tl* at the end of the word *Nahuatl* itself.) *Chocolātl* was eventually borrowed into Spanish as *chocolate,* the ancestor of the English word *chocolate* and the subject of a separate entry in this book.

The English word *cocoa* is an alteration of *cacao* under the influence of a similar-sounding English word *coco,* "coconut." As the unfamiliar products of tropical Asia and America began to arrive in Europe in the late 1500s and 1600s, the two words would have occurred in similar contexts. Nowadays, the English word *coco* is for the most part only found in such combinations as *coco palm* and *coconut* rather than used alone. People probably stopped using *coco* alone in order to prevent the confusion of *coco* with *cocoa* after the pronunciation of *cacao* was altered to *cocoa.* The word *coconut* is also the subject of a separate entry in this book.

coconut

Coconut palms grow in tropical coastal areas around the world. They are probably native to the Pacific region, but botanists are unsure exactly where the plant may have originated—coconuts float, and they can germinate even after long exposure to salt water. Therefore, if a coconut falls from a palm growing on a beach and is washed by the waves out to sea, it can be carried to distant shores and still sprout into a new tree. The Portuguese were apparently the first Europeans to encounter coconuts as they sailed around Africa to India, and when they came upon a coconut bobbing in the water beside their ship or lying on a beach, they called it a *coco*. The word *coco* was originally the name for a kind of goblin or bogeyman that had an empty gourd for a head. Masks representing the face of this creature were used to frighten children. When seen from the right direction, the three depressions or holes in the shell of a coconut form a crude image of a face, and it was this that inspired the Portuguese to give the name *coco* to the coconut.

The Spanish word equivalent to Portuguese *coco*, "bogeyman," is also spelled *coco*, and the Spanish, too, began calling coconuts *cocos*. The word *coco* begins to appear in English in the middle of the 1500s, and the first known occurrence is in a translation of a Spanish work about the plants and foods of the Americas. Nowadays, the English word *coco* is more often found in the combinations *coconut* and *coco palm* than by itself, probably to avoid confusion with the word *cocoa*, as in *hot cocoa* or *cocoa powder*. In fact, the original form of the word *cocoa* is *cacao*, and the transformation of *cacao* into *cocoa* reflects the influence of the word *coco*. The relationship between *coco* and *cocoa* is discussed further at the entry in this book for the word *cocoa*.

compliment

English has two words pronounced (kŏm′plə-mənt). One, *complement*, means "something that completes or brings to perfection" as a noun and "to complete or bring to perfection" as a verb (as in such sentences as *His tie complemented his suit beautifully*). The other, *compliment*, means "expression of admiration" as a noun and "to express admiration" as a verb (as in such sentences as *She complimented him on his excellent taste*). When writing these two words, many English speakers probably hesitate for a moment about their proper spelling, and they may wonder if the words are related. And if they are related, how did one come to be spelled with an *e* and the other with an *i*?

From the etymological point of view, *complement* and *compliment* are in fact the same word. They both descend from Latin *complēmentum*, "something that completes." The Latin word was borrowed into Old French as *complement* (now Modern French *complément*), and then, from both Latin and French, the word entered Middle English in the late 1300s with the spelling *complement*. The spelling of the word in the sense "something that completes" has been the same ever since.

Meanwhile, in Spain, the Latin word *complēmentum* became the Old Spanish word *cumplimiento*, "something that completes" or "fulfillment of a requirement." By extension, the Old Spanish word was also used more specifically to describe something, like a flowery phrase of admiration, that lends a sense of completeness to a ceremony or to a formal expression of courtesy—something, in short, that completes a protocol. As Spain was enriched by her expanding empire in the 1500s and early 1600s and her power and prestige increased in the rest of Europe, the Spanish word *cumplimiento* was carried to the rest of Europe along with the dignified formality characteristic of the Spanish nobility. *Cumplimiento*, "formal expression of admiration," became *complimento* in Italian and *compliment* (with an *i*) in French. Under the influence of *cumplimiento* and its Italian and French descendants, the English word *complement* (with an *e*) also came to be used with such senses as "something that completes the requirements of a ceremony or expression of reverence" and "expression of admiration." However, the spelling of the French word *compliment* and its European cousins also influenced the spelling of the English word *complement,* until *compliment* became the only acceptable modern spelling of the word in the sense "expression of admiration." In this way, *complement* and *compliment* came to be thought of as two words, one with the older spelling *complement* more like the original Latin word, and one with another spelling *compliment* ultimately reflecting Spanish influence.

Modern Spanish, too, has a similar pair of words, *cumplimiento* and *complemento.* The noun *cumplimiento* means "fulfilment, carrying out an order," and is the direct descendant of Old Spanish *cumplimiento* (ultimately from Latin *complēmentum,* of course). *Complemento,* on the other hand, means simply "complement" and is a direct borrowing of the Latin word *complēmentum* into Spanish.

condor

Two living species of birds are called *condor* in English, the Andean condor (*Vultur gryphus*) and the California condor (*Gymnogyps californianus*). With wingspans of about three meters (ten feet), the Andean condor is the largest flying land bird in the Western Hemisphere. (Some sea birds, the albatrosses, have longer wingspans than the Andean condor, however.) The Andean condor lives throughout the Andes mountain range in South America. The California condor is only slightly smaller than the Andean condor, and it is one of the largest flying birds in North America. The California condor once soared above Colorado, Idaho, Montana, Nevada, and Wyoming, as well as northern Mexico and Alberta in Canada, but recently its range has been drastically reduced to California, Arizona, and Utah.

Both species of condor have dull black plumage with variable amounts of white and a featherless head and neck. They feed mostly on carrion, which they locate by soaring on currents of warm air that rise from the earth when it is heated by the sun. The wings of condors are exquisitely adapted to catch these thermal updrafts, and they can soar for hours without a single flap of their wings. Just like modern observers lucky enough to see the huge birds today, the ancient indigenous peoples of California and the Andes must have stood in awe of the magnificent condor when they looked up and saw it circling gracefully high above the earth, and condors play an important part in the mythology and traditional symbolism of many indigenous peoples. At Machu Picchu in Peru, for example, the Inca created a temple out of a natural rock formation resembling a condor with outspread wings.

The English word *condor* ultimately derives from the name of the Andean condor in Quechua, the language of the Inca Empire that is still spoken by millions of people in the Andean region today. The Quechua word for the condor is *kuntur,* and this word was borrowed into Spanish as *cóndor.* In the very early 1600s, the Spanish word first begins to appear in English-language accounts of the animals of South America.

Today, the Andean condor is an endangered species, while the California condor hovers perilously close to the brink of extinction. Although the primary food of Andean condors is carrion, they will occasionally take young or sick animals, and this has given them a bad reputation among ranchers. California condors apparently feed exclusively on carrion. But in the past, if ranchers came across a condor feeding on the carcass of a sheep, they often assumed that the condor had killed it—when in fact the animal had died of other causes or had been killed by coyotes. Condors were therefore hunted by ranchers as a threat to livestock. Both condor species also suffer from loss of habitat and poisoning by pesticides. They are also poisoned by the lead in the shotgun shot that they swallow when they feed on the carcasses of animals left by human hunters. In the 1980s, the population of California condors fell to just twenty-two individuals, but intensive breeding programs has brought their numbers up to around three hundred.

Before the devastating reduction of the population of the California condor, its range once included Baja California in Mexico. The birds have recently been reintroduced to the region, and there are now more than a dozen California condors circling majestically in the Mexican sky.

conga

The conga is a dance of Cuban origin in which the dancers form a long, winding line. The name for the dance come from Spanish, and in Spanish as in English, the word *congas* can also refer to the drums that are typically used in conga music.

The Spanish word *conga* is short for *danza conga,* literally "dance from the Congo." The Spanish adjective *congo,* of which *conga* is the feminine form, comes from *kongo,* the word that means "the Kongo language and people" in the Kongo language. Kongo is the language of a Bantu people living along the lower Congo River in central Africa, and it is also a lingua franca in the southern Republic of the Congo, in the western Democratic Republic of the Congo, and in northern Angola.

coypu

Coypu, pronounced (koi′poō), is another name for the nutria, an aquatic rodent of South America that has become quite common—even to the point of being a plague—in the southern part of the United States. The word *coypu* comes from American

Spanish *coipú,* a word also found in the form *coipo.* Both forms of the word are from Mapudungun *kóypu.* Mapudungun is the language of the Mapuche people, the indigenous people of south and central Chile and southern Argentina. In Mapudungun, by the way, the word *mapudungun* itself is made up of the words *mapu,* "land," and *dungun,* "speech," while the word *mapuche* is made up of *mapu,* "land," and *che,* "people." *Mapuche* thus literally means "the People of the Land."

When the Spaniards first arrived in the Western Hemisphere, they encountered many plants and animals for which there was no name is Spanish. Sometimes they borrowed new words from the people who had long inhabited the lands that were new to the Spaniards. *Coipú* or *coipo* is an example of such borrowing from the languages native to South America. In other cases, however, the Spaniards reapplied a native Spanish word to the new animal or plant. This was also true in the case of the coypu, since the animal is also called a *nutria* in some parts of Argentina and elsewhere. *Nutria* is the Spanish word for otter. The further history of the Spanish word *nutria* is discussed at the note for *nutria* in this book.

crusade

In 1095, the Byzantine emperor Alexius I sent a plea for help to the leaders of western Europe—the Muslim forces of the Seljuk Turks were chipping away at his empire, which was located in what is now Turkey with its capital at Constantinople and stood as the only territory in the Near East still under Christian rule. Later that year, in response to Alexius's request, Pope Urban II delivered a stirring sermon to an assembly of notables at Clermont, France, and launched the first of the Crusades, a series of European military campaigns dedicated to recapturing Jerusalem and the rest of the Holy Land from Muslim control.

Urban called upon the assembly to take up the sign of the cross and attack the Muslim rulers of the Near East. Urban thought of this expedition as a kind of pilgrimage—albeit one with military purpose.

Urban commanded the pilgrims to wear the sign of the cross on their forehead or breast as they set out for the Holy Land, and after accomplishing their purpose, they were to wear the cross on their back as they returned. The pope recalled the instructions that Jesus gave to the Apostles as he sent them out to preach among the Jews (Matthew 10:38): *And he that taketh not his cross, and followeth after me, is not worthy of me.*

In 1099, the forces of the First Crusade captured Jerusalem and set up a European-ruled Christian kingdom in the region of the city, and over the course of several more Crusades, other Christian kingdoms were established in other areas of the Near East. By 1291, however, the Europeans had lost all of the territory that they captured from the Muslims. In this sense, the Crusades were a failure, but they helped familiarize Europe with the artistic splendor and scientific advances of Islamic civilization at the time.

During these two centuries of European military activity in the Near East, Crusaders from all different classes undertook the vow to recapture and protect Jerusalem, and they wore the sign of the cross as a symbol of their obligation. A few even went so far as to have the cross branded on their forehead as a reminder of their vow. The participants in the campaigns eventually came to be known in Latin as *crucesignātī*, "marked with the sign of the cross," from the Latin word for "cross," *crux*. In the various European languages, the campaigns also got their name from the sign of the cross, ultimately derived from Latin *crux*. In Spanish, for example, the word for "cross" is *cruz*, and the campaigns were called *cruzadas*, while in French, the word for "cross" is *croix*, and the campaigns were called *croisades*. The English word *crusade* ultimately derives from a crossing of

Spanish *cruzada* with French *croisade* and similar forms in Portuguese, Provençal, and Italian.

Nowadays, the term *crusade* is most often heard in the metaphorical sense, "a vigorous campaign for a cause." The *Oxford English Dictionary* notes an early use of this extended sense of *crusade* in the writings of Thomas Jefferson, who enjoins the following task upon his reader: *Preach, my dear Sir, a crusade against ignorance.*

demarcation

In the years leading up to 1492, Spain and Portugal were rivals in the struggle for control of Africa as their ships began to work their way down the African coast and the territories there began to fall under their influence. Portuguese mariners like Bartolomeu Dias, who rounded the Cape of Good Hope in 1488, were especially adventurous in their exploration of the African coast. The Portuguese hoped ultimately to reach India by sailing around Africa—if they did so, they could bypass the slow overland trade routes to India through the Mediterranean and Arabia and gain direct access to Asian goods. When Columbus's ships reached the Americas in 1492, the rivalry between Portugal and Spain became even worse—it was widely believed that Columbus had reached Asia by sailing west and had thereby established a Spanish claim to India. The only international authority that the two countries could turn to in order to solve the problem at the time was the papacy. Luckily for Spain, Alexander VI, the pope at this time, was from Valencia. In a series of bulls (papal proclamations), Alexander decreed that all lands west of a line running 100 leagues (about 260 miles) west of the Azores and Cape Verde Islands—the line lay approximately at 38° west—would belong to Spain. The notion that the people already living in the lands covered by this decree might have their own valid claim to the territory—and the legimate right to live there in peace—does not seem to have crossed Alexander's mind.

This declaration allowed Spain to claim the entirety of India, defeating the Portuguese purpose, but in 1494, Portugal and Spain met at the Spanish city of Tordesillas to renegotiate the boundary. The Treaty of Tordesillas set the boundary between Spanish and Portuguese territory at 46° 37' west. Portugal thereby received a large chunk of what is now Brazil, and later Portugal extended its portion of South America even further west into Spanish territory. Furthermore, the Treaty of Zaragoza, signed in 1529, allowed Portugal to claim all of Asia west of a line running around 145° east, including India and what is now Indonesia, China, and Japan. However, the treaty also left the entire Pacific to Spain.

The line agreed upon in the Treaty of Tordesillas eventually came to be known as the *línea de demarcación*, "line of delimitation," in Spanish, from the Spanish verb *demarcar*, "to delimit, mark boundaries." (In Portuguese, too, the line is still often called the *linha de demarcação*.) Because of the far-reaching significance of the *línea de demarcación*, the phrase was eventually translated into English as *line of demarcation*. The Spanish word *demarcación* was rendered into English as *demarcation*, and a new word entered the English language. *Line of demarcation* begins to appear in the 1700s, at first only in reference to the line set in the Treaty of Tordesillas. Later, however, *demarcation* was extended to describe other sorts of limits. The English verb *demarcate*, a back-formation from *demarcation*, begins to appear in the 1800s.

The resemblance between the Spanish verb *demarcar*, "to delimit," and English words like *mark* and *marker* (as in *boundary marker*) is no accident. *Demarcar* is derived from the Spanish verb *marcar*, "to mark," and scholars think that *marcar* is a borrowing of Italian *marcare*. Italian *marcare* in turn comes from a word in a Germanic language, and the same

Germanic word that appears in Italian *marcare* appears in Old English as *mearc,* "mark," the ancestor of Modern English *mark.*

divi-divi

The divi-divi is a tree native to southern Mexico, Central America, the northern part of South America, and the Antilles Islands. Its charming name is pronounced (dĭv′ē-dĭv′ē). The divi-divi is well known for growing in relatively dry, windswept shoreline environments, where the constant winds cause it to grow in contorted shapes. The island of Aruba off the coast of Venezuela is especially famed for its twisted, wind-shaped divi-divi trees. Besides providing interesting scenery in the Caribbean region, the seed-pods are an important source of tannin for tanning leather.

The English word *divi-divi* comes from American Spanish *dividivi,* but the tree is also known by several other names in different regions of the Spanish-speaking world, such as *cascalote* and *huatapana* (the most common name in Aruba). American Spanish *dividivi* is borrowed from one of the languages of the Carib language family, a language family including many of the indigenous languages of northern South America, the Lesser Antilles, and the eastern coast of Central America. A large number of the Carib languages became extinct during the European colonization of the Americas, and often only very incomplete written records of these languages have survived. Therefore, even though scholars may be confident that a word is of Carib origin, they may find it difficult to determine the exact Carib language from which it came.

El Niño

Climatologists use the term *El Niño* to describe a warming of the surface water of the eastern and central Pacific Ocean that occurs at irregular intervals of about four to twelve years and causes unusual global weather patterns. An El Niño is said to occur when the Pacific trade winds that usually blow from east to west off the coast of South America weaken. Under normal conditions, these winds push warm water westward away from the Peruvian coast, and this in turn causes cold water to rise from the depths of the ocean. These cold upwellings are full of nutrients, and they support a rich growth of plankton. The plankton in turn supports huge populations of fish, and the coastal peoples of Peru and adjacent regions have long depended on the abundant fish that thrive in areas of cool water off the South American coast. During an El Niño event, however, the trade winds blow less strongly, and the typical pattern of coastal upwelling that carries nutrients from the cold depths to the ocean surface is disrupted. The plankton does not grow, and the fish die off in large numbers. El Niño warming is also associated with other atmospheric phenomena that bring heavy rain to western South America and drought to eastern Australia and Indonesia. El Niño even affects the weather in the United States, but not as predictably.

When this abnormal warming of the ocean occurs, Peruvian fishermen and farmers begin to notice its effects around Christmas, and so they have given it the name *el Niño*, "the Little Boy," after the baby Jesus whose birth is celebrated during this season. With his arrival, *el Niño* drives the fish away, but he brings heavy rain that makes the deserts of South America bloom. By the end of the 1800s, Peruvian scientists had already begun to use the popular expression *el Niño* as the technical term for the warming phenomenon.

A cooling of the surface water of the eastern and central Pacific Ocean—the opposite of El Niño, so to speak—has been dubbed *la Niña*, "the Little Girl." La Niña conditions occur when the Pacific trade winds blow more strongly than usual, pushing the sun-warmed surface water farther west and increasing the upwelling of cold water in the eastern regions near the coast of South America. La Niña cooling is associated with other atmospheric phenomena that bring drought to western South America and heavy rains to eastern Australia and Indonesia. La Niña events occur somewhat less frequently than El Niño events.

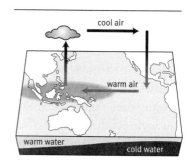

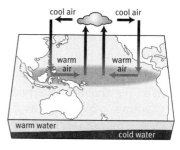

top: *normal water temperatures, with warm water concentrated in the western tropical Pacific*

bottom: *El Niño conditions, with warm water extending from the western tropical Pacific to the eastern Pacific*

embargo

When he ascended to the throne in 1556, Philip II of Spain became the most powerful man in the world. During his reign, the Spanish Empire would eventually stretch from Mexico, Central and South America, and Florida in the west to the Philippines—named for Philip himself—in the east. At this time, the Netherlands were also part of the Spanish possessions in Europe, and Philip sought to limit the spread of Protestantism in these territories. He also suspected that Elizabeth I, Queen of England, was supporting Protestantism and fomenting trouble for him in the Netherlands, and the Spanish government began to take measures to limit the power of England, cast Elizabeth from her throne, and restore Catholicism as the state religion of her island. As tensions between Spain and the other European powers rose, the Spanish governor of the Netherlands forbade the importation of cloth from England—this cloth trade was a lucrative source of income for people on both sides of the North Sea. England responded by banning the importation of Dutch goods.

The breakdown in trade and loss of income served only to make the Dutch even more dissatisfied with Spanish rule, and it became necessary for Spain to use Spanish troops to keep down the forces of rebellion in the Netherlands. In 1568, Spanish ships sailed through the English Channel bringing a large quantity of gold bullion as pay for the Spanish army, and Elizabeth had them seized, perhaps to assert her dominance in the region. Philip reciprocated by having all English merchants in the Netherlands seized, and the flow of trade between England and the territories of the Spanish Empire came to a standstill. This embargo ended in 1573, but tensions between England and Spain would continue to rise until 1585, when outright war flared up between England and Spain. Over the next twenty years, Philip assembled immense fleets, including the famed Spanish Armada of 1588, in order to isolate and invade England. But they were either defeated by the English navy or destroyed by storms. As a result, England began to gain ascendancy over Spain as the great maritime power in the world, and the Spanish word *embargo* became a familiar part of the vocabulary of English.

In Spanish, *embargo* literally means "seizure (of goods)" or "sequestration" in the legal senses of these words relating to property. *Embargo* is derived from the verb *embargar,* "to seize, to sequester, to impede." This verb developed from the Vulgar Latin word **imbarricāre*. **Imbarricāre* literally meant "to bar in, bar up, impede with a bar" and was derived from the Vulgar Latin noun **barra,* "bar." As the Vulgar Latin of Roman Gaul evolved into Old French, this same word **barra* developed into Old French *barre,* which was borrowed into Middle English as *barre,* which subsequently developed into Modern English *bar.* In this way, Spanish *embargo* and English *bar* are linguistic cousins.

The Spanish Armada of 1588 is discussed in greater detail at the entry for the word *armada* in the book.

epazote

The herb called *epazote,* pronounced (ĕp′ə-zō′tĕ) in English, is an essential ingredient in traditional Mexican cuisine. When eaten raw, some people think that whole, fresh epazote leaves taste like machine oil, but when added to a large pot of beans, a small quantity of epazote imparts a distinctive deep, earthy flavor that nothing else can replace. Many people have already known and loved epazote in good Mexican food without even knowing it. Epazote is also valued for its carminative effect—tradition has it that it makes beans more digestible and reduces flatulence.

The Spanish word *epazote*, like so many other of the culinary terms referring to the distinctive foods of the Americas, comes from Nahuatl, the language of the Aztec Empire. Beans were a staple of the diet of the Aztecs just as they are in Mexico today, and the herb was appreciated for its antiflatulent properties. The Nahuatl word for the herb, *epazotl*, makes reference to the plant's strong smell—*epazotl* is a compound made up of *epatl*, "skunk," added to *tzotl*, "filth."

Epazote is thus named like *asafetida*, another flavoring that tastes awful to many people in large quantities but adds extra kick to a dish when used discreetly. *Asafetida* means "stinking resin" in Latin, and comes from the Persian word for gum or resin, *azā*, and the Latin word *fetida*, "stinking." When used in small quantities, asafetida adds a rich oniony taste to a dish, and people belonging to the Brahmin caste in India often use it as a replacement for onions and garlic, which religious restrictions forbid them to eat. In Spanish, asafetida used to be known as *estiércol del diablo*, "devil's dung," just as it was sometimes called *devil's dung* in English, too.

F

fajitas

In Spanish, the word *faja* literally means "band," "strip," or "girdle," but in Northern Mexico and Texas, *faja* can also refer to a long and flat cut of beef taken from the lower part of the brisket, or chest, of the steer. In the United States, English-speaking butchers call this cut of beef the *skirt steak*. The *faja* or skirt steak is actually the steer's diaphragm muscle, and although the cut has good flavor, it tends to be rather tough. For this reason, butchers usually sell the *faja* quite cheap. Somewhere along the line, an enterprising cook figured out that the best way to prepare the tough but tasty *faja* easily was to cut it into strips, grill it, and serve it with tortillas, salsa, and other condiments. This dish came to be known simply as *fajitas,* literally "little strips," a word formed by adding the diminutive suffix *–ito* (whose feminine form is *–ita*) to *faja*.

farthingale

Anyone who has ever seen a portrait of Elizabeth I of England—or of any other noble lady of Elizabeth's time—has seen a farthingale, even if the word *farthingale* itself is unfamiliar. A farthingale is a support, such as a hoop made of wood or reeds, worn beneath a skirt to extend it horizontally from the waist and create the distinctive silhouette of women's formal gowns in the 15th, 16th, and 17th centuries. It was in Spain that gowns shaped by such supports first came into fashion during the latter part of the 15th century, and the style was later popularized in England by Catherine of Aragon (1485–1536).

Catherine, the youngest daughter of Ferdinand II of Aragon and Isabella I of Castile, came to England in 1501 to marry Arthur, Prince of Wales. The sickly prince died soon after their wedding, and Catherine was betrothed to his younger brother, the future Henry VIII, after giving assurances that her marriage with Arthur had never been consummated. The sad continuation of this story, including Henry's final rejection of Catherine after over twenty years of marriage, is well known—when Catherine failed to produce a male heir, Henry sought to have their marriage pronounced void on the grounds that he had married his brother's wife, but the pope refused to do this. Eventually Henry broke with the Church of Rome and established the Church of England, and the clerics in the new church obliged him by declaring his marriage with Catherine to be void. Henry then wed his mistress Anne Boleyn, the second of the six wives he would take during his eventful life. Still defiantly claiming that she was the only rightful queen of England, Catherine died in 1536 in a damp castle far from the sunny Spain that gave her birth. The fashion for far-

portrait of Queen Elizabeth I by Marcus Gheerhaerts

thingales continued in England long after her death, however, as it did in Spain and the rest of Europe for many decades more.

The word *farthingale* is a later alteration of the English word for the support in Catherine's time, which was spelled variously as *verdynggale* or *vardingale*. The English term comes from the 16th-century French word for the support, spelled *verdugalle* or *vertugade* (now Modern French *vertugadin*). The French word in turn comes from the Old Spanish word for a farthingale, *verdugado* (which is still the Modern Spanish word for this old-fashioned item). *Verdugado*, in turn, is derived from *verdugo*, which refers to a green, flexible stick of wood or the shoot of a tree. Farthingales were often made of rods of flexible wood such as this. *Verdugo* is of course itself derived from *verde*, "green," which descends from Latin *viridis*. Among other words in English that refer to the color green and come from the Latin *viridis* are *verdant*, "green with vegetation," and *verdure*, "lush greenery."

flotilla

A *flotilla* is a small fleet of ships. The word *flotilla* seems to have been borrowed from Spanish into English around 1700—at a time the power of the Spanish Empire was beginning to wane, and Spain had lost the domination of the seas to Great Britain and the Netherlands. The British and Dutch preyed upon the Spanish treasure ships that brought the gold of the Americas to Spain, and they harried Spanish merchant vessels. During this period of naval conflict between Spain and her allies on the one hand, and the British and Dutch on the other, the word *flotilla* made its way into English.

The English words *fleet* and *flotilla* are etymological cousins. Spanish *flotilla* is the diminutive of *flota*, "fleet." *Flota* in turn comes from French *flotte*, "fleet," and French *flotte* is in turn from Old Norse *floti*. (Old Norse is the name for the language spoken in Scandinavia in medieval times, the ancestor of the modern Danish, Swedish, Norwegian, Faroese, and Icelandic languages.) It is not surprising that French—and eventually Spanish—should have borrowed a word relating to the sea from Old Norse, for the medieval Scandinavians were able seamen. Their skills are well illustrated not only by the successful coastal raiding of the Vikings and the excellent design of their ship, but also by the fact that the Norse sailed across the Atlantic and set foot on North America in the year 1000. The Old Norse word *floti* is closely related to the Old English word *flēot,* and it was this Old English term that eventually developed into the Modern English word *fleet.* Both Old Norse *floti* and Old English *flēot* belong to the same family of Germanic words that also includes the English verbs *flow* and *float.* In this way, the resemblance in sound between *fleet, float,* and *flotilla* is no coincidence—the three words are linguistic cousins.

Flotilla is just one of many maritime words that English has borrowed from Spanish. Other such words discussed in this book include *armada, cargo, embargo,* and *galleon.*

galleon

Galleons were very large, three-masted wooden sailing vessels used especially by Spain from the 15th to the 17th century as merchant ships or warships. When used for war, they could be equipped with cannons. Galleons usually had two or more decks, and they were also square-rigged—that is, the principal sails of the ships were of trapezoidal shape. It was in the vast holds of galleons that immense quantities of treasure were brought to Spain from the Americas and the Far East during the days of the Spanish Empire. Galleons were the most important component of the huge naval armadas that Philip II of Spain assembled when he attempted to invade England and remove Elizabeth I from power in the 1590s, and the English navy used their own galleons when they repulsed Philip's armadas from English waters.

The English word *galleon* is a borrowing of Spanish *galeón*. The word *galeón* was formed by adding the augmentative suffix *–ón* to the word *galea*, "galley." *Galeón* thus means "big galley." The Spanish word *galea*, like the English word *galley*, designated a large, usually single-decked ship of shallow draft used in the Mediterranean during the medieval period. Galleys were propelled by both sails and oars and could be used as merchant ships or warships. The English word *galley* is a borrowing of Old French *galee*, and both Spanish *galea* and Old French *galee* ultimately come from Medieval Greek *galea*. The Medieval Greek word is probably a variant of the Greek word *galeos,* meaning "dogfish." (The English term *dogfish* can refer to many species of small sharks found around the world. The Greek word refers to the small sharks of the Mediterranean.) Galleys were swift and effective ships in their time, and they may have reminded medieval sailors of the schools of small sharks that hunt in the waters of the Mediterranean.

Since the middle of the 1700s, the word *galley* has also been used in English to refer to a ship's kitchen, and even more recently, to the kitchen of an airliner. Although this use of the word seems to have arisen from the earlier meaning of the word, "large ship of shallow draft," the details of the development of the newer meaning remain unclear.

Besides *galleon,* other words of Spanish origin relating to maritime trade and warfare are discussed in this book at the entries for *armada, cargo,* and *embargo.*

gambit

The English word *gambit* is now often used in a general sense to describe a risky maneuver or ploy used in any sort of conflict or competition. *Gambit* originates as a technical term in chess, however—a gambit is an opening move or sequence of moves in which a player sacrifices a minor piece, usually a pawn, in exchange for an advantage of some sort. The English chess term is a borrowing of Spanish *gambito,* which is in turn a borrowing of Italian *gambetto,* which literally means "sticking the leg out to trip someone up." *Gambetto* is derived from the Italian word *gamba,* "leg." This Italian word, by the way, is also the ultimate source of the rather old-fashioned slang term *gams,* "legs," nowadays seldom heard except in reruns of classic Hollywood movies.

The theory of gambits in chess was extensively developed by the Spanish priest Ruy López de Segura, who lived in the middle of the 1500s and is perhaps the first person in history who might be considered a grand master of chess. López had traveled to Italy and trounced the most famous players there, and he wrote a book, *Libro de la invención liberal y arte del juego del axedrez* ("Book of the Liberal Institution and Art of the Game of Chess"), in which he discussed various sorts of openings. It was perhaps López who introduced the word *gambetto,* "gambit," into Spanish as *gambito.* In 1575, King Philip II of Spain offered the Italians the chance to recapture their glory and organized a championship at his palace, El Escorial near Madrid. Ruy López and another Spanish master, Alfonso Cerón, played against the Italians Giovanni Leonardo di Bona and Paolo Boi. Giovanni Leonardo won, but the Spanish chess master's fame is still remembered in the name of the *Ruy López* or *Spanish game,* one of the most common openings used in chess today.

guano

The word *guano* refers to the droppings of sea birds that accumulate along certain coastal areas. The word is also used of the droppings of bats that accumulate in caves. These droppings make excellent fertilizer, and guano deposits were mined extensively in the 1800s, before the advent of modern artificial fertilizers. *Guano* is another of the many words from Quechua, the language of the Inca Empire, that have made their way into English by way of Spanish. Spanish *guano* comes from Quechua *wanu,* "dung." The largest guano deposits in the world are found in the northern provinces of Chile, in regions formerly part of the Inca Empire, as well as on islands off the coast of Chile and Peru. Despite the unsavory origin of guano, wars have been fought in modern times over the control of this important resource.

For thousands of years, sea birds have nested in the Atacama desert and on the arid islands along the Pacific coast of South America. Since little rains falls to wash their guano away, a layer of dried excrement has grown to be many feet thick in some areas. In the 1800s, these vast guano deposits had become an important source of fertilizer for the farmers around the world. The Chincha Islands are one group of guano-covered islands off the coast of Peru. Peru had effectively become independent from Spain in 1821, although the Spanish government did not recognize this officially. In 1864, after a diplomatic incident, a Spanish fleet took control of the Chinchas, depriving Peru of its main source of guano for export. Chile eventually entered the war, and the Spanish fleet suffered a humiliating defeat at Chilean hands in 1865. Spain eventually renounced its claims. This was the last gasp of the Spanish Empire in South America, so to speak. After the Chincha Islands War, Spain gave up asserting any further territorial claims on the continent, and Puerto Rico and Cuba were the only remnants of its once vast empire in the Americas.

guerrilla

The word *guerrilla* literally means "little war" in Spanish. It is formed by adding the dimunitive suffix *–illa* to the word *guerra,* "war." The word first begins to appear in Spanish in the 1500s, with the sense "small-scale military offensive." The Spanish word begins to appear in English in the first part of the 1800s, with the meaning "limited, localized war carried out by small bands of warriors." In 1837, Washington Irving used the word with this meaning in a book entitled *The Rocky mountains; or, Scenes, incidents, and adventures in the far West.* This work is an account of the expedition to Oregon carried out by the French-born American explorer Benjamin Louis Eulalie de Bonneville in the 1830s, and it refers to the intermittent warfare that broke out between the Crow and Blackfeet tribes in what is now Wyoming and Montana. The men from the United States who ventured into these territories did as much as possible, Irving notes, *to avoid being involved in these guerillas.*

The spelling *guerilla* is still quite common in English, even though it is incorrect from the Spanish point of view—in Spanish, single *r* and double *rr* represent different sounds when written between vowels within a word. Single *r* is a simple tap of the tongue behind the teeth, while double *rr* represents a heavily trilled *r*-sound. English speakers also tend to pronounce the double *ll* in *guerrilla* with the sound (l), rather than with the (y) or (y)-like sound that *ll* has in Spanish, according to dialect.

The use of the expression *guerrilla warfare* has led to a change in the meaning of *guerrilla* in English. *Guerrilla warfare* (originally meaning just "small-scale, intermittent warfare usually waged against an established military") came to be interpreted as "warfare carried out by *guerrillas.*" *Guerrilla* was then interpreted in English as meaning "a member of a warrior band conducting small-scale, intermittent warfare." In Spanish, the same meaning is instead conveyed by the word *guerrillero.*

The Spanish word *guerra* is a distant cousin of the English word *war.* Many words from the Germanic languages entered the everyday Latin spoken by the people of the Roman Empire as it approached its final collapse. Since the Roman citizenry now tried to avoid military service, the empire was forced to hire Germanic mercenaries to fight its wars, and the Romans often even paid one Germanic tribe to protect them from raids and invasions by another. In the end, the leaders of these Germanic tribes simply seized power in Roman territory for themselves and carved up the Roman Empire into smaller kingdoms. So it is fitting that the words for "war" in the modern Romance languages, like Portuguese, Spanish, and Italian *guerra* or French *guerre,* should come from a word in the languages of the Germanic peoples. In the Old French of northern France, the same Germanic word took the form *werre.* Old English apparently borrowed northern French *werre* a little before the Normans, the speakers of a northern dialect of French, conquered England in 1066. *Werre* eventually developed into Modern English *war.*

guiro

A guiro is a percussion instrument traditionally made of a hollow gourd with a grooved or serrated surface like a washboard. It is played by scraping the grooves with a stick or rod. Nowadays, many guiros are also made from wood or plastic. Guiros are frequently used in many different styles of Latin American music, such as merengue from the Dominican Republic and cumbia from Colombia. The English word *guiro* comes from the American Spanish word *güiro,* meaning "calabash gourd" and by extension, "instrument

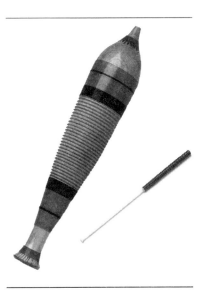

made from a calabash gourd." *Güiro* was borrowed from Taíno, the extinct language of the indigenous people of the Bahamas and the Greater Antilles.

guitar

The Spanish language has given English a remarkable number of words relating to music of all kinds, from popular Latin American styles like *mambo, rumba,* and *salsa,* to the noble *passacaglias* and *sarabandes* of Johann Sebastian Bach. Spain is also the source of one of the most important and basic terms in music—the name of the instrument called the *guitar.*

Since they are usually made of thin pieces of wood and are often delicately constructed, stringed instruments from the ancient world have rarely been preserved. Many pieces of art from ancient times, however, depict various string instruments that had a neck clearly differentiated from a wider body, one of the basic characteristics of the guitar. The performer held the instrument against the chest or abdomen and plucked or strummed the strings with one hand while pressing them down against different points of the neck with the other hand. These instruments are the early ancestors of the guitar, and from the 1400s onward, instruments resembling the modern guitar more or less closely begin to be depicted in art from various European countries. Scholars agree, however, that Spain played an important role in the evolution of the guitar. The design of the modern guitar was perfected by the renowned guitar maker Antonio de Torres Jurado (1817–1892), the "Stradivarius of the Guitar," from Almería in southern Spain.

Until the late 1500s, the guitar had languished in the shadow of the lute, which was the stringed instrument preferred outside of Spain by the nobility and the professional composers that they employed. The popularity of the guitar exploded across Europe, however, in the early 1600s, and it is then that the Spanish word *guitarra* first begins to appear in English, at first spelled just like the Spanish word. The spelling *guitar* appears somewhat later and reflects the influence of French *guitarre,* itself from Spanish.

The Spanish word *guitarra* comes from Arabic *qītāra*. (The Arabic consonant *q* is pronounced like a *k* very deep in the throat in modern standard Arabic, which is based on the language of the Koran and classical Arabic literature as it was spoken around the time of the prophet Mohammed, who died in AD 632. In many Arabic dialects, however, *q* is pronounced as *g*.) The Arabic word is in turn a borrowing of the Greek word *kitharā*, referring to an ancient musical instrument resembling a lyre and especially used to accompany songs.

In ancient times, Greek *kitharā* was also borrowed into Latin as *cithara*. *Cithara* was adopted into Old High German, the medieval ancestor of German, and it eventually developed into German *Zither*, the source of the English word *zither*.

habanera

The word *habanera* refers to a certain type of Cuban music in duple time and performed at a slow tempo. The word also refers to the dance usually performed to this music. Although the habanera originated in Cuba, sailors and laborers returning to Spain from Cuba brought the music with them, where it became an integral part of the musical tradition of Spain in the 1800s. The habanera also spread to South America, and there it became one of the principal ingredients of the tango.

The word *habanera* is the feminine form of the Spanish adjective *habanero,* meaning "of the city of Havana." The standard spelling of the Cuban capital has a *v* in English, but in Spanish *La Habana* is nowadays spelled with a *b*. This may puzzle English speakers if they do not know that the letters *b* and *v* are used to represent the same set of sounds in Spanish. Both *b* and *v* have the sound (b) at the beginning of a word and within a word after the consonant *m*. Between vowels, however, both *b* and *v* can be used to represent the characteristic *v*-like sound of Spanish, made by bringing the two lips together rather than the upper teeth and lower lip like an English *v*. Although the modern Spanish spelling system is widely admired for its clarity, Spanish spelling habits used to fluctuate quite a bit. Before the gradual standardization of the system in the 1700s, *b* and *v* were frequently interchanged—including in the name of the capital of Cuba, *La Habana*. English happened to pick up the spelling with *v.*

Although the habanera originates in the Spanish-speaking world, the melody that is perhaps the most famous habanera is usually sung with French words. This habanera comes from the opera *Carmen*, composed by Georges Bizet and first performed in 1875. The title character, a seductive Gypsy woman of Seville in Spain, introduces herself by singing a habanera about the fickle nature of love, and her song foreshadows the tragic turn that her affair with a Spanish soldier will take at the end of the opera:

> *L'amour est un oiseau rebelle,*
> *Que nul ne peut apprivoiser,*
> *Et c'est bien en vain qu'on l'appelle*
> *S'il lui convient de refuser.*

> Love's an ornery bird
> That no one can tame.
> If it's decided to refuse
> There's no use calling its name.

The melody to Carmen's aria is now a familiar tune all around the world, but Bizet himself did not write it. When he made use of it to set the words of Carmen's song, Bizet thought that he was just borrowing an anonymous Spanish folk melody. In fact, the Spanish composer Sebastián Yradier had written the tune for his song "El Arreglito" ("The Little Arrangement"). Yradier, whose original name was Sebastián de Iradier y Salaverri, is also the author of another famous habanera, the ballroom classic "La Paloma" ("The Dove"), still frequently performed today. Born in 1809, Yradier died in 1865, unfortunately too soon to hear his melody "El Arreglito" being whistled all over the world after the first performances of *Carmen*.

Habanero, an English word derived from the masculine form corresponding to *habanera,* is discussed in the following note.

habanero

The habanero is one of the hottest chili peppers. This rating is not just the personal impression of a few chili pepper connoisseurs—there is, in fact, a standard scientific system for measuring the hotness of chilies, invented by an American chemist named Wilbur L. Scoville (1865–1942). The system was originally based on a series of taste tests performed by a group of people. The members of the group tasted a solution of chili which was diluted with sugar water until a majority of the group could no longer feel any heat when tasting it. A chili had a rating of 1,000 Scovilles, for example, if it took 1,000 parts of sugar water to dilute one part of chili sample until the tasters could no longer detect it. Nowadays, however, the Scoville ratings of chilies are based on the results of a more technical test, called *high performance liquid chromatography,* that are then converted into Scovilles. On the Scoville scale, regular green bell peppers have a rating of zero. (Bell peppers contain no capsaicin, the chemical that makes chilies hot.) Ancho chilies rate between 1,000 and 2,000 Scoville units, while jalapeños can rate up to 8,000. Habaneros, on the other hand, rate from around 100,000 all the way up to 300,000 or more!

The habanero is thought to have originated in Cuba. *Habanero* is the masculine form of the Spanish adjective *habanero,* "from Havana"—the masculine form is used since *chile,* "chili," is a masculine word in Spanish. (Nowadays, however, the Yucatán Peninsula of Mexico is the largest producer of habaneros, and the distinctive citruslike aroma of the chili is an essential part of Yucateco cuisine.) The original Spanish name of Havana, the capital of Cuba, was *San Cristóbal de La Habana.* In this name, *San Cristóbal* is of course the Spanish name of Saint Christopher, the patron saint of safe travel, but no one is quite sure what *de La Habana,* "of the Habana," originally meant. According to the most widely accepted theory,

Habana somehow developed from *Habaguanex*, the name of a prominent member of the Taíno, the indigenous people who inhabited Cuba before the arrival of the Spaniards.

The feminine form of the same adjective, *habanera*, has also been borrowed into English and is discussed in the previous entry.

hammock

> *They* [the Spaniards] *also trade in those rivers for bread of* cassavi, *of which they buy an hundred pound weight for a knife, and sell it at Margarita for ten pesos. They also recover great store of cotton,* Brazil *wood, and those beds which they call* hamacas *or Brazil beds, wherein in hot countries all the Spaniards use to lie commonly, and in no other, neither did we ourselves while we were there.*

It is hard to imagine a world without hammocks, but Sir Walter Raleigh apparently does not expect many of his readers to be familiar with them in this passage from his work from 1596 entitled *The discoverie of the large and bewtiful empire of Guiana*, an account of his visit to northeastern South America. The English word hammock is a borrowing of Spanish *hamaca*, and the Spanish word comes from the language of the Taíno, the main group of indige-nous people inhabiting the Bahamas and the Greater Antilles at the time of Christopher Columbus's arrival. When the Spanish first observed the Taíno people resting in an unfa-miliar sort of net suspend-

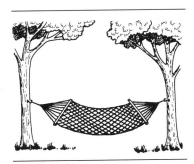

ed between hooks, they quickly recognized the comfort that hammocks provide in the humid tropics, and they took to hammocks eagerly. Hammocks keep sleepers off the ground where insects are crawling, and they are also a convenient and safe way for sailors to sleep in rough waters, since people sleeping in hammocks onboard ship are not jostled and rolled about against hard objects, as they would be sleeping on deck. Sailors eventually began to use hammocks in European navies and merchant fleets, and hammocks became standard sleeping equipment in the Royal Navy of Great Britain in the 1600s—a little after the date that Raleigh mentions them somewhat dismissively in *The Discovery of Guaina.*

hazard

The modern meaning of the English word *hazard,* "risk" or "danger," is a development dating from the 1500s. *Hazard* was originally the name for a dice game popular in the Middle Ages—a game at which one could *hazard,* or put at risk, one's money or possessions. The Middle English name for this dice game, *hasard,* was borrowed from Old French, and the Old French word in turn comes from the Old Spanish word *azar,* meaning simply "chance, fortune," and in particular, "throw of the dice."

Azar is another of the many words in Spanish that come from Arabic. It is a borrowing of Arabic *az-zahr,* "die for gaming." *Az-zahr* itself may be short for *ku'b az-zahr,* literally "cube (*ku'b*) of the flowers (*az-zahr*)". In the ancient and medieval world, dice were marked with other designs and symbols besides the dots we are familiar with today, and it is thought that a flower was sometimes painted on the winning (or the losing, according to the rules of the game) side of the die.

The *h* that appears at the beginning of Old French *hasard* and English *hazard* originated in Old French, not Old Spanish. Medieval scribes in France had the habit of writing a silent *h* at the beginning of many words of foreign origin that began with vowels—there were many native Old French words of Latin origin, like *herbe,* "herb," and *honour,* "honor," that were usually spelled with a silent *h*. However, there were also many other words in Old French that began with a real, pronounced *h*-sound, and these were spelled with *h* too, like *haine,* "hate," and *homard,* "lobster." Occasionally, medieval people made mistakes when reading unfamiliar words like *hasard,* and they began to pronounce the written *h*'s that ought to have been silent. In this way, Old Spanish *azar* became Old French *hasard* with an *h*, still heard in the English word *hazard* today. The *d* at the end of Old French *hasard* was probably added to Old Spanish *azar* as the result of the influence of the common French suffix *–ard*. This suffix is found at the end of many nouns with an unfavorable or pejorative connotation, like *brouillard,* "fog," and *couard,* "coward."

hoosegow

The word *hoosegow,* pronounced (hoōs′gou′), is a colorful old slang synonym for *jail* with a flavor of the American West: *They threw him in the hoosegaw for being drunk and disorderly.* The term was born in the lively mixture of Spanish and English spoken in the western part of the United States—it comes from the Spanish *juzgado,* "court of justice, tribunal." In many varieties of Spanish, the ending *–ado* is usually pronounced as *–ao* in everyday speech, with no *d* at all or only a very lightly articulated one. The spelling *hoosegow* thus is a pretty good representation of the American Spanish pronunciation of the word *juzgado* as it sounds to the ears of an English-speaking

American, even though *hoosegow* looks nothing like the actual written form *juzgado*. The first known occurrence of the word *hoosegaw* dates from 1909, and the word was especially associated with army slang in its early history.

Spanish *juzgado*, "court of justice," comes from the verb *juzgar*, "to judge," and *juzgar* itself comes from the Latin verb *jūdicāre*. On the way from Latin to Old French, *jūdicāre* became the Old French verb *juger*, "to judge," which was borrowed into Middle English as *jugen*. *Jugen* eventually developed into the Modern English verb *judge*. *Hoosegaw* and *judge* are thus distant linguistic cousins.

For a word similar to *hoosegaw*, see *calaboose* in this book.

hurricane

Soon after they had established colonies in the West Indies, the Spanish encountered the devastating storms that periodically ravage the Caribbean Sea, Gulf of Mexico, and Atlantic coast of North America. The Spanish writer Gonzalo Fernández de Oviedo y Valdés, who visited the Americas several times in the 1500s, describes the force of these storms—unprecedented in the experience of most Europeans—in his fascinating work entitled *Historia general y natural de las Indias* ("General and Natural History of the Indies"), first published in 1535. Oviedo gives an account of a storm that struck the Spanish colony of Santo Domingo on the island of Hispaniola (the island now comprising Haiti and the Dominican Republic), and he notes that the "*indios*" ("Indians") of Hispaniola, who are now known as the Taíno, have a special word for such storms.

> *Huracán, en lengua desta isla, quiere decir propriamente tormenta o tempestad muy excesiva....*

Huracán, in the language of this island, means specifically tempest or very strong storm.

(Oviedo's text is here presented with some of the original features of his 16th century spelling and grammar unchanged.) Oviedo even gives us the precise date of this storm he describes, Wednesday, the third of August, in 1508—right in the middle of hurricane season. The storm arrived around noon. Oviedo notes that not only were straw huts blown way, but also buildings made of stone were heavily damaged. He then goes on to describe features of the storm that make us certain it was the kind of storm that we would now call a *hurricane,* or at least a very powerful tropical cyclone. The winds change direction as the storm passes over.

> *El viento era norte e tal que, así como comenzó a cargar, entraron presto los hombres de la mar, que estaban seguros en tierra, a echar más áncoras e cables por asegurar sus naos, e como fué aumentándose más y más la tormenta, no aprovechó ninguna industria ni prudencia de los hombres....*
>
> *E cambióse después el tiempo y el viento al opósito, súbitamente, por el contrario, e no con menor ímpetu e furia. E fué tan grande el sur como había seído el norte.*

The wind was from the north and was such that, as the sky began to become overcast, the men came in early from the sea, and when they were safe on shore, to put down more anchors and fasten more cables to secure their ships, and since the storm was growing greater and greater, all the effort and foresight of the men was of no avail....

And then the storm and the wind reversed, suddenly, in the opposite direction, and with no less force and fury. And the wind from the south was just as strong as it had been from the north.

The Taíno word that Oviedo transcribes as *huracán* was borrowed into Spanish as *huracán* and Portuguese as *furacão*, and soon spread from these languages to most of the other languages of Europe. Shakespeare uses a form of the Spanish word in his play *King Lear*, which dates from around 1605. In order to live out his old age in peace, King Lear has relinquished his kingdom to two of his daughters, but since his retirement these daughters have treated him with heartless cruelty. Driven to madness by their betrayal, he wanders out into the open country in the middle of a storm, to which he addresses a speech beginning with the following words (Act 3, Scene 2):

> *Blow, winds, and crack your cheeks! Rage, blow!*
> *You cataracts and hurricanoes, spout*
> *till you have drench'd our steeples...,*

The form of *hurricane* that Shakespeare uses has had an -*o* tacked onto it—as has happened to several other Spanish words in English like *tomato* from *tomate*. English speakers were generally familiar with the fact that many Spanish nouns ended in −*o*, and so they often added an −*o* to words that knew were of Spanish origin, even when there was no −*o* on the original Spanish word. Later, of course, *hurricane*, closer to the original form of the Spanish word, becomes the usual spelling of the English word.

iguana

The word *iguana* refers to any of various species of large tropical lizards native to the Americas that usually have a large dewlap and row of spiny projections along the back. They are mostly herbivores, and some species of iguana can grow up to six feet in length. The most popular species kept as a pet in the United States is the green iguana, whose scientific name is *Iguana iguana.*

The word *iguana* first appears in English in the middle of the 1500s, in the English translation of an exhaustive report on the Americas written by the Italian-born Spanish historian Pedro Mártir de Anghiera (1457–1526). Charles V, Holy Roman Emperor and King of Spain, commissioned Pedro Mártir as his chronicler and asked him to summarize what was known about the territories that the Spanish had newly acquired in the Americas. Mártir's accounts, written in Latin, preserve fascinating details about this important period in world history—he is our one of our chief sources for information on the conquest of Mexico by Hernán Cortés, as well as of the expedition led by Vasco Núñez de Balboa that reached the

Pacific Ocean by crossing Panama. In passing, Mártir also offers much valuable information about the cultures of the indigenous peoples of the Americas that subsequently disappeared. Christopher Columbus had left some Spaniards stationed on Hispaniola to await his return from Spain, and Mártir mentions the iguana in his description of the foods eaten by the Spaniards during their stay in the unfamiliar land. (Mártir's remarks are here presented in a modern translation from his original Latin.) Mártir calls the iguanas *serpentes*, "serpents" in Latin (by which he means "reptiles"), and says they resemble crocodiles. He tells the following story about how the Spaniards came to eat them:

> [The Spaniards] later learned that these serpents were native to the island. They had not yet ventured to taste them because of their foulness, which caused not just disgust but horror. The Adelantado [a Spaniard], persuaded by the friendly banter of the chief's sister, was ready to try it, bit by bit—but when the flavor of the meat began to caress his palate and his throat, he wanted a whole mouthful, it seems. After that, they did not merely nibble at it with little bites or hardly allow their lips to touch it, but instead, they made complete gluttons of themselves, and spoke of nothing but the deliciousness of the serpents, and that their meat was more exquisite than our own peacocks, pheasants, or partridges.

Iguana meat is still eaten in parts of Mexico and Central America today, and it is credited with various powers, including the ability to restore libido. The Spanish word *iguana* itself comes from one of the indigenous languages of the Antilles that belong to the Arawak language family.

incommunicado

The English word *incommunicado* comes from Spanish *incomunicado*—the spelling of the English word was influenced by the related English word *communicate* with two *m*'s. *Incomunicado* is the past participle of the verb *incomunicar*, "to isolate, put in solitary confinement." The family of words including English verbs like *communicate* and Spanish verbs like *comunicar*, "to communicate," and *incomunicar*, "to isolate," descends from the Latin verb *commūnicāre*, "to communicate." *Commūnicāre* itself is derived from the Latin adjective *commūnis*, "common" (which is also the source of the English adjective *common* and *communal*)—etymologically, *communication* is "sharing things in common."

Spanish *incomunicado* first begins to occur in English in the middle of the 1800s. According to the *Oxford English Dictionary*, the first known appearance of the word in print dates from 1844, in a work by George Wilkins Kendall. Kendall's work is an account in a disastrous military and trade expedition to the city of Santa Fe (now in the state of New Mexico) that was attempted by men from the Republic of Texas in 1841. The men of the expedition were detained and harshly treated by the Mexican authorities and, at one point, some of them were held *incomunicado* in Mexico City.

The Texas Santa Fe expedition occurred during a period of tense relations between Texas and Mexico. Texas had declared independence from Mexico in 1835, and when Texan forces defeated the army of General Santa Anna in 1836, Santa Anna signed a treaty granting independence from Mexico to the Republic of Texas. The government in Mexico City never recognized the validity of this treaty, and poor relations simmered and sometimes boiled over between Texas and Mexico until Texas finally became one of the United States in 1845. During the short existence of the Republic of Texas, the third Texan president, Mirabeau B. Lamar, organized an expedition to the Mexican territory around Santa Fe, in what is now the state of New Mexico in the United States. The Texans hoped that the people of the settlements around Santa Fe could easily be persuaded to join the new republic. The expedition started off from Austin with over three hundred men, including merchants with trade goods in their wagons and soldiers to protect them. They even brought a cannon, hardly thinking how the appearance of a large party of armed men on the edge of their territories might provoke the Mexican authorities—with whom the war for Texan independence had never really ended.

Based upon overly high expectations, the expedition suffered from poor planning from the outset, and the Texans soon found themselves deep in a forbidding landscape with provisions running low. After suffering hunger and attacks by the indigenous Kiowa tribe, they wound up in the custody of the Mexican governor of the region, Manuel Armijo. The Texans were then marched two thousand miles to Mexico City. According to the Texans' accounts, the Mexican soldiers in charge of the march treated them brutally and killed several of them as well. The expedition members were often not given provisions and were forced to sell their clothing to buy food along the way. When they reached Mexico City, the expedition members were imprisoned until the United States secured their release in 1842.

News of the misfortunes of the expedition reached the United States and contributed to a rekindling of interest in Texas. George Wilkins Kendall's account of the expedition was widely read in the United States and may have helped make the word *incomunicado* more widely known among English speakers. Kendall was detained in several different facilities during his imprisonment in Mexico City, and at one point, he was even held in a leprosarium, for some reason. He describes his stay there as follows:

> *So long as my friends were permitted to have personal interviews with me… so long my situation was endurable… but now that I was* incomunicado—*now that all intercourse with my*

friends was cut off through some trifling caprice, my situation became irksome in the extreme.

It seems that Kendall felt that the word *incomunicado* would be unfamiliar to his readers, since he bothered to explain the term in an aside. In the days leading up to the outbreak of the Mexican-American War in 1846, the word *incomunicado* may have been helped into English during the furious debates among United States citizens about the relationship of their country to Texas and Mexico. Many people within the United States opposed the Mexican-American war as being unjust, and at the end of it, Mexico would be forced to cede an enormous amount of territory to the United States, including the states of New Mexico and California. The loss of such are large amount of territory is still a cause of national sorrow in Mexico today.

intransigent

The word *intransigent* was unknown in English before the 1870s, a time when Spain was torn apart by political strife. Isabella II of Spain (1830–1902) had worn the crown since 1836, but the real power was often in the hands of the army during her reign. Isabella was constantly engaged in palace intrigues, and she governed so badly that in 1868, there was a revolution. A coalition consisting of powerful generals and politicians of all different stripes forced Isabella to abdicate and exiled her to France. The legislative assembly of Spain, the *Cortes,* then wrote and instituted a constitution, and Spain became a constitutional monarchy—only they had to find someone to fill the job of monarch. Eventually, Amadeo, the second son of King Victor Emmanuel of Italy, was invited to take the position in 1870. This constitutional monarchy did not work smoothly at all—uprisings by various political factions and conspiracies on all sides made Spain all but ungovernable—and on February 11, 1873, Amadeo abdicated. Spain was declared a republic, and the power to govern was settled upon the *Cortes* in the First Spanish Republic.

The First Spanish Republic was the scene of a constantly shifting power struggle between the army, parties supporting the republican government, and armed factions supporting various candidates for the Spanish throne. One of these candidates was Isabella's son, Alfonso. Popular insurrection sprang up all around Spain. In 1874, the *Cortes* were dissolved and an army general, Francisco Serrano y Domínguez, Duke de la Torre, formed a short-lived government. However, the faction supporting Alfonso won out at last, and he ascended the throne as Alfonso XII in 1875, ending the republic.

During the brief life of the First Spanish Republic, the members of the political faction that upheld republican values and the constitution against the army and the monarchists were called *los intransigentes*—literally, "the uncompromising ones." This Spanish word is made up of the negative prefix *in-* and the verb *transigir,* "to compromise." Spanish *transigir* is a borrowing of Latin *trānsigere,* "to come to terms, settle, transact." (The English verb *transact* is in fact from the same Latin verb. It comes from *trānsāctus,* the past participle of *trānsigere.*) Reports of the political turmoil in Spain during the 1870s popularized the word *intransigente,* "uncompromising," in French, in which it was spelled *intransigeant. Intransigeant* came to describe any uncompromising person and attitude, not just the ardent supporters of the First Spanish Republic. By 1879, *intransigeant* has spread to English. At first the word kept its original Spanish and French spellings in English, but it soon became Anglicized as *intransigent.*

jade

Two different minerals, named nephrite and jadeite by geologists, are called *jade* in English. The color of jade ranges from deep green to pale yellowish-white, and it has been valued as a gemstone and a material for carved luxury articles by cultures around the world. Nephrite is fairly common as precious stones go, but the very hard jadeite variety of jade is extremely rare and can be found in only a few scattered geological formations around the world. The Olmec people of ancient Mexico, who flourished from around 1300 to around 400 BC and built the first of the great civilizations in Mesoamerica, prized carved objects of jade, and the Olmec jades appear to have come from sources in Guatemala. The successors of Olmecs, such as the Zapotecs and the Maya, also prized ceremonial objects of jade, and jadeite objects, probably for ritual use, were carried by trade routes far away from Mesoamerica. Jadeite axeheads brought from the mainland between AD 250 and 500 have been found as far away as the island of Antigua in the Lesser Antilles.

Among the indigenous peoples of the Americas, jade was not valued simply for its glistening green beauty and great hardness, attractive as these qualities of the stone may be. Jade was also thought to have mystical medical properties and to be particularly effective in curing abdominal illnesses and kidney stones.

In 1574, these magical properties were described by the Spanish physician Nicolás Monardes (1493–1588) in a work entitled *Historia medicinal de las cosas que se traen de nuestras Indias Occidentales,* ("Medical Study of the Things that are Brought from our West Indies"), a study of the medical applications of unfamiliar products that had begun to come to Spain from the Americas. Monardes mentions that the indigenous peoples have a stone which he calls the *piedra de la ijada,* "the stone of the loin (or flank)"—*piedra* is the Spanish word for "stone," while *ijada* means "loin" or "flank." He praises virtues of the *piedra de la ijada* in the following terms (here presented in Monardes's original 16th-century spelling):

> *Es una piedra que la muy fina dellas parece plasma de Esmeraldas, que tira a verde con un color lacteo, la mas verde es la mejor: traenlas de diversas formas hechas... unas como pescados, otras como cabeças de aves... pero todas horadadas, porque usaban los Indios traerlas colgadas para efecto del doler de yjada, o estomago: porque en estas dos infermidades haze maravillosos efectos....*

> *Tiene esta piedra por propriedad oculta... de preservar que no caygan en el dolor de la yjada, y despues de venido lo quita, o diminuye. Haze expelar arenas en mucha abondancia y asi mismo piedras. Refrena el calor de los riñones, aprovecha en dolores de estomago, puesta sobre el: y sobre todo preserva del dolor de la yjada.*

It is a stone of which the best quality looks like a plasma of emerald [green chalcedony], and it is greenish with a milky coloration, the greenest being the best. They bring them [to Spain] already carved into various shapes... some like fish, some like the heads of birds... but all pierced with holes, because the Indians have the habit of wearing them for their effect on pain of the loins or the stomach, because in these two illnesses it works wonderful effects....

This stone has the secret property... of preventing people from falling sick with pain of the loins, and after an attack of pain, it rids them of the pain, or diminishes it. It expels kidney stones, even large ones. It reduces excessive heat of the kidneys, and protects against stomachaches when placed upon the stomach, and above all, it keeps one from pain of the loins.

The supposed curative properties of the miraculous *piedra de la ijada* became well known around Europe, and as the fame of the American stone spread, the Spanish term *piedra de la ijada* was borrowed into French as *l'ejade,* "the jade." The *l'* in *l'ejade* is the form that the French definite article *le* takes before a vowel, and at some point, French speakers misdivided *l'ejade* as *le jade,* "the *jade.*" The French form *jade* first begins to appear in English at the beginning of the 1700s.

The geological term *nephrite,* the technical name for the other mineral valued as jade beside jadeite, also makes reference to the supposed magical powers of jade. *Nephrite* is a borrowing of German *Nephrit,* which was coined by the German geologist A. G. Werner in the 1700s from the Greek word *nephros,* meaning "kidney." Nephrite is, in other words, the kidney stone.

jalapeño

The jalapeño chili gets its name from Xalapa, the capital city of the Mexican state of Veracruz on the Gulf of Mexico. Xalapa is the traditional center of production for this variety of chili.

Xalapa is pronounced (hä-lä′pä). In the modern system of spelling Spanish, the sound (h) before the vowels *a, o, u,* and sometimes *i* and *e,* is usually spelled using the letter *j.* The name of the city of Xalapa, however, has kept an old-fashioned spelling in which the letter *x* is used to represent the sound (h). On the other hand, *jalapeño,* as the word for the chili from Xalapa, has come to be spelled regularly with a *j.* (The name of the country of *México*, by the way, has also kept its *x*, even though it is pronounced as if spelled *Méjico*.) The name of the city of Xalapa comes from Nahuatl, the language of the Aztec Empire. In Nahuatl, *Xallapan* means "(at the) place of the water in the sand." It is a compound of the Nahuatl words *xalli*, "sand," and *ātl*," water," with the suffix *–pan*, which means "at, in the location of."

javelina

People who have hiked and camped in the wilderness of the American Southwest may have been lucky enough to see a band of javelinas browsing in the bushes. The javelina—pronounced (hä′və-lē′nə)—is a black and gray piglike animal weighing up to fifty pounds and measuring four feet long (five, including the tail). Javelinas have a distinctive stripe of white fur extending back from their chest to their front legs, where it begins to sweep upwards until it reaches their back. The stripe resembles a collar or a yoke and gives the animal the other name by which it is commonly known in English, the *collared peccary.* Javelinas also have short, sharp tusks that they rub together to make a crunching or chattering noise as a warning to potential threats. Usually, however, they just ignore human beings or run away if they happen to meet them. In some areas of the southwest, javelinas even venture into the outskirts of cities in search of the roots, bulbs, acorns, and occasional small animals like worms that they eat. Their favorite food, however, is the prickly pear, and the best place to look for a herd of javelinas when in the Southwest is a prickly pear cactus stand.

The javelina is one of three living species of the animals called *peccaries,* which are the North and South American equivalents of the domesticated swine and wild hogs of Europe and Asia and the warthogs of Africa. Despite the close outward resemblance of peccaries and pigs, scientists classify peccaries in a family separate from swine and their relatives. Peccaries make up the family *Tayassuidae,* which is separate from the family *Suidae* that includes pigs and their close relatives. The javelina, whose scientific name is *Tayassu tajacu,* is the only species of peccary that lives in the United States. The natural range of the javelina, however, is much larger than just the Southwest of the United States—it stretches from southern Texas, New Mexico, and Arizona all the way to northern Argentina.

The word *javelina* comes from the Spanish word *jabalina,* "wild sow," the feminine equivalent of *jabalí,* "wild boar."

Spanish *jabalí* itself is one of the hundreds of words that entered Spanish from Arabic during the period of Muslim rule in southern Spain. The word comes from the Arabic expression *ḥinzīr jabalī,* literally "swine (*ḥinzīr*) of the mountain (*jabalī*)." The wild boar, of course, lives in the brush on the mountain, rather than in the sty or barn in the valley where the farmer keeps his domesticated swine. The Arabic adjective *jabalī,* "of the mountain," is made from the Arabic noun *jabal,* "mountain."

This Arabic word *jabal* can also be found in another word familiar to English speakers, the name *Gibraltar.* The British colony of Gibraltar occupies about two and a half square miles at the northwest end of the Rock of Gibraltar, a peninsula on the south-central coast of Spain. The Rock of Gibraltar commands the Strait of Gibraltar, which connects the Mediterranean Sea and the Atlantic Ocean. Gibraltar was captured by Muslim forces from North Africa on April 30, 711, under the leadership of Ṭāriq ibn Ziyād. This event opened the period of Muslim rule in the southern part of Spain, during which art and poetry flourished and scientific knowledge made profound advances. The rock where Ṭāriq ibn Ziyād began his conquest was named *Jabal al-Ṭāriq,* "the Mountain of Ṭāriq," in his honor, and this Arabic phrase eventually developed into the Spanish name *Gibraltar.* Christian Spanish forces reconquered Gibraltar in 1462, and Great Britain took control of the strategic spot in 1704 during the War of the Spanish Succession (1701–1714), the great European war fought to prevent the possibility of the same person becoming king of both France and Spain. The return of Gibraltar to Spanish control remains a sticking point in relations between Spain and the United Kingdom.

jerky

The original jerky meat may not have been beef or pork, but llama. The English word *jerky* comes from the Spanish word for "jerky," *charqui,* also spelled *charque.* Although the further origin of the Spanish word is uncertain, many scholars think that the word ultimately comes from Quechua *ch'arki,* "dried meat."

Quechua was the language spoken by the Inca, the Peruvian people that founded the Inca Empire. The Inca built an extensive system of roads to help them maintain and administer their empire, and along the roads they built inns or way stations, called *tambos,* stocked with *ch'arki* and other provisions for the people who used the roads, like military and administrative personnel. (The *ch'* in *ch'arki,* by the way, is an *ejective palatal affricate,* a sound not usually found in English or Spanish. To English and Spanish speakers, a Quechua *ch'* sounds like the English *ch* in *church* but pronounced very sharply and with a great deal of force.) Cattle and pigs are not native to the western hemisphere, and the Inca usually made *ch'arki* from their common domesticated animal, the llama. Although Francisco Pizarro and the conquistadors who accompanied him in the conquest of the Inca empire in 1532 were in search of gold and emeralds, the Spaniards were also impressed by the general magnificence and plenty of the Inca realm, including the quantities of *ch'arki* set aside in the tambos.

Other scholars, however, point out that Portuguese has a verb *enxercar,* "to dry meat," that looks like it is related to *charque.* This word is found as early as the 1400s, long before the conquest of Peru. *Charqui* may be a native Spanish word borrowed into Quechua soon after the conquest of Peru.

The word *charqui* was apparently quite widely used in the Spanish of the Western Hemisphere. Less than a century after the arrival of the Spanish in the Americas, it was borrowed into English. When *charqui* was first appears in English, it was spelled *jerkin,* a form found in the writings of John Smith (1580–1631), the English explorer who helped found Jamestown, Virginia, the first permanent English-speaking in North America. Smith is famous for his legendary love affair with Pocohontas, the daughter of the powerful chieftain of the Virginian Algonquian, the native people who lived in Virginia before the arrival of the English. Smith described the culture of this people in his 1612 work entitled *A map of Virginia, with a description of the countrey.* He compared their dried meat to the beef jerky he knew from the Caribbean:

> *Their fish and flesh they boyle either very tenderly, or broyle it so long on hurdles over the fire; or else, after the Spanish fashion, putting it on a spit, they turne first the one side, then the other, til it be as drie as their jerkin beefe in the west Indies, that they may keepe it a month or more without putrifying.*

Jerk, the verb corresponding to *jerky,* is an adaptation of Spanish *charquear,* and *jerk* first appears in the 1700s, in a description of a wild pig meat being jerked in Jamaica. And today, the growing popularity Jamaican jerked pork sandwiches has given the Spanish word even greater popularity in English.

jojoba

Jojoba is a shrub (*Simmondsia chinensis*) that grows in the Sonoran Desert of northern Mexico and the southwestern United States, as well as in the Mojave Desert of the United States. Jojoba grows about a meter or two tall and has leathery leaves and edible seeds. The seeds contain a valuable oil that can be used as a lubricant and for various other purposes. (In the technical terms of chemistry, this substance is not actually an oil but a liquid wax ester.) Jojoba oil keeps for a long time without degrading and its chemical properties are very similar to those of human sebum, the oily substance produced by the skin to keep it supple and protect it from the elements. For these reasons, jojoba oil is often used in skin moisturizers and other cosmetics.

Before the 1970s, many products now made with jojoba oil contained oil taken from the heads of sperm whales. The demand for whale oil had drastically reduced the number of sperm whales, and the hunting of the sperm whales and other whale species was eventually put under stringent international restrictions. Whale oil became entirely unavailable, but it was discovered that jojoba could provide a cheap, renewable substitute with similar or even superior chemical properties—making the whale hunt entirely unnecessary.

The word *jojoba*—pronounced (hō-hō′bə)—is a borrowing of American Spanish *jojoba*. Like many Spanish words referring to plants and animals native to the Americas, the American Spanish word is borrowed from an indigenous American language. *Jojoba* comes from one of the Uto-Aztecan languages spoken in the region where jojoba grows. (Because of the similarity of the word for "jojoba" in these languages, scholars cannot be sure exactly which particular language gave the word to Spanish.) In the language of the Tohono O'odham, one of the indigenous peoples of the Sonoran Desert, the word for "jojoba" is *hohowai.* The indigenous inhabitants of the Sonoran Desert region have long gathered the seeds as food and as an ingredient in a salve for the skin. Roasted jojoba seeds taste something like hazelnuts.

The Uto-Aztecan family of languages contains a large number of languages spoken over a broad area of Mexico and the western United States. Comanche, Hopi, and Shoshone are among the Uto-Aztecan languages spoken in the United States. The name *Uto-Aztecan* itself refers to two other members of the family. One of these is the language of the Ute people of Utah and Colorado. (*Ute* is pronounced (yo͞ot), by the way, and in fact, the name of the state of Utah is related to the Utes' own name for themselves, which means "mountain people" in their language.) Nahuatl, the language of the Aztec Empire of Mexico still spoken by over one and a half million people in Mexico today, is also a member of the Uto-Aztecan family.

K

key

The word *key*, "small island," as found in the names of such places as *Key West* and the *Florida Keys*, is also sometimes spelled *cay*. *Cay*, however, is still almost always pronounced (kē) rather than (kā) in the Caribbean and the Gulf of Mexico.

The word *key* for the device that unlocks a door is not related to the word *key* that means "small island." The first *key* descends from the Old English word *cǣg*, "key (for unlocking a lock)," while the second *key* comes from Spanish *cayo*. *Cayo* is the Spanish term for any of the numerous small, flat, sandy islands that are scattered about the Caribbean and the Gulf of Mexico and are usually covered by mangrove forests. The Spanish word is itself borrowed from Taíno, the extinct language of an indigenous people that inhabited the Greater Antilles and the Bahamas at the time of the arrival of the Spaniards in 1492.

lariat

When English speakers began to work as cowboys in the Old West, they didn't learn their Spanish out of books—they learned it from the Spanish speakers who worked beside them while roping calves, breaking horses, and doing all the other hard work that makes up a cowboy's life. When these English-speaking cowboys borrowed a Spanish word, the form that the word eventually took in English was often based on what the cowboys heard (or thought they heard) from their Spanish-speaking fellows, rather than on how the word is spelled in standard Spanish orthography. One word discussed in this book, *hoosegow,* is an example of the ways in which Spanish words were altered on their way into cowboy lingo, and *lariat* is another.

In both Spanish and English, nouns are often accompanied by the definite article when actually used in a sentence. (*The* is the definite article for all nouns in the case of English, but the Spanish definite article takes four different forms, *el, la, los,* or *las,* depending on whether the noun is grammatically masculine or feminine and singular or plural.) When actually used in a sentence, the word *reata,* "rope for tying horses to lead them in single file," was often found in the phrase *la reata,* "the rope," and at some point, cowboys therefore borrowed the whole phrase *la reata* as the simple noun *lariat,* "a rope for lassoing animals or tying them to a post." If we follow the history of many languages down through the ages, we can find other examples of the same sort of confusion about the boundary between a noun and its definite article when words are borrowed across linguistic boundaries—Old Spanish, for example, borrowed many Arabic words with the Arabic definite article, *al–*, still attached, a phenomenon that is discussed elsewhere in this book at the entries for the words *adobe* and *alcove*.

Spanish *reata* was also borrowed into English on its own, as *riata*. Both *lariat* and *riata* begin to appear in English around the same time, in the middle of the 1800s. In his dictionary of cowboy lingo entitled *Western Words,* the scholar Raymond F. Adams explains that there are certain regional preferences among cowboys and ranchers for the words *lariat* and *reata*: "The word [*lariat*] is often used in the southwest, where *reata* or *riata* may also be heard. The word *rope* is used in the Northwest.... Californians do not like the word *lariat*—they use either *reata* or *lass rope.*" Adams also notes that *lariats* are most often made of horsehair, but also sometimes of hemp or rawhide.

The Spanish word *reata* itself is derived from the verb *reatar,* "to tie again" or "to tie (horses) in single file." *Reatar* is a compound of the prefix *re–,* "again," and *atar,* "to tie." The verb *atar* descends from Latin *aptāre,* "to fit, make ready, adjust," and *aptāre* itself comes from Latin *aptus,* "fitted, fitting, suitable." *Aptus* is the source of the English word *apt,* and the words *lariat* and *apt* are thus distant linguistic relatives.

See also *lasso.*

lasso

A lasso, part of the standard equipment of the American cowboy, is a long rope knotted with a loose loop at the end that can be thrown around a horse or calf and drawn tighter around the animal in order to restrain it. The word comes from Spanish *lazo,* meaning "knot, loop, lasso," and is yet another of the many contributions that Spanish has made to the vocabulary of the Old West. The word first begins to be used in English in the very early 1800s.

The word *lasso* is pronounced in several different ways. The pronunciation (lăs′ō) closely resembles the pronunciation of the word in American Spanish, but another pronunciation, (lă-sōō′), with the *o* pronounced as (ōō), is also quite common. The same transformation of an original Spanish *o* into (ōō) in English can be heard in two other English words of Spanish origin: *vamoose* from Spanish *¡Vamos!,* "Let's go!," and *calaboose,* "jail," from Spanish *calabozo,* "dungeon."

In the early 1800s, before the spelling of *lasso* was fixed in its modern form, the word appeared in a variety of other spellings, including *lazie* and *lassau.* Judging from the different ways of writing *lasso,* there must have been a good deal of variation in the pronunciation of the word just after it was borrowed from Spanish. Such variation is only natural—whenever speakers of one language borrow a word from another language, they must adapt the foreign word, with its foreign sounds, to the sounds used in their own language. The results of this process of adaptation are often unpredictable and surprising.

The sounds of English and Spanish are quite different—in English, for example, the vowels in unstressed syllables are usually not pronounced very distinctly, whereas in Spanish all vowels are articulated clearly no matter whether they are stressed or not. English speakers also change the shape of the tongue and lips as they pronounce a vowel—they tend to "glide off" their vowels—whereas Spanish speakers maintain the same position of the tongue and lips throughout the pronunciation of a single vowel. Compare the English word *say* (sā) with the Spanish word *sé,* "I know," or English *low* (lō) with Spanish *lo,* "him, it." When saying the (ō) in *low,* many English speakers start with their lips unrounded and gradually round them into a tight circle as they pronounce the vowel. (This can be verified by saying the vowel in front of a mirror.) The end part of the English vowel (ō), in fact, sounds much like (ū) or even the sound (w). Spanish speakers, however, keep their lips in pretty much the same position while pronouncing the letter *o* in *lo.*

Because of the number and variety of such differences between Spanish and English, there would have been ample opportunity for mishearing and mispronouncing as English-speaking cowboys adopted the lingo of the Spanish-speaking vaqueros that they worked beside in the Old West. Perhaps the cowboys were trying to imitate what they heard as closely as possible, and what they heard (or what they thought they heard!) was somewhat different from what Americans of the 21st century might have thought they heard in the same situation. It was possibly in this way that Spanish *lazo* ended up being pronounced as (lă-sōō′) in English, and Spanish *¡Vamos!* as *vamoose.*

llama

The llama is the most well-known of the four species of camelids (members of the camel family) living in the Andean region of South America: the llama, the guanaco, the alpaca, and the vicuña. Two of these species, the llama and the alpaca, are domesticated animals, while the guanaco and the vicuña live in the wild. Although the exact relationships between the four species are not known for certain, many scientists think that the llama is the domesticated form of the guanaco, and the alpaca is the domesticated form of the vicuña. The indigenous peoples of the Andes had begun to domesticate camelids by at least six thousand years ago.

The llama is raised for its soft, fleecy wool and is also used as a beast of burden. The llama was in fact the largest animal domesticated by the indigenous peoples of the Americas, but it is still too delicate to be used to pull loads as heavy as those pulled by the horses and oxen of Europe, Asia, and Africa. Although children can ride llamas, an adult human being is a very heavy  load for a llama to bear. For this reason, when the Spanish conquistadors came to Peru in the 1530s, the Inca warriors had no llama steeds they could ride out to meet the Spanish warriors, who were mounted on horses.

The llama comes in a variety of colors, but its probable wild ancestor, the guanaco (gwə-nä′kō), has a reddish-brown coat with a lighter underbelly. The guanaco is also slighter and more graceful-looking than the domesticated llama. It is hunted for its hides, which are used to make high-quality leather, and for its soft wool.

Llamas and guanacos have relatively longer, more curved ears than the other two Andean camelids, the alpaca and vicuña. The alpaca is raised mainly for its silky, soft wool, and there are alpaca breeds of many different colors.

The alapaca's wild ancestor, the vicuña, is the smallest of the four camelids, and it produces the finest wool—vicuña is the most expensive variety of wool in the world. In the past, the animal was hunted for its wool, and it became very rare. The countries of the Andes worked to protect the animal, however, and set aside nature reserves for its benefit, and the number of wild vicuña has risen promisingly. Vicuñas do not thrive in captivity, so their wool can only be obtained by rounding up the wild herds and shearing them. Each vicuña only produces a relatively small amount of wool, and twenty-five to thirty vicuña must be shorn to make a single coat. The price of a man's coat of vicuña may be $20,000, while a simple scarf may cost over $2,000.

The English words for all four of these animals are borrowed from American Spanish, and the American Spanish words come from the indigenous languages of the Andes. Spanish *llama* comes from the word *llama* in Quechua, the language of the Inca people who established the Inca Empire. Spanish *guanaco* and *vicuña* come from the Quechua words *wanako* and *wik'uña*, respectively. The Spanish word *alpaca*, however, comes from the word *allpaqa* in Aymara. Aymara was the major language of the Inca Empire beside Quechua, and today, it is spoken by over a million people in the western half of Bolivia in an area centered around the city of La Paz. Aymara is also spoken by a few hundred thousand people in southwestern Peru and has other speakers in Chile and Argentina.

The word *llama* first appears in English at the very beginning of the 1600s in descriptions of Peru. The English word was also spelled *lama* and *glama*, perhaps indicating that English speakers had a hard time pronouncing the sound represented by the letter combination *ll* in Spanish. In some Spanish dialects, and in Quechua, *ll* has another sound like an (l) and a (y) pronounced simultaneously, with the middle part of the tongue against the ridge behind the back of the upper front teeth. This sound is not quite like anything found in English. In many other modern Spanish dialects, *ll* has the sound (y) so that *llama* sounds like (yä′mä). Nowadays in English, the pronunciation (lä′mə) has become standard for the word *llama*.

Since the llama and its close relatives are so important to life in the Andean region, there is even a local Peruvian and

Bolivian Spanish term that can refer to all four species of South American camelids together: *auquénido*. It was made from the Greek word *aukhēn*, "neck" or "throat," by adding the suffix *–ido*, the Spanish equivalent of the suffix *–id* as seen in *camelid*. The term *auquénido* probably makes reference to the long, graceful necks of the Andean camelids. The males of these animals "neck-wrestle" to establish their place in the social order of the herd.

loco

Since the second half of the 1800s, the Spanish word *loco*, "crazy," has been popular in American English slang as an adjective meaning "crazy" and a noun meaning "crazy person." According to the *Dictionary of American Regional English*, the first known occurrence of the word *loco* in English is found in the December 8, 1844, issue of the *St. Louis Reveille* newspaper. The paper offers the following description of an unfortunate animal, apparently a horse or mule: *He was girt about the neck with a leather bridle, and his meat was locos and wild onions.* The *loco* mentioned here is nowadays more often called by the name *locoweed*, the common term for a variety of plants growing in the Great Plains, the Rockies, and the American Southwest that are poisonous to livestock. Cattle that eat locoweed show various symptoms, including wasting, lethargy, loss of balance, and erratic and aggressive behavior—in short, cattle that eat locoweed go *loco*, to use the word that English-speaking cowboys must have picked up from the Spanish-speaking vaqueros of the American Southwest.

Loco itself is another of the many words in Spanish that were borrowed from Arabic when the southern part of the Iberian Peninsula was governed by Muslim rulers. *Loco* comes from Arabic *lawqā'*, the feminine form of the word *'alwaq*, meaning "stupid" or "foolish." *Lawqā'* first entered Spanish directly as a feminine, *loca*. The corresponding masculine, *loco*, was then created in Spanish itself, based on the pervasive Spanish grammatical pattern in which masculine nouns and adjectives ending in -*o* have their feminine counterpart in -*a* (the pattern seen in such adjectival pairs as *rojo* (masculine) and *roja* (feminine), both meaning "red"). The Arabic diphthong *aw* is pronounced somewhat like English *o* in many dialects of the language, and so *aw* can appear as *o* when Arabic words are borrowed into Spanish.

macho

In many cultures, the ideal man is imagined as physically strong, mentally resourceful, emotionally tough, courageous, and prepared to endure anything in the defense of his family's reputation and his own honor. He may even pursue a variety of amorous adventures with women. This idealized conception of the macho man plays a great role in the traditions of Spain and Latin America, perhaps even more so than in many other cultures, and the Spanish and Latin American attitude toward masculinity may explain why English has borrowed the words *macho* and *machismo* from Spanish.

In Spanish, *macho* simply means "a male animal," and by extension, "a man distinguished by qualities traditionally admired in men like strength, courage, and vigor." In English, *macho* has of course taken on a more pejorative tinge than it has in Spanish and usually means "excessively masculine," and the word is often used of the behavior of men overly concerned with proving their masculinity. *Macho* begins to appear in English in the 1920s, at first in contexts that make reference to the esteem in which traditional masculine qualities were held in Latin America.

The Spanish word *macho* is the direct descendant of the Latin word *masculus,* meaning simply "male" as an adjective and "a male" as a noun. As the everyday spoken Latin of Roman Spain slowly evolved into Spanish, the Latin word *mas-*

culus first became **masclus* in Vulgar Latin, and then the consonant cluster *–scl–* was simplified into the *ch* seen in the Spanish word *macho*. Meanwhile, as the everyday spoken Latin of Roman France slowly developed into Old French, Latin *masculus* first became Old French *masle*. Then the *s* was lost in the Old French word, and it became *male*. *Male* was subsequently borrowed into Middle English, and it eventually shows up as the Modern English word *male*. In Latin itself, *masculus* also served as the base from which a new adjective *masculīnus,* "masculine," was derived. *Masculīnus* was borrowed into English as *masculine,* and in this way, the English words *macho, male,* and *masculine* are linguistic cousins.

Machismo is the noun derived from *macho* by the addition of the suffix *–ismo,* the Spanish equivalent of the English suffix *–ism.* A person—usually a man—who espouses or exemplifies machismo is called a *machista* in Spanish. As the conception of masculinity has changed in Spain and Latin America, the meanings of the words *machismo* and *machista* have developed to reflect new attitudes. Today, there is often a pejorative sense to the word *machismo* when it refers to a system of beliefs that, besides glorifying traditionally masculine virtues like strength and stoic courage, also tries to justify the subordination of women—more or less the same meaning that *machismo* has in English today.

mambo

Mambo is a Latin American form of music and dance originated by Cuban musicians in the 1930s. Mambo music is in 4/4 time and has a distinctive syncopated rhythm. Many scholars of Latin American language and music believe that the word for this music, *mambo,* originated as a religious term in Africa. *Mambo* may originally have described communications between people and the gods, and the term may be related to the word *mambo,* "to talk," in Yoruba, a language of southwestern Nigeria.

The rhythmic complexity and drive of Cuban music is in part a heritage from Africa—many Cubans descend from people who were enslaved and brought from Africa to work in the sugar cane plantations of the Caribbean. Along with their musical traditions, these Africans also brought many words of African origin that subsequently entered the local varieties of Spanish and English as well as the French Creole of Haiti. One of these words was *mambo,* the French Creole term for a high priestess of the voodoo religion. The word *mambo* was also used among Cuban communities of African descent to mean "conversation with the gods." In the 1930s, according to Ed Morales in his book *The Latin Beat,* Cuban musicians began to use the term *mambo* as a name for the thrilling extended percussion breaks that became popular in Cuban dance music at the time—a mambo was the moment when the percussionist communicated ecstatically with the gods like a voodoo priestess in a trance.

As a name for the Cuban genre of music and dance, the word *mambo* seems to have been popularized especially by the bandleader Antonio Arcaño and the bass player Cachao López in 1938. López composed a piece he called *Mambo* which featured his propulsive repeated bass line as a ground over which his fellow musicians could improvise their elaborate percussion solos. Arcaño would call out *¡Mil veces mambo!* ("A thousand times mambo!") to tell his musicians to begin their solos. The pianist and bandleader Pérez Prado invented a dance for the mambo in the 1940s and helped export the mambo to the United States. Audiences and dancers enjoyed the thrill of mambo music and the theatricality of mambo musicians' performances onstage, and the mambo phenomenon grew steadily until it reached craze proportions in the 1950s. Mambo was also one of the many genres of Latin music that eventually contributed to the development of salsa.

mariachi

Mariachi is a style of music originating in the state of Jalisco in Mexico. The word *mariachi* is also used of the band (and of the individual band members) playing the music. A typical mariachi band includes two or more trumpets, two or more violins, a guitar, a Mexican-style *vihuela,* and a *guitarrón,* as well as other instruments. The *vihuela,* by the way, is a high-pitched, five-stringed member of the guitar family, while the *guitarrón* is a large instrument somewhat like a cross between an upright bass and a guitar. It is held in front of the body at an angle like a guitar and provides the bass line for mariachi music.

Mariachi songs typically express the joys and sorrows of love, and besides playing at a variety of other venues like weddings, mariachis are often hired by men to serenade the women they love. Tourists in Mexico are often even told that the word *mariachi* comes from the French word *mariage,* "marriage."

Why should the Mexican word *mariachi* come from French? The story begins in 1862, when French forces tried to remove the Mexican President Benito Juárez from power and install Archduke Maximilian of Hapsburg as Emperor of Mexico. Although Mexico had been independent from Spain for over forty years by this time, it had accumulated a large foreign debt owed to European countries. By installing a monarchy favorable to their interests, the French and their allies hoped to secure their interests in Mexico and guarantee access to Mexico's rich natural resources. Since the Spanish Empire had reached its greatest glory in the 1500s during the reigns of Charles V and his son Philip II of Spain, both members of the House of Hapsburg, Maximilian seemed a natural choice for the new Emperor of Mexico. The Archduke was at first reluctant to take the job, but he was told that a vote had confirmed that the Mexican people wanted him to take the throne—the vote, however, had taken place after French forces were in control of Mexico City. (There was in fact a monarchist faction in Mexican politics at the time, and the monarchists had approached Maximilian before with the offer of a crown.) The conquest of Mexico was not as easy as the French imagined, and on the fifth of May, 1862, the French suffered a humiliating defeat by the Mexicans at the Battle of Puebla. This is the battle commemorated by the Mexican national holiday *Cinco de mayo*, and the occasion is sometimes toasted with the words *¡Abajo los franceses!*, "Down with the French!" Nevertheless, it took until 1867 for Mexican republican forces to expel the French completely from the country. Benito Juárez reassumed the presidency, and Maximilian was executed by a firing squad.

During this period when Mexico struggled against foreign intervention, French troops were stationed all around the country, and—so the story would have us believe—one day some French soldiers investigated the noise and loud music coming from a wedding party somewhere in Jalisco. The music died down when the soldiers asked what was going on. At last, someone ventured to respond in French with the words *C'est un mariage*, "It's a marriage," and in the person's heavy Mexican accent, the word *mariage* came out as *mariachi*. After that, the name *mariachi* supposedly stuck.

Quaint as this story may be, it is certainly false, because traces of the word *mariachi* have been found in documents written before 1862, such as payment records for mariachi musicians. Although the true origin of *mariachi* is still much disputed, Mexican scholars now agree that it probably comes from one of the indigenous languages of Mexico. The Mexican historian and linguist Ignacio Dávila Garibi proposed that *mariachi* came from the language of the Coca, an indigenous people of Jalisco. Other scholars have proposed that *mariachi* comes from a word for a certain kind of tree in the Cora language of Nayarit, the Mexican state to the north of Jalisco. The performance platforms for mariachi or some of the instruments may originally have been made of this wood.

marijuana

The word *marijuana* comes from Mexican Spanish *marihuana,* also spelled *mariguana.* Nothing is known for certain about the origins of the Mexican Spanish word, however. In English, the term *marijuana* refers to the variety of the cannabis plant with the scientific name *Cannabis sativa* var. *indica*—the variety with a high content of the psychoactive compound in marijuana— while the word *hemp* refers to the variety of the plant with much less potent significant psychoactive properties, *Cannabis sativa* var. *sativa.* The seeds of the hemp plant can be pressed to produce an edible oil, and the fibers of the hemp plant can be used for making paper. In Spanish, the word *cáñamo* is used to refer to hemp and the cannabis plant in general, and *cáñamo* comes from the Latin word *cannabis,* which modern scientists have chosen as the genus name for the plant.

When it first begins to appear in English at the end of the 1800s, the early spellings of *marijuana* resemble Spanish *marihuana* more closely; the spelling *marijuana* begins to appear only later. It has been suggested that at the beginning of the 1900s, opponents of the use of marijuana deliberately tried to popularize the Mexican word *marihuana* as the name for the drug in English, in an attempt to demonize the drug with a foreign-sounding name. Despite appearances, the spelling of the English word as *marijuana,* however, does not originate in Spanish at all. Instead, it began in English, after English had borrowed the word as *marihuana.* The spelling *marijuana* may reflect the influence of folk etymology—some speakers of English who knew the Spanish term *marihuana* would also have known the Spanish personal name *Mari-Juana,* a popular form of *María Juana,* the equivalent of the English name *Mary Jane.* The spelling of *marihuana* in English may then have been influenced by the spelling of the name *Mari-Juana,* perhaps as a joke or as way of disguising the word. Of course, *Mary Jane* is a slang term for marijuana in English, but this slang term originates in English itself, not as a translation of a hypothetical Spanish slang term *María Juana*.

maroon

The English verb *maroon,* meaning "to put ashore in an isolated place with no hope of rescue or escape" and more generally "to abandon or leave in isolation," is derived from the somewhat archaic English noun *maroon,* "fugitive slave." The noun *maroon* originally referred to members of the remote communities established in the West Indies and southeastern South America by slaves who escaped captivity and fled into the mountains. The use of *maroon* as a verb developed from the resemblance of the condition of a marooned sailor to the isolated life of these runaway slaves. Both the noun *maroon* and the corresponding verb begin to appear in English in the 1600s, at the time when the slave trade was expanding rapidly with the establishment of sugar plantations in the Americas.

Maroon is a borrowing of French *marron,* "fugitive slave," and the French word comes from Spanish *cimarrón,* literally meaning "wild" or "feral." By extension, the Spanish adjective was also used to describe runaway slaves living in the mountains. The adjective *cimarrón* itself was made by adding the suffix *–arrón* to the Spanish noun *cima,* "summit of a mountain"—the upper slopes of mountains being the exclusive dwelling place of wild animals, as opposed to the plains where people farm and raise domestic animals.

merengue

The merengue is an energetic dance that developed in the Dominican Republic and Haiti and is characterized by a sliding step. Merengue music is in rapid 2/4 time, and the core instruments of a classic merengue band usually include an accordion, a small drum called a *tambora* in Spanish, and another small percussion instrument, called a *güiro* in Spanish, made from a gourd. The Spanish word for this style of dance and music, *merengue,* literally means "meringue (the sweet dessert)"—although it is unclear exactly how the dance might have come to be called "The Meringue." According to the *Diccionario de la Real Academia Española,* however, *merengue* can mean "mess, mix-up, rumpus, roughhousing" in the Spanish of Argentina, Bolivia, Paraguay, and Uruguay, since egg whites must be beaten vigorously in order to make a meringue. Similarly, it is possible that in the Dominican Republic, the word *merengue,* "meringue," was thought to be an appropriate way of describing the vigorous movements of the merengue dance. Merengue may in this way simply be "roughhousing."

Both the Spanish word *merengue,* "meringue, merengue" and the English word *meringue* are borrowings of the French word *meringue.* The further origins of the French word, however, are completely obscure.

See also *guiro.*

merino

Until the rise of Australia and New Zealand as wool producers in the 1800s, Spain was the most important supplier of wool to Europe. The key to Spanish success was a breed of sheep called the merino, which produced a long, fine, very high-quality wool. To keep Spain's monopoly on fine fleece production secure, it was even forbidden to export merino sheep from Spain until the 1720s. Since then, merinos have become the most widely raised variety of sheep in the world. Today the word *merino* is also used in English to describe any lightweight fabric made of fine wool. The importance of sheep herding in traditional Spain is reflected not only in the English word *merino*, but also in two other English terms of Spanish origin discussed in this book, *mustang* and *transhumance*.

The ancestors of merino sheep were probably brought to Spain by the Banū Marīn, a Berber group that in the mid-1200s extended their rule over most of the Maghreb, the area in northwest Africa that is now the modern countries of Morocco, Algeria, and Tunisia. The name of the group, *Banū Marīn*, literally means "the sons of Marīn" in Arabic. In the late 1200s and in the 1300s, the Banū Marīn also took control of some areas of Spain, but their influence in the Iberian peninsula ended after a disastrous defeat by Christian forces from Castile and Aragon in 1340. By that time, however, the Banū Marīn had managed to introduce a North African breed of sheep that the Spanish eventually developed into the merino. *Merino*, the Spanish term for the breed, probably comes from the name of the Banū Marīn dynasty. (The difference in sound between *Marīn* and *merino* probably reflects the fact that in many Arabic dialects, the vowel sound *a* approaches the sound of Spanish *e*.) The word was also probably influenced by another word pronounced *merino*, however. This word was the title of a certain kind of administrative officer who worked in the service of a feudal lord in medieval times.

The word *merino* is another example of the deep and long-lasting influence that the Maghreb, with its mixture of Arab and Berber cultures, has had on Spain. The Berbers themselves are the modern descendants of ancient inhabitants of North Africa, and they live in scattered regions from the mountains of Morocco and Algeria to oases in the deserts of Egypt. The Berber languages are distantly related to the language of ancient Egypt that was written in hieroglyphs, and they are also distant cousins of the Semitic languages like Arabic and Hebrew. Although most Americans probably think of North Africa as

Arabic-speaking, Arabic was only introduced in the region with the spread of Islam to the area after around AD 660. Despite the prestige of Arabic as the language of the Koran and Muslim culture and science, the Berber languages have flourished alongside Arabic into modern times. Even at the beginning of the 20th century, it is likely that more people in Morocco spoke Berber languages than Arabic, even though Arabic was the language of literature and traditional education.

Today, perhaps three million people in Morocco can speak the Berber language Tashelhiyt, while up to six million people in Algeria can speak Kabyle. In recent times, many Moroccans and Algerians of Berber origin have tried to expand the use of their languages in schools and daily life and to encourage their fellow Berbers to take pride in their ethnic identity, long overshadowed by Arab culture. One example of the recent upsurge of Berber ethnic pride is offered by Zinédine Zidane, the star of the Real Madrid soccer club. Zidane was born in France to parents of Kabyle origin who immigrated from Algeria, and when asked how he would describe himself, Zidane answered that he was first and foremost a Kabyle.

mesa

Mesa is another of the many words that American English borrowed to describe the land and life of the Southwestern United States, an area which was long a part of the Spanish Empire and for a while a part of Mexico. In both Spanish and English, the word *mesa* is used of flat-topped geological formations elevated from the surrounding land and edged by cliffs. *Mesa* is generally applied to formations that are broader than a butte but smaller than a plateau.

The flat top of a mesa usually consists of a layer of very hard igneous rock, like basalt, lying over layers of more erodible rock—the flat surface atop a mesa is often the remnant of ancient lava flow. Over time, rivers and streams running over the surface of the land erode the areas of softer rock, but the layer of hard rock protects the soft rock underneath—eventually, as the surrounding land is washed away, the mesa begins to emerge from the landscape.

The literal meaning of the word *mesa* in Spanish is simply "table"—compare the use of the word *tableland* in English. Spanish *mesa* descends from the Latin word *mēnsa* "table." (The consonant *n* simply disappeared before *s* as Latin evolved into the modern Romance languages like Spanish. Other examples include Spanish *asa*, "handle," from Latin *ānsa*, and Spanish *esposo*, "husband," from Latin *spōnsus*, "bridegroom.") Latin *mēnsa* is also the ultimate source of the English word *commensal*, used by biologists to describe the type of symbiotic relationship existing between two different species when one species benefits from the relationship while the other is simply unaffected. An example of a commensal relationship would be that between a small carnivorous fish that travels with a much larger predatory fish and eats the scraps that drift away from the larger fish's mouth as it feeds. *Commensal* comes from Medieval Latin *commēnsālis*, "sharing a meal, eating in common," which in turn is made up of the Latin prefix *com–*, meaning "with, together," added to *mēnsa*—commensal animals "share a table," so to speak.

mesquite

Anyone who has driven across the vast state of Texas to Mexico is familiar with small, spiny trees or shrubs called *mesquite*. There are several species of mesquite, and botanists have classified mesquite in the genus *Prosopis* in the pea family. Mesquite species are found throughout the hot, dry regions of the

Americas. Mesquite has a very long taproot that can reach down to the water table, allowing it to thrive in areas of very low rainfall. Thickets of mesquite are vital sources of food and shelter for many kinds of wildlife, and mesquite also provides forage for cattle and abundant nectar for bees. Mesquite produces very nutritious seed pods, resembling large brown pea pods, that can be ground into meal to make bread, and these pods have long been the staple food of many indigenous peoples of the American deserts.

The common species characteristic of the deserts of Texas, the Southwest of the United States, and northern Mexico is usually called the *honey mesquite* (*Prosopis glandulosa*). The pods of the honey mesquite have a particularly high sugar content. Mesquite wood burns slowly, and when used as fuel for a barbecue, it gives a distinctive flavor to the grilled food, one of the authentic tastes of the American Southwest.

The English word *mesquite,* pronounced (mə-skēt′), comes from a variant of Spanish *mezquite,* also spelled *mesquite.* The Spanish word in turn comes from *mizquitl,* the word for mesquite in Nahuatl, the language of the Aztec Empire.

moment of truth

The American writer Ernest Hemingway can be credited with introducing the idiomatic phrase *moment of truth* in English from Spanish. The earliest known occurrence of *moment of truth* is found in *Death in the Afternoon,* Hemingway's classic study of bullfighting first published in 1932. Hemingway thought that in his time the art of bullfighting had become decadent. In his book, he laments that the average bullfighter of his day kept the spectators satisfied by showing off and allowing the tips of the bull's horns to get as "mathematically close to his body as possible without moving his feet." In the past,

Hemingway writes, the thrill of bullfighting had come from the sheer danger faced by the bullfighter in front of a huge animal armed with sharp horns:

> *In the old days the bulls were usually bigger than they are now; they were fiercer, more uncertain, heavier and older. They had not been bred down to a smaller size to please the bullfighters. …The whole end of the bullfight was the final sword thrust, the actual encounter between the man and the animal, what the Spanish call the moment of truth, and every move in the fight was to prepare the bull for the killing.*

Hemingway's phrase *moment of truth* translates the Spanish expression *hora de la verdad,* "decisive moment," or, more literally, "hour of truth." This English version of the phrase caught the imagination of the English-speaking world at the time, and it soon came to be used outside of accounts of bullfights to describe any moment in time upon which much depends.

Linguists have a special name for words and expressions like *moment of truth* that are translations of words or expressions in another language—they call them *calques* or *loan translations.* Another English phrase calqued on a Spanish original is discussed at the entry in this book for the expression *blue blood.*

mosque

In the year AD 710, the Iberian peninsula was ruled by the Visigoths, the Christian descendants of a Germanic tribe that had overrun the Roman Empire in the late 400s and put an end to Roman rule in the western Mediterranean. The three-hundred-year reign of the Visigoths, however, was nearing its end. A squabble had arisen between the Visigothic king Roderic and one of his allies or vassals, Count Julian, the ruler of the Christian territory of Ceuta on the coast of Morocco across from Spain. According to the story as told in traditional ballads and the works of some medieval chroniclers, Julian had sent his daughter to be educated in Roderic's court in Toledo, and Roderic had gotten her pregnant. Whatever the cause behind the conflict—political differences or personal ambitions may have been the real motivation—Julian went to his Muslim neighbors for help in fighting Roderic.

Most of North Africa at this time was governed by the powerful Umayyad caliphate, the first of the great Muslim empires that were to rule much of the Near East and the Mediterranean world after the emergence of Islam. The Umayyad caliph ruled from Damascus in Syria, and in the early 700s, Umayyad territory already stretched from Iran in the east to Morocco in the west. The Umayyad governor of North Africa agreed to help Julian, and on April 30, 711, forces of the caliphate crossed to Spain under the command of Ṭāriq ibn Ziyad—the warrior whose fame would be preserved in the name of the Rock of Gibraltar or *Jabal al-Ṭāriq* in Arabic.

The Umayyad army, however, did much more than just intervene in Visigothic internal affairs—by the year 718, almost all of the Iberian peninsula had fallen into Muslim hands, and one of the most glorious periods of intellectual and artistic progress in the history of humanity had begun. In one form or another, Muslim rule in the south of Spain would last over seven centuries, until 1492, the year Ferdinand of Aragon and Isabella of Castile deposed the last ruler of the Muslim kingdom of Granada. Throughout much of this period, Christians, Jews, and Muslims lived side by side in relative harmony in the various small kingdoms of *Al-Andalus,* as Muslim Spain was called in Arabic. It was during this period that hundreds of Arabic words poured into the Spanish language, and among them was the word that would eventually appear in English as *mosque.*

The rulers of Al-Andalus built thousands of mosques to serve as places of worship for Muslim settlers from North Africa and also for the people who had converted to the new religion. Many of these mosques survive today, having been reconsecrated as Christian churches. The present-day Cathedral of Córdoba, for example, was in fact once the Mosque of Córdoba, one of the most brilliant of the architectural jewels of Al-Andalus. The Mosque of Córdoba was also at one time the second largest mosque in the world—a testimony to the important position that Al-Andalus held in the Muslim world. It is natural therefore that Spanish should have borrowed the Arabic word for the numerous elegant buildings that had begun to adorn the cities of Spain.

The Arabic word for "mosque" is *masjid,* a noun related to the verb *sajada,* "to bow down in worship." A *masjid* is thus literally "a place for bowing down in prayer." Arabic *masjid* entered Spanish in the form *mezquita,* "mosque." *Mezquita* was then borrowed into Old Italian as *moscheta,* and Old Italian *moscheta* developed a variant form *moschea.* This variant form of the word was then borrowed into Old French as *mousquaie,* and the Old French term eventually came into English as *mosque.* Although *mosque* first appears in descriptions of life in the Middle East, rather than in Al-Andalus, the history of the English word and its passage through Spanish reminds us that during medieval times, Muslim Spain was an important part of the larger Islamic world.

mosquito

According to the Oxford English Dictionary, the word *mosquito* first appears in English in 1572. Before that time, the word *gnat* was used to refer both to the larger biting insects we now call *mosquitos* as well as the smaller annoying creatures that are still called *gnats* today. The meaning of *gnat* was gradually restricted after the introduction of *mosquito*. In the 1500 and 1600s, of course, the Spanish Empire ruled many of the tropical and subtropical regions of the world where mosquitoes are a constant problem, and perhaps it was this that lead English adventurers and voyagers to adopt the Spanish word for these insects, *mosquito*. In Spanish,

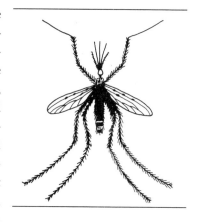

a *mosquito* is literally a "little fly"—the word *mosquito* is simply the diminutive of *mosca,* "fly."

Spanish *mosca* is the direct descendant of the Latin word *musca,* "fly." Similarly, as the spoken Latin of Italy developed into Italian, Latin *musca* became Italian *mosca.* The diminutive of *mosca* in Italian is *moschetta,* which corresponds to Spanish *mosquito* in form, except insofar as the Italian word is feminine and ends in -*a* rather than -*o.* In Italian, *moschetta* was also used to refer to the sparrow hawk, a small hawk of Europe that preys on sparrows. The meaning of *moschetta* was then further extended to "bolt for a crossbow," an extension of meaning probably suggested by the deadly darting flight of the sparrow hawk. From there, the word *moschetta* developed the meaning "small artillery piece." In the middle of the 1500s, French then borrowed *moschetta* as *mousquet* and used it to describe the guns of the period, which were fired by lighting a slow-burning length of rope leading into the receptacle that held the gunpowder. The English borrowed the French word *mousquet* as *musket,* first recorded in 1574. In this way, the English words *mosquito* and *musket* are etymologically just "little flies."

mundungus

In 1785, Captain Francis Grose, an English antiquarian and bon vivant, published a book entitled *A Classical Dictionary of the Vulgar Tongue,* a fascinating and often hilarious collection of the slang of his day. Grose's book was enormously popular—it went through several editions and was revised and expanded by other authors. Grose left nothing out that might amuse his readers—he even included some obscenities that could hardly be printed in a modern newspaper, or even in a book for the general public like this one about the Spanish words in English. Grose's book includes many words and phrases that are still familiar today, like *kick the bucket,* "to die", and *kid,* "a child"—as well as many more that have fallen out of use but deserve to be revived, like *hum durgeon,* "an imaginary illness."

Another of the fun but almost forgotten words in the *Dictionary of the Vulgar Tongue* is *mundungus.* Captain Grose's entry for this word reads as follows:

> Mundungus: *bad or rank tobacco: from* mondongo, *a Spanish word signifying tripes, or the uncleaned entrails of a beast, full of filth.*

Mundungus has been used in English since the middle of the 1600s, at first with the meaning "tripe" and then with the meaning "bad tobacco." The *-us* ending of *mundungus* was probably added to Spanish *mondongo* as a joke, making the slang word sound like a scientific term from Latin. Recently, *mundungus* has become much more well known as the name of a character in the series of books by J. K. Rowling chronicling the adventures of the young wizard Harry Potter. Mundungus Fletcher, a wizard with petty criminal tendencies, smokes a pipe whose odor is likened to burning socks.

Spanish *mondongo,* "stomach and intestines of livestock," is a variant of the word *mondejo,* the name of a dish consisting of the stuffed innards of a pig or sheep. These words belong to a larger family of Spanish words including other colloquial terms like *bandullo,* "belly, intestines," *baltra,* "belly," and *bandujo,* also the name of a dish consisting of the intestine of a pig or sheep, filled with minced meat. All these words probably descend from the Arabic word *baṭn,* "belly." (The *ṭ* represents the Arabic letter *ṭā,* which sounds like a *t* pronounced with a distinctive "low" or "dark" quality.) *Mundugus* is thus one of the large number of words that have reached English from Arabic by way of Spanish.

mustang

Mustangs are small, hardy wild horses of the North American plains. They descend from the Arabian horses brought to America by Spanish explorers—there were no horses in the Western Hemisphere before the arrival of the Spanish. When some of these Spanish horses escaped into the wilderness or were stolen or abandoned, they learned to live in the open wilderness and multiplied abundantly. Later, ranchers would sometimes let their own horses run and forage freely with mustang herds over the vast range. In this way some herds of American mustangs have constantly been infused with new blood from various other stocks. Other mustang herds have mixed relatively little with other horses, so that they faithfully preserve the characteristics of ancient breeds that have now died out in their Spanish homeland. The Native American peoples also developed their own horse breeds, like the Appaloosa, out of mustang stock. Today, there are perhaps over thirty thousand mustangs still galloping free over the American range, and they benefit from federal protection. In order to prevent overpopulation, however, mustangs are sometimes killed or captured and put up for adoption.

The word *mustang* first begins to appear in English at the beginning of the 1800s. Washington Irving used the word in 1837, in his *The Rocky mountains; or, Scenes, incidents, and adventures in the far West,* an account of the expedition to the Pacific Northwest of the French-born American explorer Benjamin Louis Eulalie de Bonneville. In the original edition of this work, the word is spelled *mestang*:

> *The first night of his march, Captain Bonneville encamped upon Henry's Fork; an upper branch of Snake River, called after the first American trader that erected a fort beyond the mountains. About an hour after all hands had come to a halt the clatter of hoofs was heard, and a solitary female, of the Nez Perce tribe, came galloping up. She was mounted on a mestang or half wild horse, which she managed by a long rope hitched round the under jaw by way of bridle.*

Irving's original spelling *mestang* gives us a clue to the origin of the word in Spanish. *Mustang* in fact comes from a mixture of two Spanish words: *mostrenco* and *mestengo,* both meaning "stray animal." Although the ultimate origin of *mostrenco* is obscure, *mestengo,* on the other hand, is a variant of *mesteño,* "stray animal." *Mesteño* is derived from the name of the *Mesta,* a medieval Spanish guild or business association of livestock owners. The *Mesta* provided a means for communal ownership and management of the large flocks of sheep and other livestock that roamed open grazing lands in Spain. Institutions like the Spanish *Mesta* were also established in some of the areas later colonized by Spain, like Mexico. The name of the *Mesta* derives from the word *mixta* in the Medieval Latin phrase *animália mixta,* literally "assorted animals."

Mixta is itself a form of *mixtus,* the past participle of the verb *miscēre,* "to mix." The resemblance between Latin *mixtus* and English *mix* is no accident—the English word in fact descends from the Latin. In Old French, the Latin word *mixtus* took the form *mixte,* and this was borrowed into English as *mixed.* Our modern verb *mix* is derived from *mixed* by a process that linguists call *back-formation.* Some other examples of back-formation in English include *diagnose* and *baby-sit,* which look like they are the originals from which *diagnosis* and *baby-sitter* were built. In fact, people used the nouns *diagnosis* and *baby-sitter* first, and only later created *diagnose* and *baby-sit* by chopping off the suffixes at the end.

English has two other words, *merino* and *transhumance,* that come from the vocabulary of livestock-raising and the *Mesta.* They are discussed as separate entries elsewhere in this book.

nachos

A Tex-Mex favorite now eaten in every corner of the United States, nachos seem like a timeless dish—what could be simpler than melted cheese over tortilla chips? In fact, nachos are a comparatively recent invention, and they are named after Sr. Ignacio "Nacho" Anaya, who came up with the idea for them on the spur of the moment in 1943.

Sr. Anaya was the maître d'hôtel at the Victory Club restaurant in Piedras Negras, a city in the Mexican state of Coahuila located on the Rio Grande across from Eagle Pass, Texas. One evening a large group of guests arrived at the restaurant, and they needed something to nibble on. Sr. Anaya could not find the chef, so he went into the kitchen to prepare something himself. He took tostadas (corn tortillas deep-fat fried until crisp), grated some cheese over them, and put them under the broiler. When the cheese had melted, he added some jalapeño pepper slices on top and emerged with the first plate of nachos ever made. His creation was a hit and came to be known locally as *Nacho's especiales* (that is, "Nacho's specials"). In Spanish, *Nacho* is a common nickname for men called *Ignacio*. Eventually *Nacho's especiales* was shortened to just *nachos*. The word *nachos* was then taken to be the plural of a common noun *nacho,* and now *nacho* is used in all sorts of phrases, like *nacho cheese flavor.*

Soon after their invention, nachos became quite popular in southern Texas, and somewhat later, in the 1970s, the well-known sports journalist Howard Cosell tasted them. He began to promote them at every opportunity, and the fame of nachos spread to every corner of the United States. To honor the creation of nachos, a nacho festival is now held annually in Piedras Negras.

noria

A noria is a water wheel with buckets attached to its rim. It is used to raise water from a stream, especially for transfer to an irrigation channel. The force of the stream turns the water wheel, bringing the buckets down to be filled with water and then lifting them up to the irrigation channel. The noria is constructed so that filled buckets will be tipped at some point as they turn above the stream, pouring water into the channel.

After Moorish forces conquered the south of Spain in the 700s and the Muslim kingdoms of Al-Andalus were born, great improvements were made to agriculture in the region, and many public works projects were built. Visitors to the region marveled at the well-watered fields and gardens of Al-Andalus—almost a paradise on earth. Norias were one kind of technology widely put to use in Al-Andalus, and Spanish *noria* itself comes from Arabic *nāʿūra*, "noria, waterwheel."

Arabic *nāʿūra* is a borrowing of the Aramaic word *nāʿurā*. Aramaic is another member of the Semitic language family, of which Arabic and Hebrew are also members. The Aramaic language was widely spoken over the Near East before the expansion of Islam in the area in the 600s—Jesus spoke with his apostles and other followers in Aramaic. Arabic eventually replaced Aramaic as the dominant language of the region, but not before borrowing many words from Aramaic, like *nāʿurā*. This

Aramaic noun is derived from the verb *nəʿar,* "to shake, roar," probably in reference to the impressive sound made by the creaking water wheel pouring out bucket after bucket of water into the irrigation channel.

nutria

Nutrias are large nocturnal rodents native to South America. They live on riverbanks and in estuaries and wetlands, where they eat the roots and bulbs of aquatic plants. The nutria, whose scientific name is *Myocastor coypus,* is very well adapted for life in the water—the female nutria even has her nipples on her sides, rather than underneath her, so that her young can continue to nurse while floating beside her as she swims along. Nutrias also have webbed feet and in general look a lot like beavers—except for their long tail, which is round and ratlike rather than paddle-shaped.

Like the beaver, nutrias also have soft fur, and in the early 20th century there was a large market for this fur in the clothing industry. Enterprising farmers all around the world started raising nutria in the hope of cashing in on the demand for their pelts. Eventually, some of the rodents escaped from the farms and took up residence in local wetlands. In the absence of caimans, pumas, and the other natural predators of the nutria in South America, wild nutria populations began to explode. The bottom had fallen out of the nutria fur market by this time, so nobody even bothered to hunt them. In many regions where they escaped or were introduced, nutrias became a serious threat to the environment—and they remain an important pest today. They eat so many plants in the wetlands where they live that the soil once held in place by the plants' roots simply washes away, and native species of animals cannot find enough to eat. Nutria damage is particularly severe in Louisiana, where the state has put a bounty of four dollars on the tail of every nutria in an effort to control their numbers. Nutria cannot tolerate very cold temperatures, however, so they have not managed to colonize the more northerly portion of the United States.

The English word for these critters, *nutria,* is actually the Spanish word for the otter. When the first Spaniards to arrive in South America encountered the nutria, they were reminded of the otters living on riverbanks back in Europe, even though otters are carnivores rather than plant-eating rodents like nutrias. In some parts of South America, the Spanish word *nutria* is still used for the rodent—rather than the otter—but nowadays the most common name for the nutria in Spanish is *coipo.* The animal is also sometimes called a *quiyá,* a word from the Guaraní language or one of the close relatives of Guaraní, which is the language of an indigenous people of Paraguay, northern Argentina, and southern Brazil. The origin of the Spanish word *coipo* is further discussed in this book at the entry for the English word *coypu.*

Just like the early Spanish explorers and settlers, the first English speakers who settled in North America also sometimes gave old names for European plants and animals to the North American species that were new to them. For example, the bird called a *robin* in North America is a large thrush with the scientific name *Turdus migratorius,* which literally means "the migratory thrush" in Latin. This bird is quite different in many ways from the smaller *robin* of England, whose scientific name is *Erithacus rubecula,* or "the little red robin" in Latin. Since the American bird has an orange-red breast and a lovely song just like the European robin, and since both species are comfortable living near human beings, the English settlers gave the familiar name *robin* to the bird that brings spring back to northern reaches of North America.

oregano

The English word *oregano* is regularly used to refer to two different herbs, one native to the Mediterranean region and another native to Mexico. The Mediterranean herb has the scientific name *Origanum vulgare* and belongs to the mint family. Other plants of the genus *Origanum,* local varieties found in various parts of the Mediterranean, are often simply referred to as *oregano* in English as well. The species *Origanum vulgare* (whose name literally means "common oregano" in Latin) is one of the essential seasonings of southern Italian cuisine—no spaghetti or pizza sauce would be complete without it.

Origanum vulgare is also used in the cuisine of other countries in the Mediterranean area, including Spain, and it is the Spanish language that has given the commonly used name for the herb, *oregano,* to English. According to the *Oxford English Dictionary,* the first known mention of the word *oregano* in English is found in writings

dating from 1771 that describe the use of the herb to preserve anchovies and meats. The author of the text notes that in the English of his time, oregano was also known as *Spanish hops*!

When, in the early 1500s, the Spaniards first began to make exploratory forays into Mexico from their bases in the Caribbean, they found that the indigenous Mexican peoples seasoned their cuisine with several herbs that tasted and smelled remarkably like the Mediterranean oregano that the Spaniards knew from home. The most common of these various Mexican herbs has the scientific name *Lippia graveolens,* and it belongs to the verbena family, closely related to the mint family to which Mediterranean oregano belongs. Today, in Mexican Spanish, the word *orégano* usually refers to *Lippia graveolens,* and no chili-powder blend could be considered authentic without the addition of Mexican oregano—one of the essential flavors of the cuisine of Mexico and the Southwest of the United States.

The Spanish word *orégano* comes from Latin *orīganum* (the same word that modern scientists use as the technical name for the genus to which the plant belongs). The Romans borrowed this word origanum from the Greeks, who called the plant *orīganon.* The Greeks sometimes spelled this word as *oreiganon,* as if it were a compound of the Greek words *orei,* "on the mountain," and *ganos,* "joy". Greek *orīganon* would therefore mean something like "joy on the mountain." Since the fragrant oregano plant thrives on the craggy landscapes of the Mediterranean shore, some Greeks tried to make the name clearer by interpreting it as "joy on the mountain." Nevertheless, it is much morely likely that this is not the real origin of the word—rather, the Greeks simply borrowed the word from some unknown language of the Mediterranean in ancient times, like many of their other words designating herbs native to the Mediterranean. These include *apsinthion* "wormwood, artemisia" (the source of the English word *absinthe*) and *minthē,* the Greek word for "mint." Latin must have borrowed its word for "mint," *menta,* from the same unknown Mediterranean source as Greek *minthē.* Latin *menta* is the ancestor of English *mint* and Spanish *menta,* "mint." However, in Spanish, mint is often referred to as *hierbabuena,* literally "the good herb."

Spanish has been the source of a number of other English words designating seasonings for food, especially since the spices of the Americas were first brought to England and the rest of Europe by way of Spanish ships. Other examples of such words discussed in this book include *chili, cilantro,* and *pimiento.*

papaya

Papayas are the fruit of a tree, *Carica papaya,* native to Central and South America and the Caribbean. The English word for this fruit, *papaya,* is a borrowing of Spanish *papaya* and possibly also of Portuguese *papaia.* (Nowadays the papaya is often called a *mamão* in Portuguese, however.) Both the Spanish and Portuguese words come from the Taíno language of the Caribbean Islands and its relatives in the Arawak language family. The Spanish historian Gonzalo Fernández de Oviedo y Valdés (1478–1557) mentions the papaya in his work *Historia general y natural de las Indias* ("General and Natural History of the Indies") among the many fruits of the Americas that were new to the Spaniards.

Oviedo y Valdés tells us that the indigenous Taíno people of the island of Hispaniola (now divided between the Dominican Republic and Haiti) called the fruit *papaya.* Similar-sounding words for the papaya are found among the indigenous languages of South America, too.

164

The papaya is also called a *lechosa* in various parts of the Spanish-speaking world because the unripe fruit exudes a milky juice when cut open—the Spanish word for "milk" is *leche*. This milky juice will irritate sensitive skin, but it is also extremely useful as a meat tenderizer. Drops of the sap can be drizzled on the meat before a barbecue to improve the quality of tough meat—a practice that probably dates back thousands of years in the Americas. (The word *barbecue* itself is also of Taíno origin and is discussed as a separate entry in this book.) The active enzyme in this juice was given the name *papain,* and papain extracted from papayas is the main ingredient in many commercial meat tenderizers.

In Jamaican English, papayas are known by the name *pawpaw,* a variant of the word *papaya. Pawpaw* is also used in the United States as the name of the fruit produced by the shrubby tree *Asimina triloba.* This kind of pawpaw is actually extremely common in the southeastern United States, and it has even been immortalized in a well-known folk song:

> *Pickin' up pawpaws, puttin' 'em in your pocket,*
> *Pickin' up pawpaws, puttin' 'em in your pocket,*
> *Pickin' up pawpaws, puttin' 'em in your pocket,*
> *Way down yonder in the pawpaw patch.*

Pawpaws are very soft when they ripen, and so they rarely appear in supermarkets. Many Americans are therefore unfamiliar with the taste of one of the most delicious native fruits of the United States, despite having heard of them in the words of the famous folk song. The flavor of a pawpaw is variously described as being like sweet potatoes, mangoes, or very ripe bananas, depending on who is tasting it. For many people, there is something vaguely tropical about it. Like papayas, pawpaws have orange-yellow flesh and many dark seeds, and this similarity probably led to the name *pawpaw,* originally meaning "papaya," being given to the North American fruit. The papaya and the American pawpaw plants, however, are unrelated.

passacaglia

The passacaglia is a musical form in 3/4 time consisting of continuous variations played over a ground bass (a bass line continually repeated throughout the composition). The passacaglia was an extremely popular form in the 1600s and 1700s, and all of the great Baroque composers of works for the keyboard wrote passacaglias, including Johann Sebastian Bach, George Frederick Handel, and François Couperin. The passacaglia was also one of the standard set of stylized dances that made up the Baroque musical form called the *suite*. Baroque passacaglias are often in minor keys and combine a dignified, stately slowness with a strong sense of forward movement.

The English word *passacaglia* is borrowed from Italian, and the Italian word is an adaptation of the Spanish term *pasacalle*. Spanish *pasacalle* is in turn from the verb *pasar*, "to pass," and the noun *calle*, "street." The *pasacalle* is thought to have originated as a lively dance performed in the street to the accompaniment of strolling musicians. In this, the passacaglia shared the fate of the sarabande, another stately form of Baroque dance music discussed in this book that originated as an animated popular dance in Spain. When these Spanish popular dances were exported to the courts of the royalty and nobility in the other countries of Europe, they were slowed down and brought into line with the general taste for majesty and refined elaboration in music that reigned among the upper classes at the time.

The Spanish verb *pasar* is of course closely related to English *pass*. Spanish *pasar* descends directly from the Vulgar Latin verb **passāre*, derived from the Latin noun *passus*, "step." As the spoken Latin of Roman France evolved into Old

French, *passāre* became *passer* in Old French, and *passer* was borrowed into Middle English as *pass*.

patio

The Spanish word *patio* refers to the roofless inner courtyard that forms the center of the house in many parts of the Spanish-speaking world. In English, however, the word has come to have a broader meaning and can also refer to paved spaces that adjoin a house. *Patio* first appears in English in the 1700s in descriptions of houses in the Spanish-speaking world.

The ultimate origins of the word *patio* in Spanish remain unclear. *Patio* has been known in Spanish since the end of the 1400s, and the word was probably borrowed from Catalan or else its close relative Occitan, the Romance language traditionally spoken in southern France that has been replaced by French to a great extent in modern times. In Catalan, *pati* means "courtyard," a development from an earlier meaning, "building plot, land with no buildings on it." In some dialects of Occitan as well, *pati* can mean "courtyard."

The original meaning of *pati* in medieval Catalan and Occitan was simply "communal pasture." Some scholars have proposed that Catalan and Occitan *pati* are derived from the Latin word *pactum*, "agreement"—the *pati* was originally the land set aside as public pasture by agreement among the members of the local community. The Latin word *pactum* is also the source of the English word *pact*.

Other scholars have seen in Catalan and Occitan *pati* a survival of one of the Celtic languages that were spoken in Spain and France before the Romans brought Latin to the region. Old inscriptions and other kinds of archaeological evidence—as well as the testimony of Roman historians—indicate that various Celtic languages were once spoken across a vast area of

Europe that stretched from central Europe in the East, across Austria, northern Italy, France, Great Britain, and Ireland, all the way into Spain. Nowadays, of course, the Celtic languages are confined to Ireland, Wales, and Brittany in France. According to these scholars, the word *pati* comes from a word for "pasture" in one of the ancient Celtic languages of Spain and the Pyrenees. The Celtic languages are actually quite closely related to Latin, and the *pa–* seen in *pati* would be the same ancient word element *pa–* meaning "to feed, let graze" that is also found in the Latin word for "pasture," *pāstūra* (the source of the English word *pasture*).

pimiento

In the time of Christopher Columbus, spices like black pepper, cinnamon, cloves, and nutmeg were extremely valuable commodities in Europe. (Black pepper, by the way, comes from a plant that is native to tropical Asia and is entirely unrelated to the plant that bears red pepper.) Although black pepper grows abundantly in Asia and is extremely cheap there, it was very difficult to get the pepper to Europe in ancient and medieval times. On one of the trade routes by which spices were transported to Europe, for example, it was shipped across the Indian Ocean to Arabia on the seasonal east winds of the monsoon, then loaded onto camels, and finally brought to the Mediterranean Sea and distributed to Europe. At each stage of the journey, the spice merchants drove a hard bargain, and as the spice passed from hand to hand, its price rose. When he sailed west in 1492, Columbus hoped to find a direct passage to Asia in order to bypass these middlemen in the trade of Asian products like pepper and cloves.

When he arrived in the West Indies, Columbus found the people living on the islands had a spice that was hot like pepper but much more powerful—the colorful, hollow, podlike fruits of a plant of the genus *Capsicum,* now called *chili peppers* or *red peppers* in English. The spice was a big hit with the Spaniards. The *Capsicum* plant and its spicy fruit podlike fruits came to be called *pimiento* in Spanish—as opposed to *pimienta,* the original, older word for "black pepper." It was perhaps even Columbus himself who bestowed the Spanish name *pimiento* on the spice since it reminded him of the *pimienta* or black pepper that he had set sail to find. Among the Taíno people of the West Indies, this plant was known as *ají,* and in West Indian and Central American varieties of Spanish, chilies are still called *ajíes.* On the mainland, the Nahuatl-speaking peoples of Mexico called the plant *chīlli,* and this is the source of the Spanish word *chile.*

The Spanish word *pimiento* eventually made its way into English in the 1600s, when it was spelled in various ways such as *piemente* and *pemento. Pimento* is still a very common spelling of the word today, and the pronunciation (pĭ-mĕn′tō) rather than (pĭ-myĕn′tō) reflects the early forms that the word took when it was first borrowed into English. The English word *pimiento* is nowadays used of the variety of the chili pepper bearing sweet, mildly hot, bright red peppers. The spice paprika is made from dried ground pimientos, and cocktail olives are traditionally stuffed with a piece of pimiento.

On their first visits to the Americas, the Spaniards also found that the people of the West Indies had another spice, the aromatic dried berries of a certain tree. These dried berries looked like peppercorns but tasted like a mixture of cloves, pepper, cinnamon, and nutmeg—all the spices that Columbus had set sail to find! Nowadays in Spanish, this spice is called *pimienta de Jamaica,* literally "Jamaican pepper," and in English, it is called *allspice.* In English, too, *pimento* was once used to mean "allspice," but this use of the word has now become rather old-fashioned.

The Spanish word *pimienta,* "black pepper," has its own interesting history. It comes from Latin *pigmentum,* which meant such things as "pigment," "vegetable juice," and also by extension "condiment"—because vegetable juices and spices add flavor and color to food. Latin *pigmentum* is of course also the source of the English word *pigment,* and *pimiento* and *pigment* are thus distant linguistic cousins.

See also the entry for the word *chili* in this book.

piña colada

A piña colada was originally a mixed drink made of rum, coconut cream, and pineapple juice, but nowadays even cakes, candies, and massage oils come in a flavor called *piña colada* that combines the taste of pineapple with coconut. In Spanish, *piña colada* means simply "strained pineapple"—*piña* is the Spanish word for pineapple, while *colada* is the feminine form of the past participle of *colar,* "to strain."

Piña literally means "pinecone" in Spanish. It comes from the Latin word *pīnea,* "pinecone," which is in turn derived from the Latin word *pīnus,* "pine tree." (The English word *pine* itself is also a borrowing of Latin *pīnus.*) The pineapple is native to the Americas, and when Christopher Columbus and his Spanish sailors came ashore after sighting the islands of the Caribbean, pineapples may have been among the fruits that the Caribbean peoples offered to their visitors. The Spanish, not having encountered the fruit before, began to call the fruit *piña.* The Spanish historian Gonzalo Fernández de Oviedo y Valdés (1478–1557) describes several fruits from the Americas in his work *Historia general y natural de las Indias* ("General and Natural History of the Indies"), a book first published in 1526 in a summary that served to introduce Europeans to the unfamiliar world that lay across the Atlantic. Oviedo y Valdés had tasted the pineapple on his voyages to the Americas, and he writes several pages extolling the marvelous color, odor, and flavor of the fruit. Here is a representative excerpt of his rhapsodic praise for the pineapple:

> *Hay en esta isla Española unos cardos, que cada uno dellos lleva una piña (o, mejor diciendo, alcarchofa), puesto que, porque paresce piña, las llaman los cristianos piñas, sin lo ser. Esta es una de las más hermosas fructas que yo he visto en todo lo que del mundo he andado.... Gustarla es una cosa tan apetitosa e suave, que faltan palabras, en este caso, para dar al proprio su loor en esto.*

> There are on this island of Hispaniola some thistles, each one of which bears a pinecone (or better said, an artichoke), as the Christians [i.e., the Spaniards] call them, because they look like pinecones without being such. This is one of the most beautiful fruits that I have seen in all the world where I have gone.... To taste it is something so appetizing and sweet, that words fail, in this case, to give it due praise in this regard.

Despite this failure of words, Oviedo y Valdés goes on to the discuss the marvels of the pineapple for several more paragraphs—he just can't get enough of it, and he regrets that all of the pineapples he tried to bring back to Spain rotted before the ships landed in Europe.

When reports of the pineapple first filtered through to the English in the 1500s, they called it a *pina*, an adaptation of the Spanish, or even a *pine*. Later, in the 1600s, *pineapple* begins to become the usual English word. In fact, the English term *pineapple* itself originally meant simply "pinecone," just like Spanish *piña*. In Middle English, *pinappel* was the usual word for "pinecone," and a *pineapple* in this sense was simply the "apple," or fruit, produced by the pine tree. By the 1700s, the word *pinecone* had begun to replace *pineapple* in its original sense, but *pineapple* has survived as the name of the tropical fruit.

piñata

Piñatas are now familiar throughout the English-speaking world as an entertainment at birthday parties. In Mexico and Spain, however, piñatas are also associated with religious celebrations, and with Lent and the Christmas season in particular. In Spain, there is often a costume ball on the first Sunday in Lent called *el baile de Piñata* that finishes with the breaking of a piñata. Although piñatas are often shaped to look like animals and caricatures of popular figures and celebrities, one of the most common traditional shapes of the piñata in Mexico is a kind of globe with seven cones sticking out at various angles. These cones represent the devil and the seven deadly sins—lust, gluttony, greed, sloth, anger, envy, and pride. The people beating the piñata joyously overcome the devil and his tricks by smashing it open to receive their just reward. While each person struggles to hit the piñata, the other people sing the following song, which exists in many different versions:

Dale, dale, dale,
no pierdas el tino,
porque si lo pierdes,
pierdes el camino.
Esta piñata es de muchas mañas,
sólo contiene naranjas y cañas.

Give it a hit! Give it a hit! Give it a hit!
Don't lose your aim
Because if you lose it
You will lose your way.
This piñata is wiley,
But it only contains oranges and sugar cane.

Piñatas were originally made from clay pots that were adorned with colorful decorations. The custom of beating the piñata is thought to have begun in Italy. The Spanish word *piñata* appears to come from the Italian word *pignatta,* denoting a kind of clay pot. These pots apparently had a squat shape like a pinecone, or *pigna* in Italian. The Italian word *pigna* is of course related to the Spanish word for "pinecone," *piña,* which is discussed in this book at the entry for *piña colada.*

platinum

After Spain conquered the Aztec and Inca empires in the first half of the 1500s, the vast mineral wealth of the Americas began to flow to Spain and helped bankroll the Spanish Empire for the next few centuries. The mines of Central America provided Spain with a huge amount of gold and silver, but the Spanish noted that another metal could also be found in the mines. When this metal was found combined with gold, it made the gold too difficult to extract and work. By itself, it could not be melted and made useful by any technique known to the Spaniards. (The ancient Mesoamericans, however, had occasionally made small objects from it using specialized techniques.) Silvery nuggets of this metal were also found in the Río Pinto, a river in what is now Columbia. The Spanish began to call this troublesome metal *platina del Pinto,* "worthless little silver from the Pinto." Local gold panners considered these hard, pale nuggets to be "unripened gold," and they threw them back into the river to ripen when they found them. The metal in these nuggets was platinum, and at the current price of platinum on the international market, they would be worth almost twice their weight in gold.

Throughout the 1600s and early 1700s, all precious metals that were exported from the Americas had to pass through Spain before going elsewhere in Europe, so little of the junk metal could reach European chemists and metalworkers outside Spain for examination. In addition, the Spanish were concerned that the silvery metal could be used to counterfeit coins, and this gave them another reason to hide the existence of the metal from the rest of Europe. However, in 1750, a sample smuggled to England led to the recognition of platinum as a new metal by two Englishmen, Charles Wood and William Brownrigg. At the same time, metallurgists could begin to put the metal to good use since it was becoming possible to attain the high temperatures necessary to melt platinum. Platinum melts at 1,768°C (3,215°F), while gold melts at 1,064°C (1,948°F) and iron at 1,538°C (2,800°F). The Spanish government subsequently allowed scientists free access to the metal—Spain was interested in finding a use for the substance, which could be polished to great brilliance but never tarnished like silver.

At first, the metal was called *platina* in English. Thomas Jefferson mentions it in a letter from 1786: *You have often heard of the metal, called platina, to be found only in S. America. It is insusceptible of rust as gold and silver are.* Soon afterwards, chemists changed the word to *platinum* to make it resemble the Latin words for metals similar to platinum like *aurum*, "gold," and *argentum*, "silver." Latin words ending in *–um* regularly develop into Spanish words ending in -o (like *oro*, "gold," from Latin *aurum*), and the Spanish word *platina* was changed to *platino* on the model of other element names ending in -o, such as *oro*, "gold."

potato

> *Let the sky rain potatoes!*
>
> —William Shakespeare,
> *The Merry Wives of Windsor,* Act 5, Scene 5

These words are spoken by Shakepeare's roguish character Sir John Falstaff after he has just met a woman that he has been trying to seduce. Sir John calls on the god Jupiter to send down a rain of sweet potatoes—in Shakespeare's day, the word *potato* referred to sweet potatoes, which were thought to possess aphrodisiac qualities. Christopher Columbus had brought back the first sweet potatoes to Europe after his first voyage to the Americas in 1492, and since then they had become widely known. The white potato, on the other hand, had only recently been introduced to England in Shakespeare's time. (*The Merry Wives of Windsor* was probably first performed in 1597.) The usual term for the white potato in Shakespeare's day was *Virginia potato* or *potato of Virginia,* despite the fact that the white potato originated in the Andes, nowhere near Virginia.

The sweet potato is the tuberous root of a vine belonging to the morning-glory family. Although the sweet-potato plant perhaps originated in Central America, it had been domesticated for thousands of years, and cultivation of the sweet potato had spread to other areas of the Americas, like Peru, by at least two thousand years ago. When Columbus arrived in the Caribbean in 1492, he found the indigenous people cultivating the sweet potato, too. The sweet-potato plant has the scientific name *Ipomoea batatas,* and the last part of this scientific name will remind Spanish speakers of *batata,* the most common word for "sweet potato" in the Spanish of Spain. *Batata* comes from the Taíno word for the sweet potato. In Mexico, the sweet potato is often called a *camote,* from Nahuatl *camotli,* while in Cuba, it is often called a *boniato.*

The white potato is the tuber produced by a plant belonging to the nightshade family, the same family that includes other important food plants like tomatoes, tomatillos, eggplants, and chilies. The white potato is native to Peru and has the scientific name *Solanum tuberosum* (literally, "the tuberous nightshade"). In Latin American Spanish, the white potato is usually called a *papa,* while in the Spanish of Spain, it is more often a *patata.* The Latin American *papa* comes from the word for the white potato in Quechua, the language of the Inca Empire that controlled the potato's homeland of Peru at the time of the arrival of the Spaniards there in 1531. The Iberian Spanish form *patata*, on the other hand, results from a blend of *batata* (the word for the sweet potato, the vegetable known earlier to the Spaniards) with the Quechua word *papa*—there was ample opportunity for confusion between the two words, since both vegetables were new to the Spaniards, and both are tubers that can be cooked in much the same way.

The same confusion extended to the English, who borrowed Spanish *batata*, "sweet potato," and *patata*, "white potato," in the middle of the 1500s—*patata*, at first meaning "sweet potato," was variously spelled in English, but eventually the spelling settled down as *potato*. (Spanish final -*a* is often replaced with -*o* in many other early English borrowings from Spanish. This and similar phenomena are also discussed at the entries in this book for the words *bastinado*, *tomato*, and *tornado*.) Both *batata* and *potato* originally had the sense "sweet potato," but *batata* was soon ousted by *potato*, still meaning "sweet potato." Later in the 1600s, as white potatoes became one of the major crops in Great Britain, Ireland, and Britain's English-speaking colonies around the world, it became possible for the simple word *potato*, rather than *Virginia potato*, to refer to white potatoes rather than sweet potatoes.

The Elizabethan usage of *potato* for "sweet potato" has survived in some varieties of English till the present day. In the southern United States, especially among older people, *potato* can still refer primarily to the vegetable that Northerners would call *sweet potato*. For Southerners for whom *potato* means simply "sweet potato," the term *white potato* or *Irish potato* usually distinguishes the white potato that originated in Peru from the orange-colored sweet potato.

See also the entries for the words *ulluco* and *yam* in this book.

puma

The puma is a large, powerful wild cat that lives in mountainous regions in both North and South America, from northern Canada to the southern Andes. Its scientific name is *Puma concolor*. The puma has tawny fur with a lighter underbelly, and it lives and hunts alone rather than in groups. It takes a variety of animals like rabbits, deer, and alpaca as prey, but it rarely attacks human beings.

Besides *puma*, the animal is known by a variety of other names in English, including *catamount, cougar, mountain lion,* and *panther*. *Puma* itself comes from the Spanish name for the animal, *puma*. Charles Darwin refers to the animal by this name in the journal of his famous expedition to South America and the Galápagos Islands, the voyage that played a large part in inspiring Darwin to formulate the theory of evolution. While traveling in the wilds of Argentina in 1833, Darwin made many observations of the puma's behavior, and he even ate one:

> *At supper, from something which was said, I was suddenly struck with horror at thinking that I was eating one of the favourite dishes of the country, namely, a half-formed calf, long before its proper time of birth. It turned out to be Puma; the meat is very white, and remarkably like veal in taste.* Dr. Shaw [a noted taxidermist of Darwin's time] *was laughed at for stating that "the flesh of the lion is in great esteem, having no small affinity with veal, both in colour, taste, and flavour." Such certainly is the case with the Puma.*

The Spanish word *puma* itself is from Quechua, the language of the Inca Empire that is still widely spoken in the Andes today. Of the other common English names for the puma, *cougar* comes from French *couguar*, an alteration (influenced by the French word *jaguar*, "jaguar") of the Portuguese word for the puma, *suçuarana*. *Suçuarana* comes from another indigenous language of South America, Tupi, spoken in Brazil and Paraguay. The Tupi word for the animal, *suasuarana,* is a compound of *suasú,* "deer," and *rana,* "like," and makes reference to its tawny color. The term *catamount,* on the other hand, is simply a contraction of *cat of the mountain.*

quirt

The cute-sounding word *quirt* refers to a kind of riding whip with a short handle and one or two lashes of braided leather. The quirt originated in Mexico and the American Southwest, and such whips are still used by some cowboys today. The

English word for this whip comes from American Spanish *cuarta*. The American Spanish term is just a specialized use of *cuarta*, "fourth." *Cuarta* is of course a word with a large variety of extended meanings, which also include "compass point, direction," and "span (the distance between the tip of the thumb and the tip of the little finger when the hand is spread out)." It remains somewhat unclear, however, just how *cuarta* came to mean "whip" in American Spanish.

Quirt is in fact a cousin of the English word *quart*. A quart is a fourth of a gallon, and the English word *quart* comes from Old French *quarte*, "fourth." When we trace the history of an English word of Spanish origin, we often discover that English has also borrowed the equivalent of the Spanish word from French, one of the sister languages of Spanish within the Romance language family. Both Spanish *cuarta*, the source of

English *quirt,* and Old French *quarte,* the source of English *quart,* descend from Latin *quārta,* the feminine form of *quārtus,* "fourth." Latin *quārtus* is in turn related to Latin *quattuor,* "four," the source of Spanish *cuatro.*

Quirt first begins to appear in English around the middle of the 1800s. The word was used by Captain Thomas Mayne Reid, an Irish-born writer who emigrated to the United States and began to write very successful novels that helped form the classic image of the Old West in English literature. A quirt appears in his novel *The scalp hunters: Adventures among the trappers,* published in 1851: *The young hunter laid his quirt to the flanks of the mustang, and started at full gallop along the Apaché trail.* This sentence vividly illustrates the wealth of Spanish vocabulary that English picked up in the Old West, for *mustang,* too, is a word of American Spanish origin. It is discussed as a separate entry in this book.

ranch

The word *ranch* comes from Spanish *rancho,* a word that has a variety of meanings in different parts of the Spanish-speaking world. For example, *rancho* can refer to the communal food served to soldiers or workers, or it can be an informal term for referring to any low-quality food in general. It can also be applied to a group of people eating such food in a mess hall. In still another meaning, a *rancho* can be a camp occupied by a few families and located at some distance from a town. And in American Spanish, a *rancho* is also a farm or rural estate where cattle are raised. It is in this last meaning that *rancho* entered American English in the 1800s, as English-speaking settlers from the United States moved into Texas, the Rockies, California, and the other areas west of the Mississippi that were part of Mexico at that time. These territories—where ranching was a most profitable way of life—eventually became part of the United States after the Mexican-American War (1846–1848).

In a work from 1849 entitled *What I Saw in California,* Edwin Bryant (who was briefly the alcalde of San Francisco in 1847) uses the word *rancho* in one the descriptions of California. Bryant's book was in fact a best-seller back east, where readers were eager for information about the gold-rich territory that the United States had just obtained from Mexico:

The Pueblo de San José is a village containing some six or eight hundred inhabitants. It is situated in what is called the "Pueblo Valley," about fifteen miles south of the southern shore of the Bay of San Francisco.... The population of the place is composed chiefly of native Californian land-proprietors. Their ranchos are in the valley, but their residences and gardens are in the town.

By "native Californians," Bryant does not mean members of the numerous indigenous North American peoples that lived in the territory before the arrival of Europeans. Rather, the ranchos were run by families descended from Spanish and Mexican settlers who arrived in the days when California was part of the Spanish Empire or of Mexico, after Mexico achieved independence from Spain in 1821. *Ranch,* the Anglicized version of *rancho,* begins to be found in the middle of the 1800s as well.

The Spanish noun *rancho,* "camp, cattle ranch," is derived from the verb *rancharse,* a variant of *arrancharse,* "to get together." More specifically in American Spanish, *arrancharse* can mean "to lodge or set up provisional living quarters (in a place)." *Arrancharse* is a borrowing of the French verb *arranger,* "to arrange," which is also the source of the English verb *arrange.*

renegade

In 711, Muslim forces from North Africa conquered much of the southern part of the Iberian Peninsula and founded the state of Al-Andalus, which later broke apart into several small Muslim kingdoms. In the early days of Al-Andalus, Christians greatly outnumbered their Muslim conquerors, and local Christian nobility sometimes even held on to their lands as vassals to their new Muslim overlords. A number of the Christian inhabitants of Al-Andalus eventually converted to Islam, however. Some may have been won over by the intellectual and artistic splendor of the civilization of Al-Andalus, while others were doubtless lured by the practical prospects of advancement in Muslim society. In addition, the persecution of Christians by Muslim authorities became more or less severe at various times in the history of Al-Andalus, and this made conversion to Islam attractive. Moreover, Christian slaves could free themselves from Christian masters simply by conversion, since Muslim law forbade the ownership of Muslim slaves by Christians. North of the borders of Al-Andalus, in the Christian-ruled areas of the Iberian peninsula, Christians generally despised these converts and called them *renegados*, literally the "ones who have denied"—the Christian faith, that is.

The Spanish noun *renegado* come from Latin *renegātus*, which is the past participle of the verb *renegāre*, "to deny." Both Old French and Middle English also borrowed the Latin past participle *renegātus*, in the form *renegat*, to mean "apostate from Christianity." The Middle English author Geoffrey Chaucer, for example, uses the word *renegat* to describe an apostate from Christianity in the Man of Law's Tale in the *Canterbury Tales*. In the 1500s, however, the Spanish word *renegado* pushes out the Middle English form of the word. At first, both the original Spanish form *renegado* and the Anglicized form *renegade* were used in English, although only the form *renegade* has survived into modern times. In the late 1500s and early 1600s, *renegado* and *renegade* came to be applied to any person who betrays or breaks away from a group.

Latin *renegāre*, "to deny," is itself a compound of the verb *negāre*, "to say no," and the prefix *re–*, which literally means "again" or "backwards" but is often used in Latin to intensify the meaning of verbs. *Negāre*, "to say no," is of course the source of such English words as *negate* and *negative*, and *renegāre* itself was also borrowed directly into English as the verb *renege*.

ristra

A ristra—pronounced (rē'strə)—is a string on which foodstuffs, such as chilies, onions, or garlic, are threaded or tied for storage. Not only do ristras help decorate bare kitchen walls, they are a good way of preserving foodstuffs that keep best in the open air. Dried chilies are likely to get musty if stored in a dark or damp place where there is no movement of air, and garlic and onions may begin to sprout. The Spanish word *ristra* descends from the Latin word *restis,* meaning not only "rope" but also "leaf of an onion or garlic." Ristras of garlic and onions have probably adorned Mediterranean kitchens since the most ancient times.

ristra of garlic

rodeo

The English word *rodeo* comes from Spanish *rodeo,* which means both "corral" and by extension "rodeo." *Rodeo* is derived from the verb *rodear,* "to surround" and "to round up cattle." In Spanish, a *rodeo* was originally just a *round-up.* The verb *rodear* in turn is derived from a word for a round object: *rueda,* meaning "wheel." *Rueda* descends from Latin *rota,* also the source of the English verb *rotate.*

The relationship between the vowels *ue* in *ruedo,* "wheel," and the vowel *o* in *rodear* is of course regular in Spanish: as the everyday spoken Latin of Roman Spain slowly evolved into the Spanish language, a Latin short *o* sound became Spanish *ue* when the stress fell upon it, but stayed *o* when it was unaccented. The effects of these two different changes are of course most clearly visible in Spanish verbs, where the vowel changes according to whether the stress falls upon it or not. *Duele,* "it hurts," comes from Latin *dolet,* stressed on the first syllable, while *doler,* "to hurt" comes from Latin *dolēre,* stressed on the second syllable. The same pattern can be seen in such pairs of related words as *bueno,* "good," stressed on the first syllable, and *bonito,* "pretty," originally an affectionate diminutive of *bueno* and stressed on the second syllable.

rumba

The style of music and dance called *rumba* originates in Cuba, although its ultimate roots are in Africa. Some varieties of rumba music are in 4/4 time with a characteristic syncopated rhythm, while others are in 6/8, and many styles of rumba dance are characterized by a distinctive swinging of the hips.

In American Spanish, the word *rumba* also means "spree" or "carousal"—rumba thus originated as "party music," so to speak. The ultimate origin of *rumba,* "spree," is probably a variant of the word *rumbo,* meaning not only "ostentation" but also "position of high social standing." In this way, the word *rumbo* meaning "ostentation" may be the same as the common Spanish word *rumbo* meaning "direction"—a person of high social standing, perhaps being one who points the way or sets a course.

The Spanish word *rumbo,* "direction," is related to the English word *rhombus.* On maps and navigational charts, there is usually a diagram, called a *compass rose* or *wind rose,* indicating the orientation of the different directions on the map or chart. The diagram resembles a many-petaled flower, with a rhomboidal "petal" for each of the cardinal compass points and the intermediate points between them. On the faces of magnetic compasses, too, the directions are also often marked as rhomboidal shapes. In Spanish, it thus became customary to refer to a point on the compass as a *rumbo,* from the Latin word *rhombus,* "rhombus," and in this way, *rumbo* became the Spanish word meaning "direction." The Modern Spanish technical term for "rhombus," however, is spelled *rombo.*

Both Spanish *rumbo* and English *rhombus* come from Latin *rhombus.* The Latin word is a borrowing of Greek *rhombos,* the technical term for the rhombus among the ancient Greek geometricians. In Greek, *rhombos* originally referred to a bull-roarer, an ancient kind of noisemaker or instrument consisting of a rhomboidal piece of wood attached to a cord. When whirled above the head, it makes a surprisingly loud, eerie, whirring noise. Apparently bull-roarers were the most rhomboidal objects that the Greek geometricians could think of. The ancient Greeks used bull-roarers in their religious rites, as do some peoples of modern times, like the aboriginal Australians.

rusk

The English word *rusk* is used of various kinds of baked goods, especially sweet raised breads that are sliced, dried, and browned in an oven. It comes from the Spanish and Portuguese word *rosca,* which literally means "coil" or "spiral" but by extension also "coiled bread, bread ring." In the 1500s, it was not Britannia, but Spain and Portugal that ruled the waves. Spanish and Portuguese ships plied the Atlantic and Indian Oceans, defending the Spanish and Portuguese territory in the Americas and Asia and bringing the products of the whole world to Europe. The ships of Spain and Portugal were provisioned with *roscas,* dried bread made from bread rings, probably like today's bagel chips but even harder. Dried bread, called *hardtack* or *ship's biscuit* in English, was the staple food of sailors on ships in those days. If kept dry, it would stay edible for years—as long as weevils did not get into it. Since the *roscas* were very hard to chew, sailors would often crumble them up and boil them with other ingredients to make their daily mess. Or they would moisten the crumbs and fry them in grease. The Spanish and Portuguese word for this type of ship's provision begins to appear in English in the late 1500s as a synonym of *biscuit.*

The Spanish and Portuguese word *rosca* not only means "bread ring," but also "thread of a screw." *Rosca,* "bread ring, screw thread" is also found in Catalan, but outside of the Iberian peninsula, *rosca* has no obvious relatives among the other Romance languages. If we simply compare the Spanish, Portuguese, and Catalan words, they look like they might descend from a hypothetical Latin word **rōsca,* but no such word is actually found in Latin. Since the word is confined in the Iberian languages, scholars hesitate to propose a Vulgar Latin word **rōsca* to account for it. Instead, some scholars have suggested that *rosca* originates as a borrowing from one of the Celtic languages spoken in the Iberian peninsula before the arrival of the Romans. *Rosca* resembles Celtic words for "bark" like Old Irish *rúsc.* How could a word for "bark" give rise to a word for "screw thread" or "bread ring"? Medieval beekeepers constructed hives for their bees from coils of bark. In French, for example, the Celtic word for "bark" became *ruche,* "beehive." On its way to modern Spanish *rosca,* the Celtic word may have undergone a similar development, from "bark" to "coiled bark beehive" to "anything coiled."

The word *rosca,* "bread ring," does not refer only to unappetizing ship's biscuit—other *roscas* are quite tasty. In many parts of the Spanish-speaking world, a rich sweet *rosca* decorated with candied fruit is eaten around the Christian holiday called *Epiphanía* or *el Día de los reyes* ("The Day of the Kings") in Spanish and *Epiphany* or *Twelfth Night* in English. The celebration of this holiday begins on the evening before January 6, twelve days after Christmas Eve. (In Medieval times, the twenty-four-hour period of the day was considered to begin at sunset, and the evening preceding a holiday was considered to be an important part of that holiday.) *El Día de los reyes* commemorates the visit of the Three Kings or Wise Men bearing gifts to the newborn Jesus in Bethlehem. To celebrate *el Día de los reyes,* in some parts of the Spanish-speaking world, children put a box full of hay or freshly cut grass under their beds for the kings' camels.

The special *rosca* prepared for the occasion is called *la rosca de reyes* ("the Kings' Rosca"), and a small object, usually a little representation of the infant Jesus, is baked into the cake. In Mexico, the person who finds the figurine when the cake is eaten is obliged to throw a party on February 2, *el Día de la Candelaria,* or *Candlemas* in English. (Candlemas commemorates the purification of the Virgin Mary according to Jewish ritual law, which stated that a woman was not ritually pure for a period of forty days following the birth of a male child.) Candlemas was traditionally celebrated by a ceremony featuring many candles and torches, during which the priest blessed candles that the congregation took back to their homes for prosperity and good luck. In many cities all over the Spanish-speaking world, Candlemas is celebrated with lively festivals, processions, and dances.

salsa

In English, the word *salsa* typically refers to a mixture of chopped tomatoes, onions, chili peppers, and other ingredients that accompanies Mexican and Tex-Mex cuisine. In Spanish, however, *salsa* is just the generic word meaning simply "sauce" or "dressing (as for a salad)"—each locality in Spain and Latin America has its own typical sauces. In fact, the Spanish word *salsa* and the English word *sauce* ultimately come from the same source.

Spanish *salsa* descends directly from Latin *salsa,* the feminine form of *salsus,* "salted." *Salsus* is the past participle of the Latin verb *sallere,* "to salt," derived from the Latin noun *sāl,* "salt." *Salsa* is in origin just "a salted thing"—in the everyday Vulgar Latin spoken by Romans around the dinner table on the farms and in the cities of the Roman Empire, the *salsa* was probably originally any salted condiment that added a little flavor to simple, everyday fare. Salt was of course an ingredient in most Roman sauces meant to accompany meats and vegetables, just as it is in modern sauces today.

Just as the local variety of everyday Latin in Spain was slowly evolving into Spanish during early medieval times, so too was the local variety of everyday Latin in France slowly evolving into Old French. In Old French, Latin *salsa* eventually developed into *sauce,* and the Old French word was then borrowed into Middle English as *sauce*, the ancestor of the Modern English word.

The similarity in sound between English *salt* and Latin *salsa* is no accident, either. Modern English *salt* descends from the Old English word *sealt*, and the Old English word is closely related to the Latin word *sāl*.

Salsa is also a popular form of Latin American dance music, characterized by Afro-Caribbean rhythms, Cuban big-band dance melodies, and elements of jazz and rock. Many salsa aficionados have pointed out that *salsa* is an ideal name for "hot" music like salsa, and the name probably originates in cries like *¡Salsa!* given by Latin bandleaders when directing their musicians to "spice it up a little." The earliest and perhaps most famous use of such exclamations is found in the song *Échale salsita* ("Throw a little sauce on it!"), a classic from the 1930s by Ignacio Piñeiro, the great master of the genre of Cuban music called *son*, one of the ancestors of salsa. Ostensibly, the song describes a vendor of thick pork sausages called *butifarras*. During a night of revelry in the town, someone saunters past the vendor's establishment and hears him cry *¡Salsa! ¡Échale salsita!* as he deals out his sausage—Piñeiro's audience was of course free to interpret the sausage-seller's cry in other ways too.

sarabande

Nowadays the word *sarabande* is most often encountered as the name for a piece of music in slow triple time, one of the standard movements that make up the standard form of Baroque music called the *suite*. The music of the sarabande was originally meant to accompany a stately court dance, and the rhythm of the sarabande is characterized by an alternation of quarter note and half note, since the notes on second and third beats of each measure are usually tied. Johann Sebastian Bach and George Frederick Handel are two of the many notable composers who wrote sarabandes, which often feature pensive yet majestic melodies. The slow, refined sarabande of the 1600s and 1700s, however, developed from a much faster dance with erotic overtones that was popular in Spain and Mexico in the 1500s.

The English term *sarabande* is a borrowing of French *sarabande,* and the French term comes from Spanish *zarabanda.* The further origin of the Spanish word is uncertain, but the noted scholar of Arabic loanwords in Spanish, Federico Corriente, supports the idea that the term ultimately derives from the Persian word *sarband* by way of Arabic. *Sarband* literally means "headband, headdress, ornament for the head" in Persian, but the word was also used as a technical term in the description of music to mean something like "refrain, chorus (in a piece of music)." The Arabic language has borrowed many words from Persian, and Arabic scholars and musicians may have borrowed *sarband* and taken it to Muslim kingdoms of medieval Spain, whose people were renowned for their refined appreciation of music and song. The Persian term *sarband* would then have become the Arabic name of a certain genre of music of southern Spain, until it eventually entered Spanish as *zarabanda.*

savanna

A savanna is a kind of flat grassland found in tropical or subtropical regions, especially those areas in which a distinct dry season alternates with a rainy season. Savannas are typically studded with a few drought-resistant trees. The word *savanna* is now used to describe this kind of landscape in hot regions around the world—including the vast savannas of eastern and southern Africa—but the term came from Spanish and in fact originated in the Caribbean. *Savanna,* also spelled *savannah,* is a borrowing of Spanish *sabana,* originally spelled *çabana* in the Spanish of the 1500s. *Çabana* itself is another of the many words that Spanish borrowed from the language of the Taíno, the original inhabitants of the Bahamas and the Greater Antilles at the time of Christopher Columbus's arrival in the Americas. Savannas are a typical feature of the islands where the Taíno lived, and the Spanish adopted the Taíno word to describe the landscapes they found as they expanded their empire elsewhere in the tropical Americas.

The Spanish historian Gonzalo Fernández de Oviedo y Valdés uses the word *sabana* several times in his description of the Americas entitled *Historia general y natural de las Indias* ("General and Natural History of the Indies"), which was first published in abbreviated form in 1526. At the time, Oviedo must not have expected his readers to be immediately familiar with the word, for he explains it in the following terms: *Este nombre* sabana *se dice a la tierra que está sin arboledas, pero con mucha e alta hierba, o baja.* "This noun *sabana* is used of land that has no stands of trees, but with a lot of tall grass, or even short grass." The Spanish word first begins to appear in English in Oviedo's own time, in the middle of the 1500s, as part of descriptions of the Americas.

In Modern Spanish, of course, the letters *b* and *v* are used to represent the same sounds. (In Old Spanish, the two letters represented distinct sounds, but by the time when *sabana* was borrowed into Spanish from Taíno, in the middle of 1500s, the letters had come to be interchangeable.) Modern Spanish *b* and *v* are pronounced like English *b* at the beginning of words, while in the middle of words between vowels, Spanish *b* and *v* have a sound like English *v* but made with both the upper and lower lips—rather than with the upper teeth and lower lip, like English *v.* When the English heard the Spanish word *sabana* being pronounced, they interpreted the sound spelled by *b* as being more like an English *v* than an English *b*, and so they borrowed the word with a *v* based on what they heard, rather than on the standard spelling of the Spanish word with *b*. (See the word *habanera* in this book for another instance of a similar phenomenon, in the English name of the city of Havana in Cuba.)

The city of Savannah, Georgia, and the Savannah River that forms the border between Georgia and South Carolina, are not thought to get their names from the Spanish word *sabana*. Instead, the name of the city and river derive from an alteration of the name of the Shawnee tribe of Native Americans, since one branch of this tribe used to live along the middle reaches of the river now called the Savannah.

sierra

In English, the word *sierra* is probably best known for the names of certain mountain ranges, such as the Sierra Nevada (in Spanish, the "snowy sierra") of Spain, the similarly named Sierra Nevada of Eastern California, and the Sierra Madre (the "mother sierra") of Mexico. The English word *sierra*, "rugged range of mountains having an irregular or jagged profile," is a borrowing of Spanish *sierra*. In Spanish, *sierra* literally means "saw," but the word is also used in the extended meaning "line or group of mountains with a jagged profile." As a further example of how a word meaning "saw" can become a word meaning "mountain range," we need only mention the *Sawtooth Mountains* of central Idaho.

The Spanish word *sierra* is from the Latin word *serra*, "saw," which is also the source of the English word *serrated*, "having teeth like a saw."

See also *cero*.

siesta

The average business day in Spain is traditionally quite different from the average American business day—company policy often requires employees to leave the office around 1:00 PM and return around 4:00 PM. They then work late, until around 8:00 PM. In this way, workers can avoid the heat of the day in summer while enjoying a leisurely lunch with their families and then resting or taking a little nap, a *siesta*. Although the English word for this custom, the siesta, comes from Spanish, the siesta is a normal part of life in many other parts of the world besides Spain and Latin America.

The average day in medieval Europe was punctuated by the ringing of bells to mark the passing time. At different times over the course of the day, monks in monasteries and clerics in parish churches would come together to chant the appropriate service in a daily cycle of prayers called the *canonical hours*. During the medieval period, the day was considered to begin not at midnight, but at dawn, around the time we would now call 6:00 AM. The first service in the series of canonical hours was sung at this time, and in Latin, this service was called the *prīma hōra,* or "first hour." Three hours later, at the time we would call 9:00 AM, they sang the service called the *tertia hōra,* or "third hour." At midday, six hours after the beginning of the day, they sang the *sexta hōra,* or "sixth hour," at the time we would call 12:00 PM. Bells were rung to call the monks to prayer, and the common people toiling in the fields or in their workshops could organize their day around the bells rung for the canonical hours.

In Spain and Portugal, it was often too hot to work in the hours right after midday, when the sun was highest in the sky, so it became the custom to eat a leisurely meal at the sixth hour and wait out the heat while resting a bit. The Spanish word for this afternoon rest, *siesta,* comes from the Latin word *sexta,* "sixth," since it was taken at the sixth hour. Similarly, the

Portuguese also have the habit of taking a *sesta,* using the Portuguese equivalent of the Spanish word *siesta.*

Besides the Spanish word *siesta,* English has another term that comes from the Latin names for the canonical hours: *noon.* Nine hours after the beginning of the day, the monks would sing the *nōna hōra,* the "ninth hour," at the time we would call 3:00 PM. Latin *nōna* was borrowed into Old English as *nōn,* and this developed into Middle English *noon. Noon,* of course, no longer refers to the time of day we would call 3:00 PM—in later medieval times in England, France, and some other areas of Europe, the canonical hours began to be celebrated earlier and earlier in the day over the course of the centuries. On certain days of fasting in the Catholic Church, the fast was broken at the ninth hour, and hungry monks may have wanted to ring the bells and sing the service of the ninth hour a bit earlier than strictly required by the rules. In this way, the ninth hour, or *noon,* came to be sung at midday.

silo

Spanish has contributed many terms relating to farming and animal husbandry to English, including the word *silo.* To most English speakers, the word *silo* calls up the image of a tall structure standing next to a barn, although it can also be used of underground installations housing missiles. In Spanish, *silo* was originally used of dry, subterranean pits for storing grain, seeds, or forage for animals. In modern times, of course, the Spanish word *silo* can also refer to structures built above ground, just like the English word. The word *silo* first begins to be used in English in the 1800s, in reference to underground storage pits rather than towers.

Underground pits have been used to store grain over long periods since the dawn of agriculture thousands of years ago. If the pits are dry and sealed to prevent moisture, fresh air, and rodents from getting in, grain can be stored in them for years. The Roman writer Marcus Terentius Varro (116–27 BC) describes how grain was stored in his day in a work called *De rerum rusticarum libri III* ("On Agricultural Topics, in Three Books"):

> Some farmers have their granaries in underground caverns, which they call *sirus,* as in Cappadocia and Thrace; others have pits, as in the country around Carthago and Osca in the eastern half of Spain. The bottoms of these pits are covered with straw, and the farmers are careful not to let any moisture or air get into them except when they are opened to be used, because no weevils will hatch if there is no air. When stored in this way, wheat will last for fifty years, and millet for more than a hundred, in fact.

The word *sirus* that Varro mentions in this passage is actually the Greek word *siros,* "pit for storing grain"—the ancient countries of Cappadocia (now in modern Turkey) and Thrace (now in southern Bulgaria, northeast Greece, and northwest Turkey) had many Greek-speaking inhabitants when Varro was writing. This name for storage caverns, which was evidently a technical agricultural term unfamiliar to your average Roman reader at the time, must have spread to the rest of the Roman world after Varro's day, for many linguists think that *sirus* is the word that eventually developed into *silo* in Spanish. Carthago and Osca, the two cities in eastern Spain that Varro names while explaining underground storage, are the cities now known as Cartagena and Huesca in modern Spain.

sombrero

The word *sombrero* simply means "hat" in Spanish, even though in English *sombrero* usually refers to a large straw or felt hat with a broad brim and tall crown, worn especially in Mexico and the American Southwest. In Spanish, *sombrero* can also mean "canopy" and even "cap of a mushroom." *Sombrero* is derived from *sombra*, "shade," by means of the addition of the extremely common suffix *–ero* that is added to nouns to make new nouns and adjectives. For example, the word *guerrero*, meaning "warrior, soldier" as a noun and "warlike, relating to war" as an adjective, is derived from *guerra*, "war," with the suffix *–ero,* while *hormiguero*, "anthill," is derived from *hormiga*, "ant."

Scholars have proposed two different, but related, etymologies for *sombra*. According to one theory, the noun *sombra* is derived from the verb *sombrar*, "to shade," and *sombrar* descends from Late Latin *subumbrāre*, "to cast a shadow upon." This Latin verb is in turn derived from the Latin phrase *sub umbrā* "in shadow"—or more literally, "under shadow." (*Umbrā* is the form that the Latin noun *umbra*, "shadow," takes after many prepositions.) The same Latin word for "shadow," *umbra*, figures in the other proposed etymology, which

is based on the Latin phrase *sol et umbra*, "sun and shadow." As the spoken Latin of Roman Spain was evolving into Spanish in early medieval times, the Latin phrase *sol et umbra* would have first become something like *sol y ombra* in early Spanish. The frequent juxtaposition of the words for "sun" and "shadow" then led to the extension of the *s* from *sol* to the beginning of the hypothetical word *ombra*, and thus Spanish *sol y sombra*, "light and shade," was born. The noun *sombra* then began to be used outside this phrase.

No matter how *sombra* came into being, it is certain that the

Spanish noun has a close cousin in French, the adjective *sombre,* "dark, dim, gloomy." This French word was borrowed into English in the 1700s—it is still spelled *sombre* in British English, even though the American spelling is now more often *somber.*

stampede

The English word *stampede* is a borrowing of Mexican Spanish *estampida.* When *stampede* first begins to appear in English in the early 1800s, it is attested in a variety of spellings, including *stampido* and *stampedo.* According to the *Oxford English Dictionary,* the first known use of *stampede* as a more or less naturalized English word (rather than simply being mentioned as a Spanish word) is found in American writings dating from 1828: *A little before daylight, the mules made an abortive attempt to raise a stampido.* Not long afterwards, in a work from 1835 entitled *A Tour of the Prairies,* the American author Washington Irving defines a *stampedo* as a *sudden rush of horses.* Perhaps the initial *e* was dropped from *estampida* because English-speaking frontiersmen associated the Mexican Spanish word with the English word *stamp.* If this was the reason for dropping the letter, then the frontiersmen were right in their linguistic analysis—as it happens, *estampida* is closely related to the English word *stamp.*

The original meaning of the Spanish word *estampida* is "loud sound, explosion, bang (such as that produced by a cannon)." The Spanish word is a borrowing from Provençal, the language traditionally spoken in southern France. The Provençal word *estampida* is derived from the verb *estampir,* "to resound," and *estampir* is most likely another of the many words that the Romance languages borrowed from the Germanic languages in the early medieval period. The source of *estampir* was a verb belonging to the same family of Germanic words that also includes the English verb *stamp,* "to put the foot down abruptly, pound." The verb *stomp,* too, originated in English simply as a variant of *stamp.*

tamale

Tamales are known by different names in different parts of Latin America. There are many distinctive regional variations of the tamale, but the basic recipe for the dish remains the same. It begins by spreading a layer of masa on a corn husk—in tropical areas, leaves from the banana tree are often used instead. Masa, by the way, is dough made from dried corn (maize) that has been soaked in limewater and then rinsed and ground into meal. (Limewater is water mixed with the alkali compound calcium oxide, which is often obtained from ashes. When the corn is soaked in limewater, the niacin in the kernels becomes more absorbable by human beings. The limewater also helps improve the nutritional qualities of the protein in the maize kernels. And not only that—it helps give the masa its distinctive enticing flavor, too.) After the masa is spread on the leaf, a mixture consisting of cooked meat, seasonings, and other ingredients is put on the masa, and the leaf and masa are wrapped around the mixture to make a tidy package. The tamales are then steamed until the masa is light and spongy.

Tamales are a daily staple in Mexico and many other parts of Latin America today, just as they have been for thousands of years. The word *tamale,* in fact, originates in Nahuatl, the language of the Aztec Empire that ruled central Mexico at the time of the arrival of the Spaniards in the Americas. The Nahuatl word for "tamale" is *tamalli*, and the Spanish borrowed this word as *tamal*. When English-speaking Americans who have learned a little Spanish travel south of the border, they are often surprised to learn this fact—that the Spanish word for a tamale is not *tamale*, but simply *tamal*. The plural of *tamal*, however, is the more familiar-looking *tamales*, and *tamales* is regularly formed according to the rule of Spanish plural formation: the plural of nouns ending in a consonant is formed by adding the ending *–es*.

The Spanish word first begins to appear in English in the middle of the 1800s, usually in the plural *tamales*. According to the *Oxford English Dictionary*, one early occurrence of *tamales* in print can be found in a somewhat patronizing and touristy description of San Francisco published in an issue of a Massachusetts newspaper, *The Boston Journal*, in February, 1884: *A queer article of food, known as 'tamales', is sold in the streets of San Francisco at night by picturesquely clad Spaniards.* One average-sized tamale is often not enough for a meal, and so tamales are seldom eaten singly. (Who was ever satisfied by just one *raviolo*, instead of several *ravioli*?) For this reason, English speakers probably heard the plural *tamales* when they first began to encounter tamales as they moved into new states of the Union, like California, that were once part of Mexico. English speakers became used to ordering and eating tamales in the plural, and they may never have heard the singular *tamal* at the time. In English, of course, the usual way of making plurals is just to add an *-s* to the singular of the noun. When circumstances forced English speakers to come up with a singular for the plural *tamales,* they simply performed this procedure in reverse and removed the *-s* to make *tamale*, pronounced (tə-mä**ʹ**lē). Linguists call this process *back-formation*, and *tamale*, back-formed from the plural *tamales*, quickly became the more common singular form in English, despite the fact that it differs from the correct Spanish form *tamal*.

After the creation of the English word *tamale,* the slang expression *hot tamale,* meaning both "a lively or brash person" or "a very attractive woman," caught on quite quickly. In the *Random House Historical Dictionary of American Slang,* the eminent scholar of American slang, Jonathan Lighter, quotes the following early occurrence of *hot tamale* from a work by Jack London written in 1895 and describing a conversation with a character called the "Frisco Kid": *Yer wants ter ast me a few questions? Den fire away. I'se yer red hot tamale.*

tango

The story of the tango begins on the shores of the Río de la Plata, the vast estuary formed by the confluence of the Paraná and the Uruguay Rivers and flanked by the cosmopolitan cities of Buenos Aires, Argentina, and Montevideo, Uruguay. One of the most important ingredients in the tango was the *milonga,* a kind of dance music in duple time typical of the Río de la Plata region. In the late 1800s, immigrants from all corners of Europe came streaming into the rapidly expanding cities of Buenos Aires and Montevideo, and from the mingling of their diverse traditions, the tango was born. Life in the wild outskirts or *barrios* of Buenos Aires is vividly depicted by the suggestive lyrics of early tango songs, in which macho characters retell the stories of their romantic entanglements. Although the birth of the tango is especially associated with Buenos Aires, the tango is also a cherished part of the traditions of Montevideo as well.

In the first few years of the 1900s, the tango spread from the Río de la Plata to Paris, and from there the passionate and erotic dance quickly conquered the whole world. During the 1920s and 1930s, in Argentina itself, the singer Carlos Gardel helped popularize the tango in all levels of Argentinian society and made the music of the tango a central part of Argentinian identity. Although Gardel's recordings are still loved today, tango continues to evolve as a vibrant form of music and dance, and it remains a vital part of life in Buenos Aires. Although *porteños* (as the inhabitants of Buenos Aires are called) will always have a special claim on the mystique of the tango, the dance is now part of world culture too—the familiar English expression *it takes two to tango*, for example, originates as the refrain of a popular song (which does not initially strike the listener as a tango) written by Al Hoffman and Dick Manning that became a hit for Pearl Bailey in 1952.

In several parts of the Spanish-speaking world, there are other styles of music and dance that are called *tango* but do not resemble the tango that has its home in Argentina and Uruguay. In the flamenco music of Spain, *tango* is a genre of *cante* ("song") in duple time, and there are traces of a dance called a *tango* in Mexico as well from early in the 1800s. In the Spanish of the Canary Islands and of certain areas of the Americas, the word *tango* can also be used to refer to festivals enlivened by dancing that are held by communities of African descent. Taking these divergent meanings into account, scholars have proposed various theories about the origin of the word *tango*, and many think that the word ultimately comes from Africa. Just like English, especially as spoken in the United States, the Spanish language of the Americas has been enriched by many words brought over by Africans who were enslaved and transported to European colonies in the Western Hemisphere. *Tango* may have come from one language or another belonging to the Niger-Congo language family in Africa. (The Niger-Congo family is one of the world's most important language families, containing a large number of languages spoken across a vast area of sub-Saharan Africa, from Senegal in the northwest to Kenya in the east and South Africa in the south.) For example, the word meaning "to dance" in Ibibio, a Niger-Congo language of Southeast Nigeria, is *tamgu*. A related word may have been borrowed from an African language in the colonial period and spread throughout Spanish, eventually to find international fame as the tango craze spread in the early 1900s.

temblor

The word *temblor,* meaning "earthquake," is most commonly heard in the southwestern United States. It is a borrowing of Mexican Spanish *temblor,* which means "mild earthquake." (In Mexican Spanish, a strong earthquake is more likely to be called a *terremoto,* from Latin *terrae mōtus,* "movement of the earth.") *Temblor* originally just meant "trembling" and is derived from the verb *temblar,* "to tremble."

It is no accident that the Spanish word *temblar* sounds like the English verb *tremble*—both verbs descend from Latin *tremulāre,* "to tremble." (This Latin verb is related to other Latin words like *tremulus,* "trembling," the source of the English adjective *tremulous.*) As the everyday Latin spoken in Spain during Roman times slowly developed into Spanish, the second vowel in *tremulāre* was dropped and the word pronounced as something like *tremlāre.* It was a little hard to pronounce the resulting sequence of consonants *ml,* so people inserted a *b* between the *m* and *l.* In addition, the *r* in the initial *tr* of the pronunciation *tremlāre* also disappeared, and in this way the Latin verb became Spanish *temblar.* A similar disappearance of *r* after a consonant at the beginning of a word has occurred in other Spanish verbs, too. *Quemar,* "to burn," for instance, comes from Latin *cremāre,* also just meaning "to burn." *Cremāre* is in fact the source of the English verb *cremate.*

Meanwhile, as Latin was becoming Spanish in Spain, the everyday spoken Latin of France was developing into French. In the history of French, the same loss of the second vowel and insertion of *b* occurred as in Spanish *temblar,* and Latin *tremulāre* became *trembler.* English then borrowed the French verb as *tremble.*

ten-gallon hat

The hollow in even the largest cowboy hats usually holds no more than three quarts. You can see for yourself by filling one of them with hard candies or dry rice (so you don't ruin the hat) and then measuring the amount. Is a *ten-gallon hat* then just another tall tale told by a cowboy? In fact, the *gallon* in *ten-gallon hat* probably didn't originally refer to an amount of liquid. Instead, the hats may have gotten their name from the decorative bands or braids used to trim the sombreros worn by vaqueros in the Old West. The Spanish name for such a braid is *galón,* a word that English-speaking cowboys eventually transformed into *gallon.* A *ten-gallon hat* was thus originally an impressively decorated piece of headgear.

The Spanish word *galón* itself is a borrowing of the French word *galon.* The same French word also entered English in the form *galloon,* a word for a narrow braid or band of lace, metallic thread, or embroidery used as trimming. The word *galloon* was perhaps not all that well known out on the range, so that cowboys ended up calling their large sombreros *ten-gallon hats* rather than *ten-galloon hats.*

Even if ten-gallon hats won't actually hold ten gallons, the term *ten-gallon hat* was probably reinforced by the fact that cowboys can use their hats as makeshift watering troughs. In his fascinating book *Western Words,* the noted scholar of cowboy lingo Ramon F. Adams lists all of the uses that a cowboy can find for his hat, including the following: *The crown makes a handy water bucket if his horse cannot get to water, and the brim serves as his own drinking cup. He starts his campfire with his hat by using it as a bellows to fan a sickly blaze, and he can use it again as a water bucket to put out that same fire when he breaks camp.*

tilde

A tilde is a diacritical mark (~) placed over the letter *n* in Spanish to indicate the palatal nasal sound somewhat like (ny), as in *cañon,* "canyon," or over a vowel in Portuguese to indicate nasalization, as in *lã,* "wool," or *pão,* "bread."

The tilde originated as a mark of abbreviation used by medieval European scribes, most often writing in Latin. When scribes wanted to save space or had come to the end of a line without finishing a word, they omitted the final letter of the word and drew a line above the letter after which the letter was omitted. In Latin, this sign of abbreviation was called a *titulus,* meaning "superscription, something written above or outside something else." The device was especially used to abbreviate Latin words ending in the consonants *n* or *m.* A Latin word like *aurum,* "gold," could be abbreviated as *aurū,* for example, and many scribes also used a curved version of the *titulus,* as in *aurũ.* The *titulus* could also be used within words. For example, a word like *annus,* "year," could be abbreviated *añus.*

How did this mark of abbreviation become a diacritical mark in Spanish and Portuguese? The Latin word *annus* provides a good example of how this occurred. In the minds of Spanish and Portuguese scribes, the *titulus* came to be just another way of writing the consonants *n* and *m* before another consonant or at the end of words. As the everyday spoken Latin of Roman Spain slowly evolved into Spanish during the medieval period, it so happened that the Latin consonant cluster *nn* (double *n*) as in *annus* became a palatal nasal sound a little like (ny). The Latin word *annus* therefore evolved into something that was pronounced like (änyo) in medieval Spanish (just as the word is still pronounced today). (There are also other sources for the sound (ny). Some are from the Latin consonant cluster –gn–, as in Modern Spanish *leña* "firewood," from Latin *lignum,* while others are from Latin –ni–, as in Spanish *cigüeña,* "stork," from Latin *cicōnia.*) The Latin alphabet had no special letter for indicating this new sound, so Spanish scribes took advantage of the *n* with the *titulus* in order to represent it, since many new (ny) sounds derived from the *nn* that they were used to writing as *ñ* in Latin. And so the word for "year" was simply spelled *año.* Similarly, the use of the tilde in Portuguese to indicate a nasalized vowel derives from the use of the *titulus* to abbreviate the nasal consonants *n* and *m.* Portuguese *lã,* "wool," for example, is from Latin *lana,* while *pão,* "bread," is from Latin *pānis.*

The Spanish word *tilde* is a borrowing of early Catalan *tilte*— to ease pronunciation, the Spanish changed the *lt* to *ld.* Catalan *tilte* comes from Latin *titulus,* "something written above another thing." The order of the *t* and *l* in *titulus* was reversed as Latin developed into Catalan, and a similar alteration of Latin consonants has also occurred in the history of the Spanish word *cabildo,* "chapter (of an organization)," from Latin *capitulum.*

In Old French, Latin *titulus* became *title.* The Old French word was borrowed into Middle English, and eventually it shows up in modern English as the word for a short inscription or name written above a written passage or at the head of a book—that is, a *title.* Etymologically speaking, *tilde* and *title* are the same word.

tomato

It is hard to imagine the cuisine of Spain, Italy, and the rest of the Mediterranean region without tomatoes, but a little over five centuries ago, no European had ever heard of a tomato. The tomato is thought to be native to Peru and the adjacent regions of South America, but it has been cultivated in Central America and southern Mexico for many centuries. The tomato does not seem to have been a staple food among the indigenous peoples of Peru, but both the Maya of Central America and the Aztecs of Mexico grew tomatoes. After the Spanish conquered the Aztec Empire in 1521, the tomato was brought back to Europe, where it quickly became a popular food in Spain, Portugal, and Italy.

The language of the Aztec Empire was Nahuatl, and Nahuatl is still spoken by well over a million people today. In Nahuatl, there is a word *tomatl* used as a generic cover-all term for various plump globose fruits including the tomato, but especially for the tomatillo. (From a botanist's point of view, a fruit is any structure that develops from certain parts of a flower and contains seeds. In this way, a tomato is a fruit just like a grape or a blueberry.) The fruits of the tomatillo plant look a bit like small green tomatoes and are produced by a plant belonging to the same botanical family as the tomato. They have seedy pulp like a tomato, but each tomatillo is enclosed by a papery covering that is the remnant of the flower calyx. When ripe, tomatillos are usually greenish with a purplish or yellowish tinge and between the size of a cherry and plum. Tomatillos are the main ingredient in Mexican *salsa verde*. The specific Nahuatl word for the tomato itself is *xitomatl*, literally "*tomatl* with a navel (*xictli*)," perhaps referring to the way the stem attaches to the tomato.

The Spanish borrowed the word *tomatl* as *tomate* and used it to refer specifically to the tomato, rather than the tomatillo. The first known references to the tomato in Europe occur in the writings of botanists in the middle of the 1500s. Subsequently, of course, the tomato spread across the world so that it is now just as at home in the rich sauces of India and the soups of Vietnam as it is in the salsa of Mexico.

In England during the 1500s and 1600s, the tomato was at first grown only as an ornamental—it was widely believed to be poisonous, or at least bad-tasting and unhealthful. The modern scientific name of the tomato is *Solanum lycopersicum*, literally meaning "nightshade wolf-peach" in Latin. The genus *Solanum* also includes the plant called *deadly nightshade*, and many of the tomato's near relatives, the other members of the genus *Solanum*, are quite poisonous. In fact, the leaves of the tomato plant itself are toxic, although the fruit of course is not. Some Northern Europeans looking at the tomato plant for the first time may have been reminded of the nightshade, and so they admired its brightly colored fruits for their appearance only and did not venture to taste them. Eventually, however, even the English and settlers in colonial North America were convinced that the tomato was good to eat, and tomatoes begin to appear in English-language cookbooks in the middle of the 1700s.

The Spanish word *tomate* is the source of the English word *tomato*. Unfortunately, knowledge of where *tomato* comes from does not really help us to decide once and for all why some people say (tə-mā′tō) while others say (tə-mä′tō). The "mah" pronunciation (tə-mä′tō) is standard in the United Kingdom, but some Americans use it as well. When the word first begins to appear in English, in the very early 1600s, it is spelled *tomate* just as it is in Spanish, and this spelling survives, in competition with the spelling *tomato*, right down to the middle of the 1800s. However, it is unclear how exactly the spelling *tomate* was pronounced over the centuries. The current spelling *tomato* begins to appear only a century and a half after *tomate*, in the middle of the 1700s. The spelling *tomato*, and whatever pronunciation was given to this spelling at the time, may reflect the influence of the word *potato*. It is interesting that the word *potato* is only pronounced (pə-tā′tō)—there is no "tah" pronunciation (pə-tä′tō) even in the United Kingdom. However, the word *potato* entered English slightly earlier than *tomato*, and we therefore cannot expect the two words to have developed in exactly the same way.

Tomato may also be another example of a phenomenon seen in several other words in this book—English speakers have been inclined, over the centuries, to add an *o* to the end of any word they know to be of Spanish origin. Ever since Spanish became one of the most widely spoken languages of the world with the rise of the Spanish Empire in the 1500s, English speakers have been familiar with the fact that a large number of Spanish nouns and adjectives end in *o*, even if they knew relatively little else about the language. In order to make words of Spanish origin conform to their preconception of what Spanish words should be like, English speakers often stuck an *o* on the ends of words of Spanish origin even where it didn't belong. The word *potato*, too, is in fact another example of this phenomenon, as is *tornado*.

tornado

The English word *tornado* looks like it comes straight from Spanish *tornado*, "turned," the past participle of the verb *tornar*, "to turn." Since the winds, clouds, and debris in a tornado whirl around in a circle, it would seem at first glance that tornados are just "turned" winds. This superficially attractive origin for the word *tornado*, however, turns out to be wrong— the word *tornado* has a far more twisted history.

The story of *tornado* begins with the Spanish word *tronada*, meaning "thunderstorm," a derivative of the verb *tronar*, "to thunder." When the Spanish began to sail regularly in the tropical waters of the Americas in the 1500s, they encountered thunderstorms far more frequent and powerful than they were used to seeing off the coasts of Europe, and they called them *tronadas*. Later on in the 1500s, when the English were marauding the tropical seas in the wake of the Spanish, they picked up the Spanish word for these storms but mispronounced and misspelled it as *ternado*. At this stage, *ternado* could be used of any of the powerful storms, including hurricanes, that are characteristic of the coasts of Africa, the Caribbean, and North America. In the first part of the 1600s, English speakers who knew a little Spanish associated their word *ternado* with the everyday Spanish verb *tornar*, "to turn," probably because of the variable direction of the gusts in tropical storms. Mariners may also have taken note of the changing direction of the winds as tropical cyclones moved over them, and the sight of twisting waterspouts and the whirlwinds we now call *tornados* may also have inspired the name. In this way, *ternado* was transformed into *tornado*. Later on, the meaning of the word in American English was narrowed, and nowadays *tornado* most often describes the funnel-shaped downward extension of a cloud generated by winds rotating in a narrow column at destructive speeds—a characteristic feature of summer weather in central and southeastern North America. The English word *tornado* has even been borrowed back into Spanish, as *tornado*—a word of English origin despite its outwardly Spanish appearance.

The resemblance between Spanish *tornar* and English *turn* is no accident. *Turn* comes from a combination of Old English *turnian* (also found in the form *tyrnian*) and Old French *torner*, both of which come from Latin *tornāre*, "to turn in a lathe." Latin *tornāre* is also the source of Spanish *tornar*.

transhumance

The word *transhumance* refers to a method of raising livestock in which herds are moved from one grazing ground to another, as from lowlands to highlands, with the changing of seasons. In

Spain, for example, shepherds would traditionally move their sheep onto the slopes of the mountains at the end of May to let them browse the fresh plant growth there, just when the lowland plains had begun to become hot and parched. In October, as winter approached and plant growth in the mountains slowed, the shepherds would bring their herds down to the plains to graze on lowland pastures refreshed by winter rains. Using such a system, the Spanish were able to put a great deal of land of marginal agricultural quality to productive use, and Spain became the world's premier producer of wool. The sheep also provided plenty of milk for making the distinctive sheep's-milk cheeses of Spain, such as manchego cheese from La Mancha. The livestock herders of Spain perfected the transhumant system to such a degree that English has even borrowed the word *transhumance* from the Spanish language. *Transhumance* comes from the Spanish verb *trashumar*, "to practice transhumant livestock raising."

The verb *trashumar* is itself derived from the prefix *tras–*, the Spanish equivalent of the English prefix *trans–* meaning "across" or "through," added to the Latin noun *humus*, "ground." The prefix *tras–* comes from the Latin prefix *trāns–*, just like English *trans–*. We may be puzzled at first when we compare the Spanish prefix *tras–*, without *n*, with English and Latin *trāns–* with *n*, but the lack of *n* in *tras–* is the result of a regular change that occurred as the spoken Latin of Spain gradually evolved into Spanish: within a word, an *n* before an *s* simply disappeared. Another example of the phenomenon is the Spanish word *mesa*, "table" (the source of the English word *mesa*, "flat-topped area of elevated land"). *Mesa* comes from Latin *mensa*, "table." The other element in *trashumar*, the Latin noun *humus*, "ground," is of course also found in English as *humus*, referring to the part of the soil made up of decayed organic matter that improves soil's fertility and helps it retain water.

The tradition of transhumant sheep-raising in Spain has also given English two other terms discussed in this book, *merino* and *mustang.*

tuna

The word *tuna* is an all-inclusive name for many species of fish belonging to the family Scombridae. Tuna have of course been caught since prehistoric times, but the word *tuna* is actually a newcomer to the English language. Before the appearance of the word *tuna* in the 1800s, the word *tunny* was used to refer to many

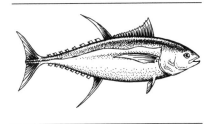

of the fish now known as *tuna,* and various individual tuna species were known by such names as *albacore, skipjack,* and *bonito,* as they still are today.

The first known use of the word *tuna* in English, according to the *Oxford English Dictionary,* dates from 1881. It is found in a report on the fish of the Pacific published in a volume of the Proceedings of the United States National Museum. The authors of the report also give the local fishermen's names for many species of fish that they describe. They describe many species of fish that now might be called *tuna,* including the albacore, a species then classified as *Orycnus alalonga* but now classified as *Thunnus alalonga.* As part of their description of the albacore, the authors mention another species of fish, similar to the albacore and living in the waters around Santa Cruz Island, one of the Channel Islands located off the coast of southern California. They had, however, been unable to acquire a specimen to examine more closely: *Another Orycnus, known as the "tuna," exists about Santa Cruz, but we failed to obtain it.* Later in the report, the word *tuna* is mentioned again, as one of the alternative names for yet another species of fish that fishermen also called the *bonito, skipjack,* or *Spanish mackerel.*

California was long a part of the Spanish Empire, and then for a while a part of Mexico, and because the English word *tuna* first appears in this state, scholars of English etymology have sought the origin of *tuna* in American Spanish. English *tuna* appears to be a variant of the standard Spanish word for "tuna," *atún. Atún* itself is one of the many Arabic words that entered Spanish when Muslim rulers governed the south of Spain. As happened with so many other Arabic nouns when they were borrowed into Spanish, the entire Arabic phrase, *al tūn,* "the tuna," including the Arabic definite article *al* (here pronounced *at* before *t*) has been borrowed into Spanish as the noun *atún.* (This phenomenon is explained in greater detail at the entry for *adobe* in this book.) The Arabic word *tūn,* "tuna," is in turn a borrowing of Latin *thunnus,* "tuna."

Since tuna are very economically important fish, it may at first seem surprising that the Spanish word *atún* should come from Arabic rather than directly from Latin *thunnus.* Tuna fishing in the Mediterranean was also an activity carried out on a wide scale by Arab fishermen in North Africa. However, a direct descendant of the Latin word *thunnus* did survive into Old Spanish times. As Latin developed into Old Spanish, *thunnus* would have become something like *toño* in Old Spanish, and although there is no word *toño* known in the history of Spanish, there is an Old Spanish word *toñino,* "little tuna," that looks like a derivative of this hypothetical *toño.* Portuguese also has a word *toninha* meaning "little tuna," and similar forms are found in Catalan and in Gallego, a language closely related to Portuguese that is spoken in the region of Galicia in northwestern Spain. Perhaps fishermen coming from the Iberian peninsula spread words in this family around the world in the days of the Spanish Empire, and these words contributed to the formation of the local Californian term *tuna*.

Although *tuna* itself does not have the meaning "tuna" in Spanish, the word is in fact commonly used in Spanish with two different, completely unrelated meanings. One kind of *tuna* is an ancient institution of Spanish universities, where a *tuna* is a group of students who sing traditional songs and play on the guitar and other instruments while dressed in the old-fashioned costumes, in imitation of the wandering minstrels of the Middle Ages. The origin of this word *tuna* is obscure, but it is often said to come from the French phrase *le roi de Thunes*, literally "the king of Tunis." This was apparently the title of a personage of some sort in medieval France, the king of the beggars and vagabonds.

The other meaning of *tuna* in Spanish is "prickly pear," the luscious fruit produced by cacti native to the Caribbean, Mexico, and the southwestern United States. This *tuna* is another of the many terms for plants and animals of the Americas that Spanish has borrowed from Taíno, the language spoken by indigenous people of the Bahamas and the Greater Antilles who met Columbus when he landed on these islands in 1492. Because both English *tuna* and Spanish *tuna*, "prickly pear," refer to foodstuffs, they are a classic pair of false friends for English speakers learning Spanish. In Spanish, however, there is nothing strange about *mermelada de tuna*—jam made from *tunas*.

U

ulluco

The Andes are the home of the potato, one of the most important food crops in the world, but the indigenous peoples of the Andean region have long grown many other tubers and root vegetables that have not succeeded in matching the huge popularity of the potato in the rest of the world. *Ulluco, arracacha,* and *oca* are the names of some important Andean root crops that are less well known than the potato outside of the Andes. The words for all these vegetables reached English by way of American Spanish, but they ultimately come from Quechua, the language of the Inca Empire that is still widely spoken in the Andean region today. Unfortunately, many of us living outside of South America have no chance to taste the grand variety of traditional foods of the Inca empire that are still enjoyed in the Andes today.

Ulluco produces edible tubers that look very much like potatoes but have a crisper yet more watery texture. The scientific name of the plant is *Ullucus tuberosus,* which is Latin for "ulluco, the tuberous." The leaves of the plant can also be eaten as a vegetable and prepared in the same way as spinach. They resemble the leaves of Malabar spinach, a close relative of ulluco from Asia that is frequently sold in Asian markets in the United States. The word *ulluco* is a borrowing of American Spanish *ulluco.* In Spanish, the word is also pronounced and spelled *olluco*. Both forms come from the Quechua name for this vegetable, *ulluku*.

Arracacha, also sometimes known as *racacha*, belongs to the same botanical family that includes carrots and celery. Its scientific name is *Arracacia xanthorrhiza*, "arracacha, having yellow roots." It has a fleshy whitish or yellowish taproot like a parsnip, but somewhat thicker, that is eaten cooked. Cooked arracacha root has a very fine celery-like flavor, and the vegetable is popular in South America in the area where it can be grown. Unlike carrots and parsnips, however, arracacha cannot be stored for very long. The word *arracacha* comes from Spanish *arracacha*, and the Spanish word comes from Quechua *rakacha*.

Oca belongs to the same genus of plants as wood sorrel, a common plant in North America with tiny yellow flowers. The scientific name of oca is *Oxalis tuberosa*, "wood sorrel, the tuberous." Its tubers that can be cooked and eaten like potatoes after peeling. The tubers come in many colors, but one widely grown variety is pink. The word *oca* comes from Spanish, and the Spanish word comes from Quechua *uqa*. The consonant *q* in this word represents a sound that linguists call a voiceless uvular stop. The sound reminds English speakers of a *k* made very deep in the throat.

Oca is picky about its growing conditions—it will only produce tubers when the days become short in autumn. But the plant may also be killed by too much cold. These requirements have limited its spread outside of the Andes, but since at least the 1920s, oca has been popular in New Zealand. New Zealanders usually call the vegetable simply by the name *yam*, and some New Zealanders do not even know that *yam* refers to an entirely different vegetable in other parts of the world.

vamoose

The verb *to vamoose*, "to leave hurriedly," has a full range of tenses and grammatical moods in English, and it can be used with all grammatical persons: *He vamoosed, I'll vamoose, Let's vamoose, You had better vamoose, She told them to vamoose.* However, *vamoose* comes from the Spanish first person plural command form *¡Vamos!*, "Let's go!" of the irregular verb *ir*, "to go." The verb *vamoose* originated in America and comes into use in the middle of the 1800s, although the Spanish word *¡Vamos!* was occasionally used as an unassimilated foreign expression in English somewhat before that time. The word had a variety of spellings when it first appeared in English— *vamosed* and *vamosing* were common ways of spelling the past tense and the present participle, and other spellings like *vamous* and *varmoose* were found as well.

Much like the English expressions *Let's go!* or *Come on!*, Spanish *¡Vamos!* can be used to tell a person to "get a move on"— not only when leaving a place and going somewhere else but also when some task needs to be done. The transformation of *¡Vamos!* into the English *vamoose* probably occurred in situations like the one represented in the following hypothetical exchange: *"What are you still doing here? Vamos!" "Just a minute." "Come on! Vamos!" "All right, I'm vamosing."* Later on, the first speaker could have described the exchange as follows: *I told* him *to vamos, and he vamosed.*

On the pronunciation of *vamoose*, see *lasso*.

vanilla

The marriage between chocolate and vanilla is an ancient one—the indigenous peoples of Mesoamerica, such as the Maya, flavored their drink of ground chocolate beans with vanilla, the pods of vines belonging to the orchid family. Most vanilla comes from the species native to Mexico and Central America, *Vanilla planifolia,* although vanilla is also produced from other members of the genus *Vanilla.*

The production of vanilla is a labor-intensive process. In the wild, the plants are usually pollinated by a certain species of bee native to Mexico and Central America, but in cultivation, human workers must pollinate each flower by hand. The vanilla vine has attractive whitish-green flowers that mature into thin pods around twenty centimeters (eight inches) long. These pods have no vanilla aroma while they are still green—in order to develop the distinctive flavor of vanilla, the pods must be cured in a moist, hot, closed environment. The pods are picked by hand and then their growth is stopped by laying them out in the sun, boiling them, or putting them in a hot oven. Bundles of pods are then wrapped in cloth and placed in wooden boxes, and the boxes are heated to more than 50°C

(120°F) for a week or more, when they develop their rich aroma. The beans are then removed from the boxes and allowed to dry out gradually, during which time they shrink somewhat.

When the Spanish arrived in Mexico and Central America and found the indigenous peoples flavoring their food with the pod of the vanilla vine, they called it *vainilla,* literally "little pod, little husk," a diminutive of the word *vaina,* meaning "sheath, scabbard for a sword" and by extension, "pod (as of peas)." The Spanish word *vaina,* "sheath," in turn comes from Latin *vāgīna,* "sheath." The loss of a *g* between two vowels on the way from Latin to Spanish (as seen in *vaina*) is a regular phenomenon—other examples of the same processes can be seen in Spanish *real,* "royal," from Latin *rēgālis,* and *liar,* "to tie up, bind" from Latin *ligāre.* The Latin word *vāgīna,* "sheath," by the way, is also the source of the English anatomical term *vagina.*

The Mexican drink made of chocolate flavored with vanilla was an immediate hit when the cocoa beans and vanilla pods were taken back to Spain in the first part of the 1500s. It took some time, however, for vanilla and chocolate to catch on elsewhere in Europe—the Spaniards guarded the delicious secrets of the Americas jealously. Vanilla first begins to be mentioned in English around the middle of the 1600s—at first, the word is spelled *vaynilla,* similar to Spanish *vainilla,* but later on the altered spelling *vanilla* wins out in English.

vinegarroon

The vinegarroon (*Mastigoproctus giganteus*) is a member of a group of eight-legged arthropods called whip scorpions, which resemble scorpions but have whiplike tails with no poisonous stings. Vinegarroons have blackish-colored carapaces, and they have pincers that they use to catch crickets and other insect prey. They can grow to be up to five or six inches long, and they look very fearsome, somewhat like a cross between a lobster and a scorpion. Vinegarroons do not pose much of a threat to human beings, however—although their unique defense mechanism can be quite annoying. When it feels itself to be in danger, the vinegarroon will whip its tail toward the threat and

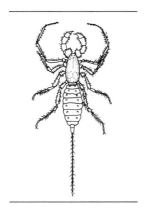

spray it with a secretion containing acetic acid—the same acid that makes common household vinegar sour. The acid produced by vinegarroons is twenty times more concentrated than vinegar, and it is an effective deterrent to rodents and other animals that might try to eat them. If human beings get too close to the vinegarroon's spray, it can burn their eyes and nose as well. The vinegary smell left by the vinegarroon is also quite strong.

The vinegarroon lives in Mexico and the southern United States, and the English word *vinegarroon* (also variously spelled *vinegaroon* and *vinegarone*) is a borrowing of American Spanish *vinagrón*. The animal is also more often called *vinagrillo* in American Spanish. Both words are derived, one with the common *–ón* and the other with the common suffix *–illo*, from the Spanish word for vinegar, *vinagre*. *Vinagre* itself comes from Latin *vīnum ācre*, literally "sour wine."

Even when bottled, wine will quickly turn to vinegar if substances are not added in order to stop bacteria from turning the alcohol in the wine into acetic acid. In the past, substances like pine resin were added to prevent this process, and even today, wine flavored and preserved with pine resins is still drunk in Greece, where it is called *retsina*. Nowadays, chemicals called sulfites are most often used instead. Vinegar can also be made from alcoholic liquids based on barley (*malt vinegar*) or rice (*rice wine vinegar*), but the ancient Mediterranean was a wine-drinking region—the people in Roman Spain and the rest of the Roman Empire, for instance, stored wine in big jars, and when one of these jars went bad, it provided enough vinegar to last a household for a year.

The English word *vinegar* also comes from Latin *vīnum ācre*. As the spoken Latin of Roman France developed into Old French, Latin *vīnum ācre* became *vinaigre*. The Old French was then borrowed into Middle English and eventually developed into Modern English *vinegar*.

volcano

The word *volcano* ultimately comes from the name of the Roman god of fire and metalworking, *Vulcānus*, who is known as *Vulcan* in English. The Romans thought that the chimney to Vulcan's underground workshop was located on one of a group of very active volcanic islands north of Sicily in the Tyrrhenian Sea, now known as the Aeolian Islands. The Romans called this ash-covered island, where they believed Vulcan shoveled out the cinders from his forge, by the god's name *Vulcānus,* and it is still called *Volcano* in Italian today.

In AD 829, Sicily was invaded by an Arab force, and from AD 832 to 1072, Sicily flourished under Muslim rulers. Arabs conducted a great deal of maritime trade in the area, and they borrowed several local Sicilian and Italian words. These included the word descended from Latin *Vulcānus,* and in Arabic, this word took the form *burkān.* (In Modern Arabic, *burkān* is still the generic word for "volcano.") According to some scholars, the Spanish word for "volcano" is a borrowing of the Arabic form of the word, rather than being a direct descendant of the Latin word. The intermediate transmission of the word through

Arabic would explain the fact that the Spanish word does not end in -o as would be expected if it descended directly from a Latin word ending in -us. (According to this theory, the spelling of the Spanish word *volcán* must then reflect the influence of the original Latin word.) In any case, by the 1200s, the Latin word *Vulcānus* had taken the form *volcán* in Spanish. *Volcán* was subsequently borrowed into French as *volcan,* and then from both French and Spanish at once, the word entered English as *volcan.* According to the *Oxford English Dictionary,* the first known use of the word *volcan* in English is found in work by John Frampton from 1577, *Monardes' Ioyfull newes out of the newe founde worlde,* which refers to *sulfur found nigh unto the Volcan of Nicaragua.* Frampton's work, by the way, is a translation of Nicolás Monardes's work *Historia medicinal de las cosas que se traen de nuestras Indias Occidentales* ("Medical Study of the Things that are Brought from our West Indies"), a description of the many new products reaching Spain from its conquests in the Americas.

Later on, *volcano* becomes the most common spelling of the English word, under the influence of Italian *volcano.* (Italian *volcano* itself, used in the generic sense "any volcanic mountain," is in fact thought to derive from Spanish.) The English, safe on their nonvolcanic isle, often heard reports of Italian volcanoes like Aetna on Sicily and Vesuvius near Naples, as well as volcanoes on the Aeolian Islands like Stromboli, and the fame of Italian volcanoes eventually led to the predominance of the Italian form of the word.

warsaw

English has at least one word of Spanish origin beginning with *w*, even though the letter *w* is only used in foreign words in Spanish. The word *warsaw* refers to a very large grouper (*Epinephelus nigritus*) that lives in the warm waters of the Atlantic from North Carolina southwards, through the Gulf of Mexico and the Caribbean, all the way to the northern coast of South America. Warsaws can grow to over six feet long and weigh over five hundred pounds, and they are good to eat, too.

The origin of the word *warsaw* referring to the fish has nothing to do with the name of the capital city of Poland. Rather, it is an adaptation of American Spanish *guasa,* a word typical of the Spanish dialects of Cuba and Venezuela. *Guasa* refers to a relative of the warsaw, the goliath grouper or jewfish (*Epinephelus itajara*).

The English names of several other kinds of fish come from Spanish. Other fish names discussed in this book include *barracuda, cero,* and *tuna*.

xoloitzcuintle

Despite the fact that English has very few words beginning with the letter *x*, it is possible to find a few words beginning with *x* that have passed through Spanish on their way into English. One of the most interesting of these is *xoloitzcuintle*. The xoloitzcuintle is a small- to medium-sized breed of dog with a very striking appearance—the dog's dark-colored, smooth skin is hairless, although it often has small tufts of hair on the head, tail, and feet. The breed was developed in pre-Columbian Mexico and is sometimes also called the *Mexican hairless* in English. After the Spanish conquest of Mexico, xoloitzcuintles became relatively uncommon, and the breed survived only in remote areas. In more recent times, the breed has undergone a considerable revival in Mexico as well as in other countries.

The English name for the breed, *xoloitzcuintle,* is usually pronounced (shō-lō-ēts-kwēnt′lä). The word reached English by way of Spanish, but it ultimately comes from Nahuatl, the language of the Aztec Empire. In Nahuatl, the name of the breed is *xōloitzcuintli,* a compound of *itzcuintli,* "dog," with another noun, *xōlotl. Xōlotl* has a variety of meanings, including "servant," "slave," "boy," and "pet." *Xōlotl* is also the name of an Aztec god, the companion or double of the god Quetzalcoatl. Just as Quetzalcoatl was associated with Venus as the morning star, Xōlotl was identified with Venus as the evening star, and he guarded the sun during its nighttime journey through the underworld. In art, Xōlotl is often depicted with a dog's head that looks rather like the head of a xoloitzcuintle. In the religion of Nahuatl-speaking peoples, dogs were thought to help guide the souls of dead people to the otherworld. Xōlotl's depiction as a dog is probably related to the role of the dog as guide and protector of people in Nahuatl-speaking cultures.

The use of the letter *x* to represent the sound (sh) in Nahuatl, and occasionally Mexican Spanish, is actually a relic of the pronunciation of the letter *x* in the Spanish spoken by Spaniards at the time of the conquest of Mexico between 1519 and 1521. At that time, the letter *x* was pronounced (sh) in Spanish. Words like *dixo,* "he said," and *caxa,* "box," were pronounced (dē′shō) and (kä′shä). Nowadays, these words are spelled *dijo* and *caja* and pronounced (dē′KHō) or (dē′hō) and (kä′KHä) or (kä′hä). This change from (sh) to the raspy sound (KH)—or to a simple (h) in many dialects—began in the 1500s, and by the middle of the 1600s, most of the words that had once had an *x* pronounced (sh) in Spanish now had a (KH) or (h) sound spelled with a *j,* or with *g* when before *i* and *e.*

Nevertheless, a few Spanish words kept the old spelling with *x* out of respect for tradition. One of these is the name of the country *México* itself, pronounced (mĕ′hē-kō). Before the change of (sh) to (KH) or (h), the name *México* was pronounced approximately (mĕ′shē-kō). *México* ultimately derives from

Nahuatl *mēxicah,* the name of the group of Nahuatl speakers whose capital was the city of Tenochtitlán, now Mexico City. The word *mēxicah* has also been borrowed into Spanish as *mexica,* usually pronounced (mĕ-shē′kä), and it is used by some Nahuatl speakers and people descended from Nahuatl speakers as a name for their own ethnic group.

Before the arrival of the Spanish in Mexico, Nahuatl speakers had their own pictographic writing system. The traditions of the indigenous writing system perished with the conquest of the Aztec Empire, and the Spanish introduced the Roman alphabet. The sound (sh) is often used in Nahuatl, and in the new alphabetic writing system based on Spanish spelling, the letter *x* was used to spell this sound just as it was in the Spanish of the 1500s. At the time when Spanish was changing the sound (sh) to (KH), Nahuatl simply kept it as (sh), despite the fact that many Nahuatl speakers were bilingual in Spanish. In this way, the Nahuatl word *xōloitzcuintli* preserved its (sh) until it was borrowed into Spanish and English.

yam

Yams are the starchy tubers produced by various species of a tropical vine belonging to the genus *Dioscorea.* They are a staple food in many tropical regions around the world. Some varieties of yams are poisonous when raw—they contain crystals of calcium oxalate, which can irritate the mouth and the digestive tract. Cooking, however, breaks the crystals down. The flesh of yams ranges from whitish to bright orange. In the United States, the word *yam* is also used for another vegetable with orange flesh, sweet potatoes. Sweet potatoes are the tuberous roots of a vine with the scientific name *Ipomoea batatas* that belongs to the morning glory family.

The English word *yam* comes either from Portuguese *inhame* or from the earlier form of the Spanish word for "yam," *iñame.* The modern form of the Spanish word, *ñame,* has dropped the initial vowel. Descriptions and reports of the yam written in English begin to appear in the 1500s and early 1600s, drifting in from the tropical regions that were mostly governed by Spain and Portugal at the time. During this period, yams were still a foreign item to most English speakers, and they spelled the name for the vegetable variously as *inany* or *ini-amo,* for example. Later, by the middle of 1600s, the Spanish or Portuguese word had become naturalized in English as *yam.*

Spanish *ñame* and Portuguese *inhame* are ultimately borrowed from a word in one of the languages of West Africa, but which one exactly is hard to say because words similar to *ñame* and *inhame* occur in various West African languages. These include *ñam*, "food, to eat" in Wolof (one of the major languages of Senegal and The Gambia), *ñambu,* "manioc," in Bambara (one of the major languages of Mali), and *nyami,* "to eat" in Fulani (spoken across a vast area of West Africa stretching from Senegal to northern Nigeria).

See also *potato.*

yerba mate

Yerba mate is a South American evergreen tree (*Ilex paraguariensis*) closely related to holly. It is widely cultivated for its leaves, which are dried and used to prepare a tealike beverage extremely popular in Brazil, Uruguay, Argentina, Paraguay, Bolivia, and Chile. For instance, among the gauchos—the Argentinian and Uruguayan equivalents of North American cowboys—the day begins not with a pot of coffee set on the fire and drunk out of a little tin cup, but rather with a *mate* (a deep cup made from a hollowed-out dried gourd) full of *yerba mate.* Dried yerba mate is usually sold already broken into small bits, which are light grayish-green and look rather like dried oregano. To prepare the yerba mate, a quantity of leaves is measured out into the *mate* cup and hot—but not boiling—water is poured into the cup. (If water at the boiling point is used, the tea will be too bitter.) The beverage has a grassy, intensely "green" flavor, and it contains caffeine as well as various other active compounds. Many people besides South Americans prefer the stimulant properties of yerba mate, perceived as being gentler, to those of tea or coffee.

Yerba mate is traditionally drunk through a *bombilla,* a tube of silver or other metal that is open at one end like a straw, but fitted at the other end with a sort of filter, a bulbous, strainer-like cap perforated with many holes. The end with the filter is put into the cup, and the beverage sucked up through the straw, keeping the leaves in the cup. Yerba mate leaves can be infused many times without losing flavor.

The *yerba* in the Spanish word *yerba mate* is a variant spelling, frequently used in Argentina and elsewhere, of the word *hierba*, "herb, green plant." (The letter *h* is always silent in Modern Spanish.) Spanish *hierba* is in fact the same word as English *herb*, from an etymological point of view. *Hierba* descends from Latin *herba*, meaning "grass, a growth of green plants." Although an *h* appears in the spelling of the Latin word *herba*, your average Roman pronounced the word as *erba*. Speakers of Latin had already ceased to pronounce the letter *h* in the days of the Roman Empire. In the streets of Rome and the farms of the Roman provinces, Roman soldiers and farmers dropped their *h*'s just like a modern Cockney in the streets of London, and it is the speech of these average Roman citizens that eventually evolved into the modern Romance languages like Spanish. In this way, the spelling *yerba* without the *h* is historically justified.

Next door to Spain, over the Pyrenees, the spoken Latin of Roman Gaul gradually evolved into Old French, and Latin *herba* became Old French *erbe*. The Old French word was then borrowed into Middle English as *erbe*, still usually spelled without the *h*. Under the influence of the original Latin spelling *herba*, however, medieval English scribes sometimes tacked an unpronounced *h* back onto *erbe*, and this eventually led to the Modern English spelling *herb* with a silent *h*—silent in the United States, at least (most speakers of British English pronounce the *h* in *herb* under the influence of this spelling).

The word *mate* (mä′tā) in *yerba mate* is pronounced with two syllables and refers to the *mate* in which the beverage is prepared and served. *Yerba mate* is thus literally "*mate*-cup herb." The Spanish word *mate* comes from the Quechua word *mati*, "vessel or dish made from a dried gourd." In English, the word *mate* is often written *maté*, with an acute accent on the *e*. This spelling is doubtless intended to suggest that the word has two syllables, and to prevent people from misreading it as the common English word *mate*, "companion." However, in Spanish itself, the word is spelled simply as *mate*, without an accent. *Mate* is stressed on the first syllable, and an erroneous spelling *maté* in Spanish would indicate an accent on the second syllable. (*Maté* is a real Spanish word, though—it means "I killed"!) Many English speakers do in fact pronounce the English word *maté* with the stress on the second syllable, probably under the influence of similarly spelled English words like *café*. Many people who know Spanish, however, object to this way of pronouncing *maté,* since it strays unnecessarily far from the pronunciation of the original Spanish *mate* in *yerba mate* and is based purely on English spelling.

yuca

Yuca is another word for *cassava* in English. Like *cassava*, it comes from Spanish, but in Spanish, *yuca* refers to the cassava plant and to its root, the source of a kind of flour widely used in many parts of the Spanish-speaking world. On the other hand, *casabe,* the source of the word *cassava,* usually refers to a kind of bread made with yuca flour. Both Spanish words come from Taíno, the extinct indigenous language of the Bahamas and Greater Antilles. *Yuca* comes from the Taíno word for the root itself, while *casabe* (formerly spelled *casabi*) comes from the Taíno word for the bread prepared from the root.

Cassava or yuca is also called sometimes *manioc* in English, and this word is related to another Spanish word for *yuca, mandioca.* Both the English and the Spanish ultimately come from a word in Tupi or one of its close relatives among the languages of South America. The Tupi are the indigenous people whose ancestors lived along the coast of Brazil, in the Amazon River valley, and in Paraguay at the time of the arrival of European explorers. Many Tupi groups were driven extinct after the Europeans took control of the region, while other Tupi groups have been assimilated into general Brazilian society. Nevertheless, Tupi and its close relatives have contributed a large number of words to the Portuguese of Brazil, and some of these words have made it into English, such as *toucan* (the bird) and *piranha* (the fish). One of the close relatives of the Tupian languages is the language of the Guaraní, an indigenous people of Paraguay, northern Argentina, and southern Brazil. Spanish *mandioca* probably comes from Guaraní *mandiog.*

The round pearls of tapioca in tapioca pudding are made of the starch of cassava, and *tapioca* itself is another word of Tupian origin. English *tapioca* comes from Portuguese, and the Portuguese word comes from Tupi *typióca.* In Tupi, this word is a compound of the words *ty,* "juice," *pyá,* "heart," and *oca,* "to remove." Cassava roots contain cyanide, and the useful cassava starch has to be separated from the roots by arduous processing. The roots are ground up, the pulp is washed in water to separate the starch granules, and then the mixture is wrung out and dried to produce starchy flour.

The word *yucca* refers to several species of plants growing in the warm regions of North America. Yuccas have swordlike leaves growing densely around a short trunk, and their large white flowers are borne in a cluster on a long spike. They are attractive plants, often used in landscaping, and the yucca has been designated the state flower of New Mexico. The English name for these plants, *yucca,* comes from the scientific name of the genus to which they belong, *Yucca.* It is thought that the genus name *Yucca* derives from the word *yuca,* "cassava." However it remains completely obscure why a botanist might have used the Taíno and Spanish word for "cassava" in coming up with a scientific name for yucca plants—yucas and yuccas are completely unrelated, and the plants look nothing like each other.

See more at *cassava.*

zocalo

In Mexico, the vibrant center of life in a large city is often the public square or plaza, which is usually adorned with imposing churches and civic buildings. The Mexican Spanish word for such a plaza, *zócalo,* has been borrowed into English as a word to describe this institution of Mexican life. The usual English pronunciation of the word, as (sō′kä-lō′) with an initial (s), remains fairly close to the original pronunciation of the word in Mexican Spanish.

The grand zocalo of the capital of Mexico, *La Plaza de la Constitución,* has been the heart of the city since Aztec times—the city cathedral on the zocalo occupies a site near the great temple of Tenochtitlán, as Mexico City was once called in Nahuatl, the language of the Aztecs. In fact, this plaza was the first zocalo actually to be called a *zócalo.* The original meaning of the word *zócalo* in Spanish was "socle"—that is, a plain square block that serves as a pedestal for a sculpture or column. At the beginning of the 1800s, the Plaza de la Constitución was occupied by a statue depicting Charles IV, king of Spain from 1788 to 1819, seated on horseback. In 1843, General Antonio López de Santa Anna, then president of Mexico, ordered that the old statue be removed and replaced with a grandiose monument commemorating the independence of Mexico. (This is the same Santa Anna, by the way, who is remembered in the United States for ordering the deaths of

234

all Texan militiamen captured at the Battle of the Alamo in 1836, during the Texas rebellion against Mexico.) A huge block of marble for the socle of the statue arrived and was put in the middle of the square. Soon after, the Mexican government was distracted by political upheavals and the Mexican-American War. Funds for the construction of the monument ran short, and the project was put on hold, indefinitely. The block of marble, however, stayed put. It became a local landmark, and people began to refer to the whole plaza as *el Zócalo*, "the Socle." Eventually the socle was removed, but the name for the plaza stuck. In time, this use of the word *zócalo* spread to the rest of Mexico, and now the central plaza of any Mexican city can be called a *zócalo*.

It is no accident that the Spanish word *zócalo*, "socle," and the English word *socle*—pronounced (sō'kəl)—sound a bit alike. Both words come from Italian *zoccolo*, originally meaning "wooden shoe" and later "socle." (If the development of a word meaning basically "shoe" to a word meaning "pedestal" seems a bit bizarre, consider the word *pedestal* itself. It comes from Italian *piedistallo*, literally "stall for the feet.") The source of the Italian word *zoccolo* is the Latin word *soccus*, which was the name of a kind of Roman slipper or socklike shoe. In medieval times, the Latin word *soccus* was also borrowed into Old English as *socc* and eventually developed into the everyday

late 19th century engraving of the Plaza de la Constitución, Mexico City, featuring the statue of Charles IV

English word *sock,* meaning "stocking." In this way, *sock* and *zocalo* are distant linguistic cousins.

Zocalo is not the only word in English whose history has been influenced by the actions of General Antonio López de Santa Anna. The Mexican general and president also helped introduce *chicle* into English, and this word is the subject of a separate entry in this book.

Glossary

American Spanish: The Spanish language as spoken and written in the Western Hemisphere.

Arawak language family: Any of a large family of indigenous languages in South America and the Caribbean, spoken by a widespread group of peoples living in an area that includes parts of Colombia, Venezuela, Guyana, the Amazon basin of Brazil, Paraguay, Bolivia, Peru, and formerly most of the Greater Antilles. Taíno was an Arawak language.

augmentative: Relating to a suffix that indicates large size or great force in the word to which it is added. The word *augmentative* is also used to indicate a noun formed with an augmentative suffix. For example, the Spanish word *hombrón*, "big, tough-looking man," is derived from the word *hombre*, "man," by means of the *augmentative* suffix –*ón*.

Aymara: An indigenous people of highland Bolivia and Peru. The Aymara language is the most widely spoken language in the Aymaran family.

back-formation: The process by which a new word is created by removing a word element, such as a suffix from an already existing word, as *vacuum clean* from *vacuum cleaner*.

calque: A form of borrowing from one language to another whereby the semantic components of a given term are literally translated into their equivalents in the borrowing language. The English term *world view*, for example, is a *calque* of German *Weltanschauung*, made up of *Welt,* "world," and *Anschauung,* "view." Also called *loan translation.*

Carib: Any of a large group of indigenous peoples inhabiting nothern South America, the Lesser Antilles, and the eastern coast of Central America. The languages of the Carib people belong to the Carib language family, a large language family that also includes many languages of northern South America.

Catalan: The Romance language of Catalonia in northeastern Spain, also spoken in the small country of Andorra in the Pyranees, in the region of Rousillon in the southwest of France, in the Balearic Islands off the Mediterranean coast of Spain, and in a small part of Sardinia. Although most Catalan-speaking territory is located in the modern country of Spain, Catalan is in some ways more similar to Occitan and Provençal, the traditional languages of southern France, than it is to Spanish. Catalan literature flourished in Medieval and Renaissance times, but use of the language was subsequently discouraged by the central government in Spain. Catalan speakers, however, never ceased trying to promote the use of their language despite official discouragement, and in recent decades they have been successful in restoring their right to use their language in schools and for other official purposes.

Classical Latin: The Latin language and literature from around 200 BC to around AD 200.

Coptic: The language of the Copts—that is, the Christian Egyptians of pre-Islamic Egypt as well as their later descendants. Coptic descends from the Ancient Egyptian language that was written in hieroglyphs. Arabic has replaced Coptic as the everyday spoken language of modern Copts, but Coptic is still used as the liturgical language of the Coptic Church. Coptic and its ancestor Ancient Egyptian belong to the Afro-Asiatic language family, a large language family in which the Semitic language family is also included.

diminutive: Relating to a suffix that indicates smallness in the word to which it is added, or by extension, other related qualities such as youth, familiarity, affection, or contempt. The word *diminutive* is also used of nouns formed with a diminutive suffix. The *-let* in *booklet* and the *–kin* in *lambkin* are *diminutive* suffixes. Some of the the diminutive suffixes of Spanish include *–ito*, *–illo*, and *–ino*. See the entries for the words *mosquito* and *albino* in this book for examples of the use of diminutives in Spanish.

folk etymology: A change in the form of a word or phrase resulting from a mistaken assumption about its composition or meaning, as in *shamefaced* for earlier *shamfast*, "bound by shame," or *cutlet* from French *côtelette*, "little rib."

Germanic: Belonging to the branch of the Indo-European language family that includes English and its closest relatives. (Indo-European is a very large language family that also includes Latin and its descendants, the Romance languages, as well as most of the other languages of Europe, Iran, Pakistan, and northern India.) The modern Germanic languages include English, German, Yiddish, Dutch, Afrikaans, Flemish, and Frisian (the closest relative of English, spoken in the Netherlands and Germany), Norwegian, Icelandic, Faroese (the language of the Faroe Islands between Scotland and Iceland), Swedish, and Danish. The Visigoths, who established a kingdom in Spain at the fall of the Roman Empire, also spoke a Germanic language.

Late Latin: The Latin language as used from around AD 200 to around 700.

loan translation: See *calque* above.

Medieval Latin: The Latin language as used from around AD 700 to around 1500.

Middle English: The English language as spoken and written from around 1100 to 1500. Middle English borrowed a very large number of words from Old French and Medieval Latin.

Middle French: The French language as spoken and written from around the middle of the 1300s to around 1600.

Modern English: The English language as spoken and written since around 1500.

Modern French: The French language as spoken and written since around 1600.

Modern Spanish: The Spanish language as spoken and written since the middle of the 1500s.

Nahuatl: The language of the indigenous Nahua people of Mexico. One group of Nahuatl speakers founded the empire, usually known as the Aztec Empire but now often called the Triple Alliance, that ruled much of central Mexico at the time of the arrival of the Spaniards in the Americas. The Nahuatl language belongs to the Uto-Aztecan language family, a large language family that also includes other indigenous languages of the United States such as Hopi, Comanche, and Ute.

Old English: The English language as spoken and written from the middle of the 400s to the beginning of the 1100s.

Old French: The French language as spoken and written from the 800s until around the middle of the 1300s. Middle English borrowed a very large number of words from Old French.

Old Spanish: The Spanish language as spoken and written before the middle of the 1500s.

Old Provençal: See *Provençal* below.

prefix: A word element that can only occur attached to the front of a word and that is used to form a new word or indicate the grammatical role of the word in the sentence, such as *dis–* in *disbelieve*.

Provençal: The Romance language of the region of Provence in southeastern France. It is is closely related to Occitan. (The term *Occitan* refers to the group of dialects of the Romance language family spoken in southwest France.) Some linguists consider Provençal and Occitan to be one language. In medieval times, Provençal and the various Occitan dialects were referred to as a group by the term *Langue d'oc* (from the word for "yes," *oc*, in this group of dialects in southern France), and the medieval forms of these dialects were the medium of expression for a rich body of poetry that was influential throughout Europe. For convenience, linguists often refer to the medieval forms of these dialects under the blanket term *Old Provençal*.

Quechua: An indigenous language of the Andes, the most widely spoken member of the Quechuan language family. Quechua was used as the administrative language by the Inca, the ethnic group that formed the ruling class of the Inca Empire, which was conquered by the Spanish between 1531 and 1533. Today, Quechua is the indigenous language of the Americas that has the most speakers.

Romance language: Any of the languages that developed from Vulgar Latin. The most well-known Romance languages are national languages of the modern nation-states of Europe, including Portuguese, Spanish, French, Italian, Rhaeto-Romance (one of the four official languages of Switzerland), and Romanian. However, the Romance language family also includes many other regional languages of Europe, and in recent times, these regional languages have received more recognition and support from the central government. These regional languages include, for example, Galician (spoken in the northwest corner of Spain), Catalan, Gascon (spoken in the region of Gascony in France), Occitan (spoken in southwest France) and its close relative Provençal (spoken in southeastern France), Wallon (a language spoken in Belgium and closely related to French), Sardinian (the language of most of the island of Sardinia), Friulian (spoken in northeast Italy), the many other regional languages of Italy and Sicily, and several varieties of Romanian spoken throughout the Balkan peninsula. Many of the regional Romance languages have rich literary histories dating from medieval times.

standard: Of or relating to the variety of a language that is generally acknowledged as the model for the speech and writing of educated speakers. Sometimes the term *Standard English* is used in this book to distinguish the speech and writing of middle-class educated speakers from the speech of other groups and classes, which are termed *nonstandard*. The term *standard* is highly elastic and variable, since what counts as a standard variety will depend on both the locality and the other varieties with which it is being contrasted. A form that is considered standard in one region may be nonstandard in another, and a form that is standard in one variety may be considered nonstandard in the context of other varieties. In Spain, for instance, the letter z and the letter c before i and e are pronounced as (th) in the Castilian variety of Spanish that is considered to be the educated norm and is most often heard in the media. In the regional dialects of Spain, however, some speakers pronounce z and c before i and e as (s), and when considered in the larger context of the society of Spain, this pronunciation (s) is nonstandard. In the Spanish-speaking countries of the Americas, on the other hand, the vast majority of people of all levels of education regularly pronounce z and c before i and e as (s) in all social circumstances. Thus, in American varieties of Spanish, the pronunciation (s) is standard, while the Castilian pronunciation as (th) is nonstandard—the opposite of the situation that exists in Spain. Despite the fact that what is considered standard varies by circumstance, the term *standard* remains a useful term in describing the way a language is spoken and written in a society, but the context of its interpretation must always be made clear.

suffix: A word element that can only occur attached to the end of a word and that is used to form a new word or indicate the grammatical role of the word in the sentence, such as *–ness* in English *gentleness*, *–ing* in *walking*, or *-s* in *sits*.

Taíno: The indigenous people living in the Bahamas, Cuba, Hispaniola, and Puerto Rico at the time of Columbus's arrival in 1492. The term *Taíno* is also used to refer to the language spoken by this people. By the end of the 1500s, the language and culture of the Taíno had become extinct because of the effects of colonization. Many people in the Greater Antilles and the Bahamas, however, are at least partly of Taíno descent. Since the Taíno were the first indigenous people encountered by the Spaniards, the Spaniards learned to name many of the plants, animals, and cultural artifacts of the Americas from the Taíno, and the Spanish language preserves a large number of borrowings from Taíno. Most of what we know about the Taíno language comes from words that were borrowed into Spanish. The Taíno language belonged to the Arawak language family, a large language family also including many languages of South America.

Vulgar Latin: The everyday speech of Latin speakers in the late Roman Empire and the period just after the disintegration of the Roman Empire in Western Europe. Vulgar Latin differed in certain respects from Classical Latin—that is, the Latin used in Roman literature. It is Vulgar Latin, rather than literary Latin, that is the direct ancestor of the individual Romance languages. Roman graffiti as well as inscriptions written by uneducated people sometimes give us direct evidence of everyday Roman speech, but Roman literature for the most part conforms to literary norms that eliminated all evidence of the changes that were occurring in everyday spoken Latin. By comparing the forms of words in the Romance languages, however, linguists are able to reconstruct what Vulgar Latin words and sounds were like even though they are not preserved in surviving Roman documents. The entries for the words *bonanza, embargo,* and *salsa* in this book discuss examples of the way in which linguists reconstruct Vulgar Latin words and use them to explain the history of words in the Romance language family. Linguists call attention to the fact that the existence of Vulgar Latin words is hypothetical by putting an asterisk in front of them. For convenience, however, linguists often say that a word in a Romance language simply comes from Latin, rather than from Vulgar Latin, when evidence indicates that the Classical Latin word and its counterpart in Vulgar Latin were essentially the same. (The word *vulgar* in *Vulgar Latin,* by the way, does not indicate that this Latin was notably obscene. Instead, *vulgar* is here being used in a sense closer to its etymological meaning. The English word *vulgar* comes from Latin *vulgārius,* literally meaning "of the common people," which is itself from *vulgus,* "the common people.")

A Note on Sources

Many different editors of the American Heritage Dictionary have worked over the years to gather the etymologies that are detailed and discussed in the word history notes collected in this volume. The sources of evidence that they have used in compiling this book are the great historical dictionaries of English and other languages, and readers who would like to know more about the history of English and Spanish are encouraged to consult these works for further enlightenment. Most important among these sources is the *Oxford English Dictionary* (OED Online, http://www.oed.com, Oxford University Press, 1989–). Also essential are the *Middle English Dictionary*, edited by Hans Kurath, Sherman E. Kuhn, et al. (University of Michigan Press, Ann Arbor, 1952–2001), the *Dictionary of American Regional English*, edited by Frederic G. Cassidy and Joan Houston Hall (four volumes, A–Sk; Belknap Press of the Harvard University Press, 1985–2002), and the *Random House Historical Dictionary of American Slang*, edited by J. E. Lighter (two volumes, A–O; Random House, 1994). When we have given the dates at which words or meanings are thought to have entered the English language, we have often given the dates recorded in these large historical dictionaries.

In researching the history of Spanish words, the online version of the *Diccionario de la lengua española, vigésima segunda edición* (http://buscon.rae.es/), produced by the Real Academia Española, has also often been consulted. In particular, the *Diccionario de arabismos y voces afines en iberorromance* by Federico Corriente

(Gredos, Madrid, 1999) has been a rich source of information on the history of Spanish words of Arabic origin. For the further etymologies of words in other languages besides English and Spanish, we have also consulted the *Trésor de la langue française informatisé* produced by the Centre National de la Recherche Scientifique (http://atilf.atilf.fr/tlf.htm). To the authors and editors—past and present—of all these great works, we are heavily indebted.

Other Works Consulted

alligator: The quotation is from *The rare travailes of Job Hortop*, a facsimile reprint of the first edition with an introduction by G.R.G. Conway (Mexico: 1928).

armadillo: The quotation is from Nicolás Monardes, *Historia medicinal de las cosas que se traen de nuestras Indias Occidentales* (Sevilla: Padilla Libros, 1988), page 81.

barbecue: The quotation is from William Dampier, *Dampier's Voyages*, edited by John Masefield (London: E. Grant Richards, 1906), Volume 1, page 51.

barracuda: Valencian *barracó* is recorded, for example, in Antoni Maria Alcover et al., *Diccionari català-valencià-balear* (Palma de Mallorca: Impr. de mn. Alcover, 1930–1969).

blue blood: The quotation is from Maria Edgeworth, *Helen* (New York: Macmillan Co., 1896), page 157.

booby trap: The quotation is from Gonzalo Fernández de Oviedo y Valdés, *Historia general y natural de las Indias,* Book 14, Chapter 1, page 69, in *Biblioteca de autores españoles,* Volume 118 (Madrid: Ediciones Atlas, 1959).

calaboose: The quotation is from Mark Twain, *Life on the Mississippi* (New York and Oxford: Oxford University Press, 1996), pages 548–549.

chicle: The story of the invention of chicle chewing gum is told in Michael Redclift, *Chewing Gum: The Fortunes of Taste* (London and New York: Routledge, 2004), pages 24–29.

chocolate: The quotation is translated from *De orbe novo decades octo* in Petrus Martyr de Angleria, *Opera* (Akademische Druck- und Verlagsanstalt: Graz, Austria, 1966), fourth part, Chapter 4, page 179.

cockroach: The quotation is from John Smith, *The generall historie of Virginia, New England & the Summer isles, together with The true travels, adventures and observations, and A sea grammar* (Glasgow: J. MacLehose and sons, 1907), page 337.

guerrilla The quotation is from Washington Irving, *The Rocky mountains; or, Scenes, incidents, and adventures in the far West; digested from the journal of Capt. B. L. E. Bonneville and illustrated from various other sources* (Philadelphia: Carey, Lea, & Blanchard, 1837), Volume 2, Chapter 49, page 233..

hammock: The quotation is from Sir Walter Raleigh, *The discoverie of the large and bewtiful empire of Guiana*, edited by V.T. Harlow (London: Argonaut Press, 1928), page 33. The spelling has been modernized.

hurricane: The quotation is from Gonzalo Fernández de Oviedo y Valdés, *Historia general y natural de las Indias*, Book 6, Chapter 3, pages 146–147, in *Biblioteca de autores españoles,* Volume 118 (Madrid: Ediciones Atlas, 1959).

iguana: The quotation is translated from *De orbe novo decades octo* in Petrus Martyr de Angleria, *Opera* (Akademische Druck- und Verlagsanstalt: Graz, Austria, 1966), first part, Chapter 5, page 59.

incommunicado: The quotation is from George Wilkins Kendall, *Narrative of the Texan Santa Fé Expedition* (New York, Harper, 1844), pages 254–255.

jade: The quotation is from Nicolás Monardes, *Historia medicinal de las cosas que se traen de nuestras Indias Occidentales* (Sevilla:

Padilla Libros, 1988), pages 23–24.

jerky: The quotation is from *A Map of Virginia, with a Description of the Countrey, the Commodities, People, Government and Religion,* reprinted in *Travels and Works of Captain John Smith Edited by Edward Arber,* edited by A. G. Bradley (New York: Burt Franklin, 1966), page 63.

lariat: The quotation is from Ramon F. Adams, *Western Words: A Dictionary of the American West* (Norman, Oklahoma: University of Oklahoma Press, 1968), page 173.

mambo: The African origins of the word *mambo* are discussed in Ed Morales, *The Latin Beat: The Rhythms and Roots of Latin Music from Bossa Nova to Salsa and Beyond* (Da Capo Press: 2003).

moment of truth: The quotation is from Ernest Hemingway, *Death in the Afternoon* (New York: Scribner, 2003), pages 67–68.

mundungus: The quotation is from Francis Grose, *A Classical Dictionary of the Vulgar Tongue,* edited by Eric Partridge (New York: Barnes & Noble, 1963), page 239.

mustang: The quotation is from Washington Irving, *The Rocky mountains; or, Scenes, incidents, and adventures in the far West; digested from the journal of Capt. B. L. E. Bonneville and illustrated from various other sources* (Philadelphia: Carey, Lea, & Blanchard, 1837), Volume 2, Chapter 19, page 194.

piña colada: The quotation is taken from Gonzalo Fernández de Oviedo y Valdés, *Historia general y natural de las Indias,* Book 7, Chapter 14, in *Biblioteca de autores españoles,* volume 118 (Madrid: Ediciones Atlas, 1959).

puma: The quotation is from the entry for September 16, 1833, in Charles Darwin, *Journal of researches into the natural history and geology of the countries visited during the voyage of H.M.S. Beagle round the world, under the Command of Capt. Fitz Roy, R.N.,* 2d edition (London: John Murray, 1845), pages 116–117.

quirt: The quotation is from Thomas Mayne Reid, *The scalp hunters: Adventures among the trappers* (New York: G. W. Dillingham, Publisher, 1891), page 189.

ranch: The quotation is from Edwin Bryant, *What I Saw in California,* (Palo Alto: Lewis Osborne, 1967), page 313.

silo: The quotation is translated from Marcus Terentius Varro, *De Rerum rusticarum libri iii*, Book 1, Chapter 57.

ten-gallon hat: The quotation is from Ramon F. Adams, *Western Words: A Dictionary of the American West* (Norman, Oklahoma: University of Oklahoma Press, 1968), page 205.

Index

This index lists in alphabetical order the words and phrases that appear as headwords or are discussed as words in the text. The index is also sorted by language. English and Spanish words are listed first, followed by Arabic, French and Old French combined, Greek, Italian, Latin, Mayan, Nahuatl, Portuguese, Quechua, and Taíno, and finally the words from other languages besides these. English headwords are indicated by small capitals.

SPANISH

gambetto 97, 98
marcare 84, 85
mosca 152
pigna 173
volcano 222, 223

LATIN

MAYAN LANGUAGES

may 67
sik'ar 68
sīk' 68

NAHUATL

āchiotl 3
āhuacamolli 22
āhuacatl 21, 22
ātl 65, 66, 122
cacahuatl 74
camotli 175
chicolātl 65, 66
chicolli 65, 66
chīlli 63, 169
chocolātl 65, 66, 67, 74
epatl 91
epazotl 91
itzcuintli 226
Mēxicah 227
mizquitl 148
molli 22
tamalli 201
tomatl 208
tziktli 61
tzotl 91
xalli 122
xictli 208
xitomatl 208
xococ 66
xōloitzcuintli 226, 227
xōlotl 226

PORTUGUESE

alcatraz 8
coco 75
demarcação 84
inhame 228
rosca 187

QUECHUA

ch'arki 124-125
kuntur 78
llama 134
mati 231
papa 176
puma 177
rakacha 217
ulluku 216
uqa 217
wanako 134
wanu 98
wik'uña 134

TAÍNO

casabi 56, 231
hamaca 107
huracán 112

OTHER

allpaqa (Aymara) 134
aulun (Ohlone) 1
ḏbt (Egyptian)
hohowai (Tohono O'odham) 127
kongo (Kongo) 79
kóypu (Mapudungan) 80
mambo (Yoruba)
ñam (Wolof) 229
ñambu (Bambara) 229
nyami (Fulani) 229
rúsc (Old Irish) 187
tamgu (Ibibio) 203
tōbe (Coptic) 5

Picture Credits

abalone © Houghton Mifflin Company, School Division

alfalfa Laurel Cook Lhowe

armadillo Chris Costello

breeze Elizabeth Morales

castanet © PhotoDisc, Inc.

chicle The San Jacinto Museum of History, Houston

cockroach Laurel Cook Lhowe

divi-divi Chris Costello

El Niño Elizabeth Morales

farthingale Art Resource, NY/National Trust

guiro © Houghton Mifflin Company, School Division

hammock Laurel Cook Lhowe

iguana © PhotoDisc, Inc.

javelina Getty Images, Fototeca Storica Nazionale/Photodisc

llama © PhotoDisc, Inc.

mosquito Cecile Duray-Bito

oregano © PhotoDisc, Inc.

papaya Chris Costello

quirt Laurel Cook Lhowe

ristra Getty Images, C Squared Studios/Photodisc

sombrero © PhotoDisc, Inc.

tuna Chris Costello

vanilla Chris Costello

vinegarroon Cecile Duray-Bito

xoloitzcuintle © Houghton Mifflin Company, photo by Evelyn Shafer

zocalo Corbis/Archivo Iconografico, S.A.

258